EX Libris

S0-ALM-823

NEW
WORLD
OF THE
MIND

NEW
WORLD
OF THE
MIND

JOSEPH
BANKS
RHINE

WILLIAM SLOANE | ASSOCIATES

COPYRIGHT 1953 BY JOSEPH BANKS RHINE

PRINTED IN THE UNITED STATES OF AMERICA

ALL RIGHTS RESERVED

PUBLISHED SIMULTANEOUSLY IN THE DOMINION OF CANADA

BY GEORGE J. MC LEOD, LIMITED, TORONTO

CONTENTS

EX LIBRIS

To the Memory of DR. WILLIAM PRESTON FEW
First President of Duke University

and PROFESSOR WILLIAM McDOUGALL, F.R.S.
Founder of the Department of Psychology

Whose sponsorship and assistance made
possible a laboratory devoted to the
explorations reviewed in this book.

FOREWORD:

ON NEW WORLDS

■ This book is about a new world that science has discovered, a region within what we call the mind, a world that has throughout the past been shrouded in dark mystery and superstition.

Many new worlds have been discovered by man—worlds that lie outside himself. He has been less successful within. His new worlds of the past range from deep within his own planet—and even inside the atom—to far beyond the visible spectrum and beyond the visible stars. But the great discovering human mind has never yet thoroughly explored its own puzzling complex nature.

It now looks very much as though here and there a few pioneer explorers have broken through to a truly new world within man, a world of distinctively mental reality. The larger outlines are discernible, however, only when the scattered findings are brought together and considered as a whole. This book is an attempt to bring those fragments together, to show where they belong in the book of knowledge, and to appraise their meaning for human life.

How do explorers tell when they find a new world? Like Columbus, they usually do not know at first themselves. When, however, they report what they have found to their fellows, especially to their own professional group, and receive the response, "Impossible. We have never heard of it; there isn't any such world," they may know at least that what they have found is *new*. If, then, they can successfully meet the criticisms received, survive the scoffing rejection of their findings for a decade or two, and finally establish their case among those few who will look at it carefully, they know their "world" is both new *and* true. It is not an illusion.

When, it may next be queried, is a discovery big enough to be called "a new world"? Whenever the new outlook changes distinctly and profoundly the way we look at the world we already know; when it exerts a permanent influence on our way of life. Let us see if this new world of the mind can measure up to these criteria.

New worlds, of course, are never discovered all at once. A new hemisphere may be glimpsed first only as a few small islands, or an electrical universe as a few tiny sparks. The remaining parts of the whole factual reality have to be found and put together bit by bit. This task of completion is commonly a long one.

At a certain stage of discovery, as in gathering the pieces of a puzzle, hints of the hidden design flash across the minds at work on it. In the studies here reviewed of some of the strange, unrecognized powers of the human mind, we who are working in this field have only recently come to that stage of seeing the signs of a pattern in the odd pieces that have been found. The import of that pattern for the human situation today seems so great that we cannot wait for the full factual picture to emerge. We need, and for many reasons we want, to share it as it develops. It has, therefore, been gratifying to find that others wish to watch with us the advancing exploration of this truly new and significant world within the bounds of the personality of man.

Advances of new world magnitude are, of course, never made entirely by one individual. As a rule there is much teamwork and the coordinated effort of many helping hands, too many to be credited by routine acknowledgements. That is especially true of the work with which these pages deal. It is so much a group achievement, the labor of so many individuals, that it would be vain to attempt to identify the credit lines. Rather, the work itself is the thing; the main rewards are in the doing.

But in the reading, let no one forget that far back behind the mere tale of the deeds stands a long line of doers, distributed widely over the globe and back through the years, many even whose names will not appear in so brief and general an account, but whose fine, patient efforts were an essential part of the accomplishment.* This compromise with brevity is made with the understanding that those who are led by these less documented pages to wish to go beyond them to the original sources will have every aid extended to them.† For every reader may this new world excursion be but the first of a series of voyages, each one advancing further the boundaries of discovery in the realm of what men vaguely call the human spirit!

* In the preparation of the book I have been aided most devotedly and capably by my wife and colleague, Dr. Louisa E. Rhine. Miss Elizabeth McMahan, Dr. J. G. Pratt, and Mrs. Farilla David of the Parapsychology Laboratory at Duke have been of great assistance, as have Miss Frances Phillips and R. Mc-Lean Campbell of the editorial staff of William Sloane Associates. To all these and to others who helped, I am deeply grateful.
† The small index numbers found here and there in the book refer to appendices to the various chapters; these are at the end of the book, and for the most part give references to further reading matter or sources.

Part **I**

EXPLORATIONS

IN THE NEW WORLD

Chapter **1**

A CHART OF

THE AREAS DISCOVERED

■ This new world is new only to the sciences. It has, of course, always been here. Its spontaneous manifestations have thrust themselves under the eyes and ears of men in all the human cultures of which there is any record. Almost everyone is in some degree familiar with them; they are popularly called "psychic" experiences, or, more professionally, *psi* occurrences. The branch of science that grew out of the study of these psychic phenomena was first known as psychical research; it is now called parapsychology. These spontaneous experiences still serve as an introduction to the field, even though by themselves they are not taken to prove anything.

Here are a few examples of common types of psychic experiences . . . §A student once came to see me to tell me that during the previous night her roommate had awakened, emotionally upset, hearing her grandmother calling her name. She felt certain this meant there was something wrong at home, and she wanted to telephone. She was persuaded, however, to wait until morning. When she did get in touch with her family, she learned that during the night her father had had a heart attack and that in the excitement her grandmother, who lived with the family, *had* called for the girl, forgetting that she was away at college. ∫A little boy of four in Springfield, New Jersey, awoke from a nightmare screaming; he thought his father was struggling to get out of water and that there was tall grass around it. Two days later the father and his brother-in-law capsized on a marshy lake in trying to retrieve ducks in a bad wind. The brother-in-law drowned and the father saved himself only after a desperate struggle through the tall grass. He recalled the child's dream as he frantically battled his way through the water and reeds. ∫A dear friend whom I have known well for twenty-five years spent the night, along with her little daughter, in the house of a friend she was visiting. In the night the child, frightened, awoke her by clinging to her and crying, "Mommy, make that old man go away." The child described the old man as carrying a chain. In the morning my friend told her hostess about the experience; the latter disclosed that others had seen an old man with a chain in that room. She had hoped he would not "return" again. ∫A woman in Ohio wrote that on the morning on which her seven-year-old grandson died, a geranium plant, which had been on her window sill in the breakfast room all winter, fell off, breaking the pot into several pieces. There was no jar or any other evident reason why it should fall at the time. She found that it must have fallen at the exact moment of her grandson's death. Some other members of the family had intended to take a geranium to him that morning. The next afternoon the grandmother and the boy's mother were sitting in the breakfast room eating lunch and talking about the child. They were both looking toward the same geranium plant, which had been replaced on the window sill. "Mother, did you see the plant?" the daughter exclaimed. "The plant just seemed to take a jump." The grandmother replied, "Yes, it was just as if Jeffrey were trying to talk to us." Before either one of the two women could get over to see whether the plant was sitting firmly, it toppled over again and fell.

Let no one get off course at this point in trying to explain these examples of psychic experiences in some nonpsychic fashion. That would be missing their point. Such experiences should not be taken as adequate evidence of anything by themselves. They are emphatically not the kind of stuff of which proof is made in any of the studies considered in this book; but without making any attempt to come to conclusions about them, something can still, with perfect safety, be learned from them. At the moment, however, the only purpose these examples are intended to serve here is to illustrate what people mean when they refer to "psychic" occurrences.

Two characteristics combine to make an occurrence "psychic": First, the event has to be attributable to some sort of personal agency or causation. It is more than an impersonal happening like a flash of lightning; some personality must be involved. Second, there must be no reasonable explanation as to how the event could have been produced, no explanation, that is, in terms of the orthodox science of today. A psychic experience, then, is a kind of miracle—that is to say, an inexplicable phenomenon—but not attributed to divinity.

In each of the examples given, something happened that was quite unexplainable. How could the girl have known that her grandmother was calling? How could the little boy have foreseen, if he did, that his father was going to be nearly drowned? How could my friend's little daughter have seen the same apparition that others had seen before in the same room? And what known principle could have pushed the geranium over twice, once with the two women watching it? Even while making all kinds of reservations, as we must do, about uncertainties of observation and reporting and the like, we can still see that such experiences have something in common. They satisfy both of the two criteria: They are unexplainable and in each case the agency appears to have been personal; the event, if it happened as related, did not just happen by itself.

But there are a great many things in nature, and especially in human nature, that are still unexplainable. In fact, as the reflective psychologist would be the first to concede, there is precious little really known about the fundamentals of persons and personality; that is, little of all there is to know. What, then, is it that makes these psychic phenomena so unique and challenging that the investigation of this particular area of the vast unknown has opened up a new world?

The answer to this question requires a further word about the way psychic events happen. They are not merely unexplainable; such occurrences are downright impossible if the standard textbook ideas about the world and man are correct. The point is that these experiences, if there is anything at all in them, are not merely baffling; they are revolutionary. Either many thousands of reports in the collections are entirely misleading or else the philosophy of man currently dominant among the conventional sciences is wrong; for, according to that philosophy, nothing like what is implied in these occurrences could possibly happen.

Let us look carefully, then, into what it is that is so contradictory about psychic experiences. What is so revolutionary about them? Why are they not readily explainable? The answer lies in the fact that the scholars of our culture have only two general sorts of explanations for things that happen: All their theories of the fundamental causes of events have to fall under one of the two headings, natural or supernatural. Man's first theories of what goes on in his world largely involved the supernatural, but later, as the effort to find the most rationally acceptable causes succeeded, science advanced into one area after another and supernaturalism had to give way before it. Since progress was naturally greater and easier in the more objective areas like those dealing with matter and its motion, knowledge accumulated most rapidly in the physical sciences. On that account the standards of scientific thought were taken from physical law, physical concepts of causation, and the physical properties of things. Since physical nature came under control first, the pattern was thus set for the intellectual habits of science as a whole.

To most students of science natural law came, therefore, to mean physical law. Physicalistic modes of thought and explanation dominated the studies of nature everywhere, even in psychology, the beginning science of human nature. Most schools of psychology became and remain today more or less frankly physicalistic. The only alternative they knew, or know even yet, was the supernaturalism from which they had delivered their science. Supernaturalism had thus become the very antithesis of science, and anything that challenged physical explanation smacked of supernaturalism.

Yet there are these thousands of unexplainable experiences that people say have happened to them—events that seem to defy physical interpretation. They appear to be natural, even though they are spontaneous and puzzling. The girl heard her grandmother calling her when she was several hundred miles away. The little boy foresaw his father's accident in the water two days before it occurred. No physical stimulus imaginable could have evoked the experience of the little girl who said she saw the old man with the chain, and no energy is known that could have upset the geranium plant on the window sill where it had sat securely for many months. Even though these are simple non-evidential illustrations of experiences that serve only to raise questions, it is clear that if they are considered at all they cannot be explained in terms of physical processes.

Rather, this type of experience takes one well out of the world with which physics deals. Accordingly, if there is anything genuine in psychic occurrences, it must represent a different world so far as physics is concerned. But physics provides the only kind of descriptive terms scientists have developed in dealing with the worlds that have been conquered in the past. Parapsychology is, therefore, science's first new world beyond physics.

It will be granted, then, that the world of phenomena we are approaching is *new*. It is unquestionably new, at least, to natural science. If adequately established as real, it could profoundly alter the conventional views of man and his universe. Anything that does that must surely affect his conduct of life; and that would be novelty enough, indeed! But before taking up in the following chapter the question of how well established is the hold or claim that has been made on this new world, I shall outline first the main divisions of what has already come into clear scientific perspective.

Such an outline should begin with the corner of the research field that has lent itself best to scientific investigation. For purposes of illustration, examples of typical spontaneous psi experiences will be cited, experiences that first raised the questions the researches are attempting to answer. For many people the commonest type of psychic experience is that in which the person to whom it occurs, the subject, seems to know what is going on, to perceive some real objective event, even though he is far away from the scene where it occurs and could not possibly be relying on any of the known senses. Such experiences of the extrasensory perception (ESP) of objective events, commonly called clairvoyance, take many forms. One of the most familiar is the intuitive impression or hunch or compulsion to act. ¶An old friend, a business executive, told me that once his mother had gone off on a week-end visit with friends some miles away in the country, leaving her husband at home alone, slightly indisposed. Suddenly she experienced a compelling impulse to return home, even though she could give no rational explanation and the hour (late at night) was unusual and inopportune. She had only a general feeling that there was something wrong at home. She found on arriving there that the house was on fire from a spark from the fireplace. Her husband was asleep upstairs, totally unaware of his danger. ¶Sometimes, especially in dreams, the scene may be viewed with almost photographic clarity. During World War II a Philadelphia woman saw in a dream the S. S. *Oregon* rammed by a naval vessel, off Nantucket, and she saw her son, who was second mate on the *Oregon*, clinging to a raft along with only a few others. She awoke the family with her screams. The morning papers confirmed the dream picture very much as she saw it. Her son was one of the few survivors. ¶It is not often, however, that the individual when awake has so clear a conscious vision of the scene involved. Such a rare person, however, was the distinguished Swede, Emanuel Swedenborg, who, in Gothenburg in 1759, watched and reported the progress of a disastrous fire several hundred miles away in Stockholm. At another time, during dinner with a manufacturer, Swedenborg warned his host that a fire had broken out in his factory; the warning proved to have been both correct and timely. ¶Vivid flashes of clairvoyant perception are often experienced even by children. During World War I a child of three and one-half years stopped in his play one day (November 7, 1918), acting as though hurt, and cried, "My daddy is choking. He's down a hole and he can't see." After the father's return from

France it was found that at the very hour of the child's experience
he had been gassed while in a cellar and as a result had been
blinded for three weeks.

It is clearly suggested (I did not say "proved"!) by these and
the multitudes of similar cases on record that some persons have
on occasion a perceptual awareness that brings them knowledge
or a compulsion to act or an appropriate emotion—often without
their getting the full meaning of the event at the time. However,
only certain individuals report such experiences. The majority of
people do not have anything of the kind happen to them. Some
of those who do may have only one case in a lifetime while others
may have a great many. But all such experiences are spontaneous
and not under the control of the person concerned. They are
likely to slip up on the individual when off guard, as in dreams
or when, during waking hours, he is not strongly concentrating
his thoughts.

Through the ages there have been countless attempts to control
and use some such power as clairvoyance. The various kinds of
fortunetelling and occult counseling that have abounded in every
culture are too numerous even to list. What stands out, however,
is that none of these has borne up through the years sufficiently
well to become an established practice that could be handed down
as a well-developed art. In no culture has there been such mastery
over clairvoyant perception that it could be passed on to posterity.
The nonexperimental psi occurrence, then, is a completely spontaneous type of experience and one that throughout the past has
never been well enough understood or sufficiently mastered to be
utilized in any reliable way.

The spontaneous flashes of clairvoyant perception, however,
have at last been subjected to experimental investigation. It
should not be expected that anything that occurs so spontaneously
and uncertainly as do these phenomena would have been caught
and controlled at an early stage of scientific research, for spontaneity and lawfulness are opposite characteristics. Experimental
conditions that take the uncertainty out of natural operations are
difficult to impose on a type of occurrence as fugitive as this one.
At any rate, without going into the long history of the slow development through which tests of such extrasensory modes of

perception as clairvoyance have progressed, I will proceed to the type of experiment that has enabled the scientists concerned to decide whether or not clairvoyant ESP (extrasensory perception) really does occur beyond legitimate dispute. That decision was a necessary and basic first step in itself.

I will describe an experiment[1] which was conducted at Duke University in 1933 in what has come to be known as the Parapsychology Laboratory. Even though it has often been mentioned in print, I chose this particular work because it served to satisfy all who had a part in it that ESP of the clairvoyant type really can occur. This experiment was something of a turning point or a milestone, at least, for the Duke Laboratory. Before I describe it, however, I should give some of its background.

My research assistant at the time of this experiment was J. G. Pratt, a graduate assistant in psychology. In a long series of experiments, most of them exploratory in character, Pratt and I had as our principal subject a student, Hubert E. Pearce, Jr. In most of these experiments Pearce was instructed to try to identify the order of cards in a pack of twenty-five, with the card faces hidden from him. He knew the five symbols or suits (star, circle, square, cross, and waves) that were on the cards, and either recorded his response ("guess") or called it aloud. His scoring was sufficiently high to indicate the operation of something more than chance. Then the test procedure was modified so as to increase the safeguards against error or sensory cues. For example, the cards were completely screened from view during the more advanced tests and even removed to another room; but even after these precautions were added Pearce (and other later subjects like him) continued to score at a rate of success that was significantly above that to be expected from chance alone.

The test and the pack of cards used in it (now known as ESP cards) had been designed to make it easy not only to measure the rate of success but to know how much would have to be allowed for the effect of chance alone. In the run of twenty-five card trials, with five cards of each design in the pack and when the subject did not know his successes or failures until the end of the run, chance alone would give, in a series of sufficient length, an approximate average of five hits or 20 per cent. (We tested chance theory itself on this procedure to the extent of half a million trials.[2])

Pearce, an outstanding subject, would average from six to eleven hits per run (that is, from 24 to 44 per cent) at an experimental session. Several times, however, in runs of twenty-five trials, he got a score of zero; that is, he missed *every* card in the deck. Once, too, in an informal but nonetheless impressive set of circumstances, he scored a perfect run of twenty-five successive hits. At the time of the particular experiment now to be described his average score had been approximately eight hits per run over a series of seven hundred consecutive runs.

In this experiment which Pratt and I carried out with Pearce in August and September of 1933, the aim was to set up conditions thoroughly adequate to exclude all the factors that could produce extrachance scores except ESP. Pratt handled the target pack of cards in one building (now the Social Science Building on the Duke campus), while Pearce was located in a reading cubicle across the quadrangle in the stacks at the back of the Duke University Library. Thus he was situated approximately 100 yards away from the cards.

At the start of each session, before Pearce departed for his cubicle, the two men synchronized their watches. After he left, Pratt shuffled the cards and placed the pack at a left-hand corner of his table. At the agreed-upon starting time Pratt removed the top card and, without looking at it, placed it face down on a book in the middle of the table and left it there for a minute. He then removed the card, still keeping it inverted, to the right-hand corner of the table and immediately picked up the next card and put it on the book. This routine was continued until all the cards were transferred, one at a time, to the other corner. Thus twenty-five minutes were taken for each run of twenty-five trials. Pratt then recorded the order of the cards in duplicate and, as a safeguard, before he met with Pearce, sealed one copy in an envelope for delivery to me.

In the meantime, over in his cubicle in the other building, Pearce had put down on his record sheet during each minute the symbol which he thought was on the card that Pratt had in position at the time. At the end of the run he, too, made a duplicate of his record of the twenty-five calls and sealed one copy in an envelope for my records before checking his duplicate with Pratt. I was thus able to make an independent check from my duplicate records and the two men together made their own checkup as to the number of hits scored. In this way any question of the individual good faith of any one of the three of us was obviated.

Two runs through the pack were made per day and the total series consisted of 12 runs or 300 trials. The number of hits expected on a theory of pure chance was 20 per cent of 300 or 60 hits. Pearce obtained a total of 119 hits or just one short of double the number expected from chance. His average run score was 9.9 hits per 25 or 39.7 per cent of the total trials made. A score as large as this one of 119 hits in 300 trials would be expected to occur by chance only once in approximately a quadrillion (1,000,-000,000,000,000) of such experiments; we knew, therefore, that every reasonable man would, without further argument, join us in dismissing the chance explanation.

There are no known sensory processes that could be supposed to operate under these conditions. No type of rational inference could apply to a case of this kind. Examination of the order in which the cards fell showed no peculiar recurrence of symbol pattern into which Pearce might have fallen by accident or by the discovery of such a pattern in earlier runs. We, therefore, were forced to decide that, whatever clairvoyance or the extrasensory perception of objects *is*, this was a case of it. It was a case in which results were obtained under the strictest control.

The above conclusions had, of course, some very definite limitations; certainly, Pearce's experimental demonstration did not establish everything that may occur in spontaneous cases. It did not tell what clairvoyance is or even just how to produce a similar result. This successful experiment was a necessary first step, but only one step. We had simply found that it was possible to demonstrate clairvoyant perception under well-controlled test conditions. It was another question how it was done, how the demonstration could be repeated, how many other people could do it, or how well the average subject would do it, et cetera. It had been shown that clairvoyance occurred on this occasion with this subject and experimenter and situation; that was one safe conclusion that could be drawn from this experiment; it was an experiment that could stand by itself, leaving the other questions for other researches.

However, even pared down to this, such a demonstration was in itself a new and radical development for science. There were echoes to that effect in the reaction which the publication of the results received from the psychology profession, the general field to which the experiment belongs. The report of these researches (in a book entitled *Extrasensory Perception*) initiated what is doubtless the most heated controversy American psychology has ever experienced. Some reflections of this heat may still be felt in the following chapter; at least, it indicates, to put it mildly, that the findings were not "old stuff."

Clairvoyance seems simple, however, compared to the kind of experiences that come next—those involving the future. These are presented next because they appear again to be clairvoyance, different only in being directed toward events ahead in time instead of present or past. It is, in fact, the most bewildering thing about this next type of psychic case that they show no relation to time. In approximately half of the general run of Dr. Louisa E. Rhine's large collection of spontaneous cases,[3] the scene or event connected with the subject's experience has not actually taken place at the time. In other words, if the reporting and interpretation are correct, the perception is prophetic or *precognitive*.

Again, while it is doubtful if any fair-minded person could read these cases by the hundreds without being profoundly impressed, I repeat that to the investigator in parapsychology such anecdotes are valued not as evidence but for suggestions they give of still undiscovered areas that offer possibilities for further researches.

The best approach to these cases of ESP of the future is to ask first: What about the effect of space? In fact, it was the successful attack on the question of distance that led up to the investigation of time in relation to ESP. It is plain enough from the experiences as well as from the experiments that ESP is not limited to short distances. Swedenborg, as has been said, was at least three hundred miles from the fire which, according to the account, he was able to perceive. The child who "saw" his father being gassed in France in 1918 was three thousand miles away. A review of the thousands of cases in the Duke collection shows *no relationship* at all between distance and the number or type of psychic experiences.

Research results from the laboratory confirm this observation. Pearce, in his distance experiments, was located 100 yards from the target cards. The score average he obtained at that distance was approximately the same as that secured in similar tests in which the cards were on the table in front of him. It may be concluded, therefore, that distance in itself is not a factor of importance in ESP, spontaneous or experimental.

But the world of modern physics is invariably a space-time system. It should be expected, then, that psychic phenomena would be found to be as independent of time as they are of space. Time should not be expected to show a limiting relationship if space fails to do so.

And time does not. Curiously enough, the person who has a clairvoyant experience often does not know whether or not the event that comes to his consciousness has happened yet. This is especially likely to be the case where distant events are involved. There is no time arrow along with the experience to mark it as past, present, or future . . . ¶An old schoolmate of mine once told a friend of hers that she had seen a notice in the paper of the death from a heart attack of one of their mutual friends. The other woman expressed surprise and incredulity. What paper? Where? When they searched the papers they found no such announcement. My friend was puzzled indeed. Had she dreamed the whole thing? The next day, however, the person they had been so much puzzled about did have a heart attack and the paper of the following day did contain the notice which my friend had fancied she had seen earlier. It could well have been that she had dreamed she had read it and, as sometimes happens, had not remembered it as a dream.

Precognitive experiences more often than not do come as dreams. Such dreams may not be exact. Often they are fragmentary, sometimes dramatized and elaborated. Sometimes they have interesting substitutions as this one does . . . ¶A woman in Youngstown dreamed that she had injured her right hand. She did not dream *how* she did it, but only that she was in great pain. She thought she tried to find a doctor, but they were all out when she called. At last, however, she found one and he said, "Don't worry. It will be all right." But she kept repeating, "Doctor, it hurts." The dream so impressed her that she related it to her sister. The next morning her five-year-old daughter caught her right hand in the automatic wringer. With the child screaming with pain the mother called two doctors, only to find they were out. But she found the third one in. He examined the child and said: "Don't worry. It will be all right." The child kept saying on through the day, as the mother had done in the dream, "It hurts!" . . . It is the thought-provoking effect that is the main value of such accounts; but it is a value that can hardly be overestimated. The case just cited, for example, involves what looks like pre-cognitive telepathy, for the mother seemed to suffer the same pain that her child did later on.

One would naturally think that if precognition occurs, however spontaneously, and has any practical value, it would save people from some of their impending dangers. There are numerous cases that suggest that it does . . . ¶The day after a disastrous hotel fire in Atlanta a few years ago, a Duke student came to see me to relate the following story. She said that a few hours before the fire had occurred her mother and father, who had retired for the night in that hotel, had arisen about 2:00 A.M., dressed, and driven home. According to the account nothing external had disturbed them. The mother had simply had an uneasy feeling. She insisted that they get up and go on, and she finally prevailed over the protests of her sleepy husband. Perhaps she may have had a dream that she did not remember. At any rate, the impulse to act was all that could penetrate her waking consciousness.

Many people merely have warning hunches, apparently without dreams or other more detailed impressions . . . ¶The wife of one of my colleagues believes she often knows of the advent of danger in time to escape it. One night she and her husband were about to motor home from Norfolk, Virginia, when she had a hunch that there was danger ahead. Consequently, instead of driving home late at night, they spent the night in Norfolk. On their way to Durham the next morning, while coming through the lonely area of Dismal Swamp, the drive shaft of the car broke.

The predicament they were in would have been a very uncomfortable one had it happened in that isolated region late at night.

He would be a mentally inert person, indeed, to whom experiences like these would offer no challenge. The questions they raise radiate in all directions, but the paramount issue is whether or not they involve any true precognition, whether the mind can in some way transcend the barriers of time and acquire reliable impressions of events to come, things that, as we ordinarily think, are still awaiting their place in the seriality of causal developments. If the mind could do that and true precognition really occur, the consequences of the discovery for human thought would surely be beyond description.

From this introduction it can be seen that the hypothesis of precognition is strongly suggested, and once it was clear that it could be tested, the suggestion was enough. Nothing, in fact, seemed as urgent and important as bringing the question of prophecy down to controlled experimental test. The beginning was made back in the fall of 1933, right on the trail of the Pearce and Pratt distance tests. Even so, experiments in precognition are still quite recent even for this new science of parapsychology. Indeed, one wonders why, in view of all the many practices that claim to involve prophecy that have gone on in every land and time, no one before ever took the trouble to bring the matter to a systematic test. Apparently no one had ever even attempted to develop a test for precognition. Probably all those who were analytic enough to consider what kind of test would be necessary to examine it were too critical of the sketchy evidences and claims for prophecy to make the considerable effort required for an experiment.

An experiment in precognition, however, followed logically after Pearce's demonstration of ESP at a distance in 1933. The method that had been in use for testing clairvoyance was easily made over into a preliminary test of precognition. All that was needed was to ask the subject to indicate on his record sheet, not what the card order in the pack was at the time, but what it would be after the deck was shuffled. The results obtained in this kind of prediction test turned out to be above the chance average. The test method was then further improved and conditions imposed that would preclude any imaginable type of error or other counterhypothesis. For example, different types of randomization of the card order were brought into use to insure that a chance arrangement was provided.

For tests of precognition it is important to make sure that the series of events which the subject is to try to predict is truly random. We found at an early stage that shuffling by hand was not adequate; in fact, it was later found possible to combine ESP and shuffling so as to make a pack of cards match a series of calls to a degree beyond chance—a "psychic shuffle." On that account shuffling by hand was discontinued and shuffling machines introduced. But even the use of such mechanical devices did not satisfy all of us. Finally, by 1941, a fair amount of agreement was reached when the following plan was evolved and the tests carried out. The target deck of cards would be cut on the basis of a routine use of maximum and minimum temperature figures published in a certain newspaper on a certain day in the future specified, of course, in advance. The subjects were then asked to predict what the order of the cards would be when such a cut was made in specified packs of cards.

As it happened, most of the subjects that were used in these tests were naive,[4] and no doubt that was a happy circumstance, for they did not question the method by which the targets would be selected. At any rate, they could not be supposed to have given the details much, if any, rational consideration, a fact that was probably a key to their success. The more successful subjects were the children and adolescents. The task we put before the subjects was made as simple as possible. Record sheets were given them on which there were five short double columns each having five spaces. The subjects were told that later certain symbols would be put in the right-hand spaces in the columns, and their task was to write in the spaces on the left the symbols that would later appear on the right. Nothing was said about how these target symbols would be selected.

The scores secured in these tests were not greatly beyond the average expected from chance. For one thing, there were no exceptional subjects like Pearce available to us then. Also, we were making a point of using unselected subjects, in fact, all the children, adolescents, and adults we could attract into the test by the use of parties and small rewards. Further, since the subjects could not be promised any knowledge of their scores and, accordingly, could not be given any rewards until the check-up period which would be from one to ten days following the test, most of the incentive and excitement value inherent in the clairvoyance tests was probably lost. However, the first series we carried out did give significant or extrachance results (by a sensitive measure known as salience-ratio covariation described in the original report). The odds against getting score effects of the kind we obtained were of the order of 500 to 1. That figure is well beyond the standard criterion for considering that something lawful is taking place, something beyond chance itself.

It was a beginning well worth following up. We were encouraged sufficiently to do a second experiment;[5] and this was conducted also in 1941 with the help of Miss Betty M. Humphrey, then a graduate student in psychology. In this second research, under essentially the same conditions as far as the precautions and methods went, we still obtained significant results. In this case the odds again ranged to the order of 500 to 1 that our subjects would get as far as they did from the kind of results expected from chance alone. With the two experiments combined we were satisfied that we were not dealing with mere accidental results. The children especially were doing something that related in some reliable way to an order of cards that was not to be determined until from two to twelve days later, and then would be selected by methods that assured random targets. The only counter-possibility would have been that the cards had been shuffled or cut so as to make the order fit the call record sheet. Neither the subject nor the experimenters had any conceivable opportunity to do that unless they influenced the temperature (or the thermometer or the observer who made the readings) by the process of psychokinesis or PK, that is, the direct action of mind on matter. We will come back to this question in a later chapter.

We were, and we still are, much too close to this first new rough-hewn evidence of precognition to assess it very accurately. We had some appreciation of the fact that we were swinging far out over the old conventional walls of centuries of scientific orthodoxy and dimly discerning the broad outlines of a world fantastically novel and strange to those who live beneath the standard ceiling of traditional ideas. Otherwise we would hardly have persisted in experiments so difficult in themselves and so surely foredoomed to stubborn rejection by those who determine the prevailing beliefs in the sciences. Now, however, the age-old question of precognition had been brought to test. A method had been developed and results obtained under conditions adequate to meet the counterhypotheses of the time. The way has been opened for others to go further and to improve on what has been done.

What the experiments indicated was that ESP could, under controlled conditions, be made to transcend space and time. That was about all that could be concluded from them. It had not been demonstrated that the effect could be produced with just anybody at any time under any conditions. In baseball terms, we had only got to first base in showing that an effective relation can be established between some individuals and a future order of events.

Even a restrained statement of these limited results on a topic as important as this, however, is about as revolutionary to the established scientific philosophy of today as could be imagined. Not only is there no current physical theory to account for such results, but their very occurrence is a hard and irreducible fact that defies every reliable concept of physical causation that man had ever had. So there cannot be any doubt that what has been uncovered in these experiments is novel, indeed, to the world of science.

The most familiar psychic experience of all is that involving *telepathy*. This type has also excited most popular interest and is the one given most attention by the societies for psychical research. And telepathy, too, has had the most curious research history among all the odd capacities of the psychic order that have thus far been investigated.

In part, the attention that had long been given to spontaneous thought transference was due to the natural interest attaching to anything that links people together, especially when long distances separate them. But there is also the fact that cases of what appear to be mind-to-mind contact over the barriers of space suggest, even more than does clairvoyance, that there is something in the mind that is not bound down by the physical limitations that restrict sensory functions. They suggest some degree of separability of mind from body, at least in function. Accordingly, when, in the middle of the nineteenth century, the impact of materialistic science fell hard on the spiritual thought of the Western world, many intellectuals turned to the investigation of telepathy for evidence from nature itself that would refute the claim that all human life is bound by the purposeless forces of matter. Telepathy, in fact, was the chosen topic of investigation by the founders of the British Society for Psychical Research, although later the claims of mediumship took precedence and all but crowded it off the stage.

To a great many people, telepathy is not a very uncommon occurrence in daily life. There are many types of it, but only a few need be illustrated here . . . ¶I will choose an example from a casebook kept by my wife on our children's experiences. She found that up until the children reached school age there were frequent unspectacular instances of what looked like telepathy between her and them. For example, one day as she was ironing she fell to thinking silently, with some regret, that it had been a long time since she had been to visit Mrs. McDougall. One of the little girls, aged between two and three, was playing with blocks on the floor. She looked up and said, "Mommy, why don't we go and see Mrs. 'Dougall?" ¶Telepathy occurs rather commonly between dreamers, too. Again I will turn to my wife's notebook. She was awakened one night from a nightmarish dream by a call from our three-year-old daughter in an adjoining room. In her dream my wife had been terribly frightened by some vague, undefinable pursuer, and when she asked the child what was the matter the reply was, "I'm scared." "What scared you?" The child had to think. "I guess it was a—a bear." She, too, was not sure what she was afraid of. (Had my wife cried out in her sleep and given the child a fright? I have never heard her do so in thirty-three years.)

There are cases of telepathic dreams reported in which it seems as if the two persons concerned actually communicate with each other . . . ¶For example, a woman whose son was in military service on a Pacific island during World War II dreamed one night that a palm tree was being blown over onto his tent. Terrified, she called his name aloud and woke up. Later he wrote that in his sleep that night he thought he heard her call. He got up and ran out of the tent to see where the voice was coming from. Just then a tree fell, crushing the cot on which he had been sleeping. He was sure, he wrote her, that his dream had saved his life. He did not know, of course, until he received her letter that she had actually called as she dreamed of his peril. ¶In one of the most striking types of telepathy one person experiences another's suffering as if the two minds were really one unit. In a family that I know very well, the following happened. One day the father was driving home by automobile along a New Jersey highway. Suddenly, with no warning, he felt a crushing pain, so severe he thought he would die, shoot through his chest. He somehow managed to stop the car. After a short while he recovered. There seemed nothing the matter with him then and he drove home. While telling his wife about this strange experience, the like of which he had never had before (nor, for that matter, during the many years that have passed since), and discussing the need for a medical examination, the telephone rang. It was a message stating that his son in Colorado had been killed in a head-on collision of the car which he had been driving. The time of his son's death coincided closely with that of his own violent chest pain. The son was crushed against the wheel. ¶During the war, under the stress of the exceptional anxiety that then prevailed, telepathy seemed more frequently than usual to break the barriers of separation. One day a Duke student, daughter of one of my friends, came in to tell me that during the Italian campaign she had had a dream in which she saw her fiancé, who was in the U. S. Army in that sector, get off the train at the Durham station. Everything appeared all right except that he was completely white-haired. The dream puzzled her and she told her mother about it. Her mother persuaded her to write to him about it. She showed me a few lines from the letter she received in reply: "I have been trying to think for a month how I could bring myself to tell you of this thing that has happened to me. The night we landed on Anzio Beach my hair did turn white. I just couldn't tell you. This must have been God's way of breaking the news to you."

There is no way of being sure in cases of this kind that there is any direct mind-to-mind transfer of thought. However, it is obviously quite possible that in the case just given, the dreaming girl might have picked up by clairvoyance the fact of her fiancé's sudden graying. Although I could not prove it, to me it seems more likely that his own anxious thoughts projected themselves into the subconscious matrix of her dreaming mind . . . ⟨Even in the following case of Dr. C., the actual explanation must remain in doubt. She wrote me that while in China she was awakened from sleep one night during the war by hearing her mother calling her name. As she later learned, the mother in New England was at that very time dying and asking for her daughter. Of course, there is no way of knowing whether it was the mother's thought and emotion that, halfway around the world, broke into the sleeper's consciousness. Dr. C. could instead, for all one knows, have got the message by clairvoyant knowledge of the objective calls. . . . The general tendency of most interested individuals in the past when any question of this kind arose has been to prefer the telepathic interpretation as against that of clairvoyance. As will be seen, however, there is no scientific ground for this preference.

In turning to an account of the experimental work on telepathy, it will be wise to keep in mind that, from the first coining of the word "telepathy" by Frederic W. H. Myers more than fifty years ago, the phenomenon has generally been thought of as a direct mind-to-mind contact, not involving any physical intermediation of either the bodies of the two subjects or anything else.

The experimental study of telepathy has already gone through a number of major stages and it is safe to say that it will go through at least one more. The first experimenters to deal with telepathy were so much interested in it, to the exclusion of any other kind of extrasensory perception, that they did not consider it worth while to distinguish between various kinds. If they designed an experiment in which the possibility of any kind of sensory perception was excluded, and if they then got positive results, these were credited to telepathy. If the person who was the sender in a telepathy experiment made a drawing which the receiver was to try to reproduce, or if the sender looked at a playing card or other object which the receiver then tried to identify without the aid of the senses, for the results to be ascribed to telepathy it was necessary only that the receiver's responses check with the sender's items. Obviously, however, the receiver could just as well with the aid of clairvoyance directly perceive the object itself at which the sender was looking. Thus clairvoyance was in no way ruled out in any of the experiments of the first fifty years or more of investigation. This same indefiniteness prevailed, too, in the "telepathy" researches carried out in the psychology laboratories of a number of universities in Europe and America.

By 1930, however, clairvoyance had come sufficiently into the focus of thought that, when the experiments began at the Laboratory at Duke, an effort was made to distinguish between the two processes, telepathy and clairvoyance. The earlier telepathy tests were recognized as having produced evidence of some form of extrasensory perception, but it was considered necessary to use new methods to find out whether there was any evidence that the telepathic type of ESP could be obtained when the possibility of clairvoyance was ruled out.

In the new tests (for "pure telepathy," as they were called) that were then made,[6] the subject was asked to identify a symbol present only in the sender's thoughts (with no card or other objective target on which clairvoyance could operate): a symbol which the sender had not yet recorded. The sender waited until the receiver signaled that he had recorded his call. Only then did he record the symbol that had been selected for the trial. The result of all the comparisons was that there was no essential difference in scoring rate, whether the pure telepathy type of test or the old-style procedure of undifferentiated ESP was used. It was found that the results were about the same, whether the sender looked at the card or not.

Comparisons that were made with the third condition (clairvoyance) of having no sender at all also showed no different order of result. In these tests, of course, there was merely a random card order. These tests showed that subjects who were capable of either pure telepathy or the undifferentiated ESP of the old telepathy tests were, likewise, capable of scoring in the pure clairvoyance tests in which there was no possibility of telepathy. These similarities in results, regardless of the variety of ESP presumably involved, were findings of the early years at the Parapsychology Laboratory. Since that time there have been subjects who did not do equally well in both telepathy and clairvoyance tests, but these later exceptions do not disprove the earlier results. They only indicate that other factors than the abilities may influence the results, such factors, for example, as the subject's or even the experimenter's beliefs about the abilities in question.

It seemed increasingly probable that in all these various operations there is only one basic general psi capacity involved. This suggestion came from the growing evidence that the same general conditions seem to affect success in one kind of ESP test as in another. Accordingly, the expression "extrasensory perception" was adopted to include telepathy and clairvoyance and precognition as well.

With the tests outlined above, however, the case for telepathy was far from settled. A third stage of research on that problem began when the question was raised as to whether or not a pure telepathy test was really as pure as had been supposed;[7] whether clairvoyance was ruled out by merely having the sender delay in recording his thought until after the receiver signaled that his response had been recorded. What if the receiver had precognitive ability? It was necessary to presume that he had, if, as now seemed likely, precognition was just another aspect of ESP. What was to keep the receiver, then, from going ahead to the moment after the sender had made his record and precognitively perceiving what it was? In doing so he would not have to draw upon the thought processes of the sender at all. Accordingly, then, telepathy had not, after all, been conclusively established as a type of ESP distinct from clairvoyance. There was, in fact, no evidence for telepathy in which all reasonable possibility of precognitive clairvoyance was excluded.

The realization of this loophole in the evidence for telepathy at once set off another project of exploration. And, as a result of some even more discriminatory experiments, telepathy was again established on a new basis designed to meet the new requirements. This work was done both in the Parapsychology Laboratory, primarily by Miss Elizabeth McMahan,[8] and in England by Dr. S. G. Soal[9] of Queen Mary College, University of London. In order to get this new basis the experiment had to be designed so that the sender would *never* make any objective record of his choice of symbol that clairvoyance, even precognitive clairvoyance, could reach. Yet he had to make this choice of symbol in such a way that someone else could independently check his symbol order; otherwise there would be no independent check on the reliability of his scoring. Such independent checking is required by the standards maintained for the more decisive research in parapsychology, the only kind from which conclusions regarding debatable issues are drawn.

After some careful thinking about the matter, several ways were devised to enable an assistant experimenter to check the sender's target order without making any objective record. But these methods would be too complicated to describe here, and they must be studied in the original reports by those who wish to examine the procedures critically and thoroughly.

After these successful experiments it appeared that telepathy had passed its third test. It is worth saying again, however, that as far as it meets the requirements for good experimenting, all the evidence from all the telepathy tests from the beginning of research on the topic is a part of the general stock of evidence for extrasensory perception. It can still be evidence of a general or undifferentiated ESP, but ESP nevertheless. There have not as yet been very many of the highly select, third-stage, twice-refined tests for telepathy, although what there is was obtained under some of the most stringent conditions that have been developed in this field, and the field is one in which, of necessity, methods have had to be especially well controlled.

But, alas, in spite of all, the telepathy problem is still not completely solved. It is even hard to see how anything more can be done about it just yet; sooner or later, however, there will have to be at least a fourth stage before it is known whether anything like telepathy as it was originally conceived is possible or whether, eventually, the definition will have to be changed and the older concept of it as mind-to-mind contact given up. As it is, there is no assurance, not even any high order of probability, that what is being dealt with here is a direct mind-to-mind transfer. Until it can be determined whether or not there is a mind that functions with such independence, no answer can be made. And even if it is found that the mind is such that it can act independently in any way, there will still be the question as to whether telepathy does operate in a direct mind-to-mind transfer.

Perhaps the most plausible alternative to the original hypothesis (one of several outlined by Drs. R. H. Thouless and B. P. Wiesner[10]) would be that the receiver mentally interacts in some way with the sender's nervous system, much as the latter himself does when he remembers something. This would be a kind of clairvoyance, though it might be of a special kind. Or the sender could be operating in some way directly on the nervous system of the receiver, something like the way he operates on his own in bringing about motor responses.

As it is, the evidence on hand for telepathy can be explained only as a general sort of extrasensory person-to-person exchange. We shall have to wait until someone can think of a way to refine the procedure further before we can get beyond that. Probably it will be necessary to wait until more is known about what the concept of *mind,* as distinguished from the whole *person,* really represents before the problem can be further pursued. Many psychologists, such as the behaviorists, have been trying by verbal magic to make the concept of mind vanish from the stage of scientific reality, as those of soul and spirit have already done. However, the concept of mind does not stay "vanished." This very difficulty about the mind helps to keep the problem of telepathy an important one. If a method that fully meets these new questions could be found to prove the case for telepathy now, showing *direct* intermental reaction to be possible, it would be going a step beyond the present frontier in the psi researches. The field of psychology as a whole needs this challenging problem of telepathy to help to keep attention on the fact that no science yet has a theory of how a mind could influence a body let alone how it could affect another mind. As can be seen, the explorers in parapsychology have pursued the telepathy problem back to that darkest corner of all the sciences of man, that which concerns the fundamental nature of personality itself. There they are stuck for the time being because nobody knows whether, in the sense implied, there *is* a mind.

But in spite of all the difficulty encountered, there is no reason to give up on the telepathy question now, any more than there was in earlier stages. It may, perhaps, be an advantage to go back to spontaneous experiences and consult a wider range of orienting ideas in search of the new approach that is needed. It would be too bad to have to wait before getting on with this problem of telepathy for the conservative, orthodox psychologist to make up his mind about his mind at the slow tempo at which he has for decades been cerebrating about his cerebrum.

What, now, about *physical* effects? What about the effect of mind on the physical universe? All the types of psychic experience so far discussed have contributed to the individual some kind of knowledge or guidance. The experiences I have related have left effects that have been principally mental or subjective. These very happenings and the experiments they encourage raise the question whether there may not be psychic experiences that are to ESP what the normal *motor* responses in the human being are to *sensory* experience. Are there any physical effects of psychic origin that still come within the classification of parapsychology; that is, that defy explanation in terms of physical causation?

As a matter of fact, there are observable physical effects, although they are noticed and reported much less commonly than are perceptual psi experiences. At the same time, even though more infrequent, the psi experiences having physical effects that are reported are likely to be more dramatic and, on first acquaintance and without a supporting rationale, even to approach incredibility.

In my book, *The Reach of the Mind*, I ventured to relate one very dramatic case reported by the internationally known Swiss psychiatrist, Dr. C. G. Jung.* he states that when he was a young man working on his medical thesis, which dealt with mediumship, two unexplained physical effects occurred in his house, both taking place when no one was in the house. The first was the "explosion" of an old steel bread knife, leaving the blade broken into five pieces. The other involved the splitting of a round table top.

---

* I did not identify him then, and I do so now in view of his frank stand on these psychic problems, as, for example, in his recent book (with Prof. W. Pauli), *Naturerklärung und Psyche*.[11]

Both events were accompanied by a pistol-like report that was heard outside in the garden. The medium was not present. There is not even a plausible theory of the agency in this case, as there is in a great many instances.

Many of the physical effects reported are associated with death. The clock stops, a picture falls, a window shade flies up, or a vase breaks, all in some unexplainable fashion at the time a person connected with the object dies . . . ∫The wife of one of my professional friends reports that her father, while listening to the radio, died suddenly of a heart attack. Although the radio was beyond his reach and he was unable to walk, it stopped when he died. No one was in the room with him at the moment. The radio was in good repair and the program uninterrupted on the air, but its sudden cessation attracted the attention of his son-in-law in an adjoining room, who came in and found the father dead. . . . This association of the physical event with death does not really explain how the effect, if genuine, was produced. It only raises the question, and that is all this type of incident can be expected to contribute.

Even when the event is not associated with the moment of death, it often may be attributed to the agency of a deceased individual . . . ∫A professor and his wife whom I have known for years had this experience: A neighbor woman had died the day before. Both families had been interested in proof of spirit survival and before the woman had died she had been asked by the professor and his wife to give them evidence of her continued existence if she could. The night after her death they were both awakened at 1:00 A.M. by the coming on of an old flashlight. It was one that would no longer function and had been lying unused on a shelf nearby. Although when the professor turned it off it would not light again, even the next evening, yet at 1:00 A.M. that night the light came on once more and was seen by both persons a second time. They thought their friend had something to do with it.

This purposive theme of seeming to give assurance of continued survival runs through a lot of these unexplainable cases of physical effects . . . ∫A very puzzled woman tells that one day she and her mother heard a sharp explosive report localized in a glass drinking set in their dining room. The pitcher and all six of the glasses were found to have been cracked. The daughter stated that she saw her deceased grandmother standing in the doorway at the time of the noise.

Yet it is not only when someone dies or when a deceased personality is apparently associated that such things happen. A picture may fall or a clock stop back home, it seems, when a man in the service gets word he is returning home or is liberated from prison. Or it may be coincident with an injury . . . ∫A woman wrote that her aunt with whom she was living had a son in Korea who was badly injured when his jeep hit a mine. Within a few minutes of the time of his injury the kitchen clock unaccountably fell off the mantel and a pile of dishes fell out of the cupboard. One of the two women was present in one case and the other in the second. The two events were some minutes apart and there was no jar or vibration to explain them. The mother was immediately worried about her son.

Perhaps I have not yet said often enough that it would be scientifically unthinkable to consider any of these reports of spontaneous occurrences as acceptable proof of anything. It is quite enough to take them as things that people say happen to them; and when enough people say the same kind of thing, no matter how strange and incredible it may be, it is wise to look into the facts, letting the interpretation wait. There are always perfectly *safe* ways of looking into such matters. Such looking and the follow-up researches make up the advances of science. How can progress be made if all the puzzling things that occur in nature are ignored and if scientists refuse to study what they cannot at once explain and what some people call impossible? It is conceivable, even likely, that the less striking physical effects of psychic origin are mostly overlooked and consequently only the spectacular ones get reported. To search for the unspectacular would mean to analyze occurrences in the physical environment, beginning with the body itself. Next, it would be in order to study the effects that human beings exert on their material surroundings— their overt behavior. Small unconscious effects would naturally be easily overlooked in such gross, unanalyzable activity; they would even be hard to find and identify.

Still, there *are* many unexplained physical effects experienced. Many puzzling observations have turned up in medicine, psychology, and anthropology. In all these areas effects have been reported that would seem possibly to be the result of some sort of psychic causation, although at this stage it is impossible, of course, to say what the explanation is. Take, for example, the raising of blisters by hypnotic suggestion. In this type of phenomenon the hypnotized subject is told that he will have a blister in a certain place. In a great many cases, in some even with careful control over the conditions, it is reported that one appears. For such an effect medical science has as yet no explanation.

Similarly, in psychosomatic medicine, both orthodox and unorthodox, many completely puzzling physical occurrences are reported. It has been the established practice in many clinics to treat warts purely psychologically and the treatment has a large measure of success. How the cure is actually effected remains to be discovered, but there is ample evidence now of its successful use. The treatment of burns by suggestion, like that of warts, began among untutored folks who had the "gift" passed on to them by another who possessed it. Not only is the pain evidently removed by this magic treatment, but the injury is greatly reduced; for example, in many cases, as reported by competent observers, blistering is avoided. As in the instances of the sudden graying of hair, an actual phenomenon does occur, no matter how impossible it may seem. And there is no known way for the mental state of the individual (usually fright or anxiety) to bring about the physical change. The point here is that there may be a problem for parapsychology involved.

When cases of folkway practice involve animals, it is still more difficult to explain them by conventional theories . . . ∫According to one of my most respected friends, a learned and responsible woman, her family once owned a purebred heifer that became so badly marred with warts as to make the animal unsalable. A man locally reputed to be able to remove warts gave the stable boy some words to say as he fed the heifer (the man stressed the fact that the boy's belief in the power of the cure was essential) and soon afterward the warts all disappeared—soon enough to impress the family, although the exact timing was not noted. . . . This is a type case, not an isolated one, suggesting areas in which a physical effect of psychic origin might play a part, though one cannot be sure whether or not it does. To the open mind such cases should serve to raise a question, a question that is important, even if not an easy one to answer.

To continue raising questions: Is there an element of direct mental action operating at times to influence results in games of skill and chance? Many people believe that sometimes, by strongly thinking of and willing a certain result, a physical effect may be made more likely to occur. Many an athlete, including some athletic coaches and a number of performers in various kinds of skilled action, more or less secretly believe that they have some direct mental influence as they watch the basketball or the arrow or the dice leaving the hand of the player.

Such belief is more prevalent among those who play with dice; perhaps it is because, in a proper game, the element of skill is not supposed to enter into the result. It is a not uncommon belief among dice throwers that they can exert a direct influence upon the fall of the dice. They believe it is true especially when they get into a certain state of high concentration generally described as "hot." Even without supposing that all the stories told of the marvelous and consistent results obtained are true, one can recognize that these reports raise a question. That is the question of whether the mind could possibly exert a direct effect upon the falling object. Fortunately, the throwing of dice can easily be made into a suitable technique for a test that could answer the question. It was, in fact, by that handy technique that the experimental work on the problem of the direct influence of the mind on matter had its beginning. This action is known as *psychokinesis* or PK, a word that had currency before the experiments began.

The suggestion for this technique of testing for PK ability came, incidentally, from a young gambler. This young man had visited the Duke Laboratory to discuss what he considered the role of ESP in gambling practice. He also asserted stoutly his confident belief that he could mentally influence the fall of dice under the right conditions and accepted the challenge to demonstrate the point. He succeeded well enough to justify a thorough test of his claim; he called it, "The Law of Mind over Matter."

The experiments in throwing dice, however, were not the first attempt at a study of the "mind-over-matter" problem. Historically a really vast but largely unrewarded expenditure of effort had already gone into the investigation of the physical phenomena of mediumship—effects produced in the séance room purportedly as a result of spirit agency. The Spiritualist movement was initiated a little over a century ago. It was associated from its beginning with mysterious physical manifestations, with unexplained rappings and lights and the movement of objects. Such movement of objects, assumed to be caused by spirit personalities without physical contact on the part of the medium, had been called *telekinesis*. It became one of the most investigated phenomena of mediumship during the late nineteenth century and the first quarter of the twentieth. A number of scientists of distinction became interested and some of the investigations even penetrated, temporarily, at least, the university laboratories of psychology (for example, that of Harvard, in the investigation of the Boston medium, Margery).

The effort was made to allow the medium sufficient freedom that the phenomena under study might be produced but to try to impose, at the same time, such conditions that the origin and nature of any phenomena that might result could be interpreted. The range of types of manifestation was extremely wide and varied. There were less striking effects such as slight movements of objects (supposedly without contact) under dim illumination or in complete darkness with luminous bands on the objects. Claims that independent spirit voices had been produced were common. There was "spirit photography," too. One of the most frequent effects claimed was the materialization of the deceased spirits who presented themselves as visible bodies, supposedly built up from a sort of "spirit matter" called "ectoplasm."

The testing of such a claim presented a delicate and difficult problem. It was necessary to apply just enough and not too much control over the conditions. Few people on either side of the issue were ever satisfied with the controls, and in no instance of the many investigations in Europe and America was there ever reached a sufficiently clear-cut demonstration of the telekinetic effect to satisfy the requirements for a sound scientific judgment. No large group, even of those who were seeking to discover whether such effects are possible, to say nothing of the wider public, was ever convinced. Accordingly, while many cases of alleged telekinesis were investigated, cases on which it is not possible now to reach a conclusion one way or the other, the great amount of time and energy devoted to exploratory effort in this area failed to establish the occurrence of telekinesis.

On the other hand, the tests of psychokinesis made by throwing dice had from the beginning many advantages. One great virtue in this technique lay in the fact that everyone was able to throw dice. No special persons had to be sought out as mediums; in fact, my wife and I began early in 1934 by testing ourselves, our family members, our friends, students, and even our casual visitors. It became a game with a serious justification, a social pastime that had full intellectual license. It lent itself to scientific control without unwarranted concessions to the subjects' whims or beliefs. It was not hard for the subject to get the feeling that he *could* influence the dice; he could usually watch the results as he went, and doing so added much to his interest.

Like the telepathy experiments, these in psychokinesis have gone through several stages.[12] In the first, these tests consisted of trying to influence one or more dice by willing a certain face or combination of faces to turn up on the final fall. A great many variations of test conditions were introduced during the course of experimentation. The dice might be merely thrown from hand or cup, or they might be released by some trip arrangement and allowed to roll down an incline under the influence of gravity. They might be put in a rotating box or cage and the apparatus driven by electric motor. The throwing of various numbers of dice at a time was tried. The number ranged widely; beginning with one die per throw, then with a pair; eventually 6, 12, 24, 48, 96, or even more might be released at a time. If one die was thrown, the target had to be one of the six faces; if a pair, it might be a designated face or it might be a combination such as 7's, or high dice (a total of 8 to 12), or low dice (a total of 2 to 6).

Since the computation of the number of times a given face or combination would be expected to turn up as a result of chance alone is not difficult, and since almost everyone finds it interesting to throw dice, the method turned out to be sufficiently popular that there was no trouble in getting subjects to cooperate.

Most of the subjects got results in some degree above the average expected from chance. Generally speaking, most of the experiments carried out at the Parapsychology Laboratory, and elsewhere with some degree of collaboration with the Laboratory, yielded results sufficiently different from chance to be interesting. More and more the realization grew that some other factor than chance was operating, and it was a factor that could not be attributed to errors in recording or faulty dice or skill in throwing. The test was designed so that these factors could not affect the conclusions. However, even on the basis of extensive work which was carried on over a period of eight years, no final publishable conclusion was drawn until a second phase of the research had been reached, one that afforded a still more definite control over all the alternative explanations and possible errors.

This second phase began in 1942 when my research assistant, Miss Humphrey, and I began a re-examination of the PK test data that had accumulated, that is, the record sheets on which had been recorded the original results of experiments, most of which had been completed years before. By that time certain curves of hit distribution had shown up so often in ESP test results that the idea occurred to us to see what kind of hit curves might be produced in PK data. It was beginning to appear that PK might be a sort of Siamese twin of ESP, so many common features had been discovered in the two bodies of evidence. It had been the ESP results that had suggested the hypothesis of PK with sufficient seriousness to lead to its investigation. Therefore the suggestion seemed reasonable that if in ESP the subject derived something reliable from the object, some counterinfluence of subject upon object in return might be expected. Such an effect would merely be an application of the Law of Reaction.

If ESP and PK were basically closely related processes, it was argued, then similarities in test conditions might bring about similar effects such as curves of hit distribution in both ESP and

PK data. Hence the PK records were examined for distribution curves.

It was found that the subjects did generally tend to decline in scoring rate as they continued through a run, whether the runs were of 12 throws or 24 or 36. When the record column was divided into halves, so that the rate of success could be compared for the top and bottom halves, it was found that there was a highly significant top-bottom difference. This decline was found when the results of the work as a whole, that is, all the available data which could be adapted to this analysis, were pooled. There was a similar decline in scoring rate across the record page from left to right. The columns on the left half showed higher averages than those on the right. When everything available was pooled (a total of 18 research series), there was still such a consistency in the decline from left to right and from top to bottom that when the record page was divided into four quarters so that the upper left quarter could be compared with the lower right, there was a diagonal decline that was strikingly significant.[13] In this study of the quarter distribution of the page the odds against the chance occurrence of an effect so great are of the order of millions to one.

A kind of double-clinching further analysis was then found possible to apply to 12 of the 18 series. This consisted of a quarter-distribution (QD) analysis of the set, which is a smaller division of the record page. It was found that if the subject was doing the test in small sets of, let us say, six columns of six throws each, several sets on the page, as a rule the top half of the set averaged higher than the lower, and the left half of the set was generally higher than the right. There were exceptions, but they were few. The upper left quarter again had most of the hits and when compared with the lower right it showed as significant a difference as had the page as a whole. Thus we had an independent confirmation of this effect.

The significance of these hit distribution data, found long after the tests had been made, was so great that we were at last fully convinced that the PK effect was a real one. For these differences could not be attributed to factors in the dice, since the dice were always the same throughout the set (and, with minor exceptions, over the page, too) in which the differences were found. The same was true of the recording methods and the way in which the dice were handled. The only factor that did differ across the page was the psychological one. That hit distribution was understandable in terms of the variation of the psychokinetic principle as it had operated under the complex conditions of the subject's personality and the structure of the test. Such effects are similar to certain ones already familiar in general psychology. Compare, for example, gradient effects in memory and learning tests.

We could see no alternative to PK as the explanation. In some way which was difficult to understand but which probably involved a reversal of the same psychophysical principle required for ESP, the subject had been able to influence the movement of the object. Even though the effect produced was very slight, it was no more delicate and elusive than the traces of perceptual activities that had been caught in the ESP tests.

There was no hint as to how far this PK effect could be generalized, nor could anyone state with confidence the conditions under which the effect might be demonstrated. It had been a long and tedious task by which tentative conclusions had finally been reached. The collaboration of many experimenters and a large number of subjects had been involved. Into the task had gone the cumulative knowledge and experience and wisdom of a great many people. But even so, it was recognizably just a beginning and its greatest value lay in the possibilities it opened up and the procedure it provided for further exploration.

Further controls than are mentioned here were imposed. There will be more on these in the next chapter. And there is now even a further stage of the PK research program in action, a third period of development. The effort is currently being made to branch out in the testing of PK to include a range of other methods. In the main, these ventures are still too new and unconfirmed to be brought specifically into the present review. They extend in scope of target material over the familiar classification of "animal, vegetable, and mineral," and even get down to electrons and cosmic rays. The one repeated and confirmed departure from dice that should be mentioned is that of the several PK test series reported by Dr. R. H. Thouless[14] of Cambridge University and by Miss McMahan,[15] using flat objects (discs) with two target faces.

One of the main new developments in the present stage of PK research is the introduction of PK "placement" tests. These represent a change in method rather than in target object. Sufficient work has been done by several different investigators using this method (first introduced by Wm. E. Cox) that it can now be considered as an established method.[16] In placement tests the subject, instead of trying to make the test objects land with a given face turned up, tries to make them fall or roll into a designated target subdivision of the total area over which they can range, let us say the left half of a table. For the most part a two-division area has been used and the objects are released from a stationary neutral point and in a neutral manner. The two divisions are used as target an equal number of times so as to equalize any differences in the target areas. The fact that objects can be influenced to fall so as to indicate a placement effect has already been demonstrated in a number of researches. (See especially the papers, in the *Journal of Parapsychology*, by H. Forwald, the Swedish engineer who has contributed most of the PK placement researches.)

It has been shown possible, then, not only to make selected faces of cubes and discs turn up as the objects fall, but also to influence the direction the object will take. This psychophysical influence is the PK effect. It has been found possible to produce these effects to an extent statistically significant over long series of trials. If even these limited and necessarily fragmentary findings are sound, as we are now convinced they are, there is no need to ask that the discovery be new to the body of knowledge of the natural sciences. Outside the halls of science the idea may be as old as civilization itself, but the methods used have now finally brought the PK phenomenon under the control of science, at least to the point of establishing its occurrence.

In all the above researches we are dealing, of course, with normal average human beings as subjects and are using the methods of investigation characteristic of the sciences. In the spontaneous experiences cited I have merely considered a range of phenomena that are reported to occur in nature all over the habitable globe, occurrences that natural science in the past has left for explanation to supernaturalism. The explanatory hypotheses that I have entertained have hitherto been considered as reasonable only in the field of religion. Yet as far as these hypotheses have been tested, it has been by the strictest methods of experimental inquiry. If, however, this world of psychic operations such as ESP and PK is new to science by reason of its *findings*, it is equally new to the realm of supernaturalism on account of its *methods*, the methods by which the results have been obtained. The basic ideas are familiar enough to the supernaturalistic disciplines, but not so the methodology, the analyses, the evaluations, and the generalizations to which they lead. The method of dealing with the phenomena is entirely new to those disciplines.

These discoveries, these glimpses of all that may be involved in ESP and PK, are, then, the first toe contacts, the first small outlying islands of a new world. Will the physicalistically oriented scientist follow or even look? Or will he continue to be convinced by the old charts of the past that tell him there cannot be any such new world? Will the supernaturalist, the religionist, the theologian be interested, or are these discoveries, the first results of a slow and difficult research, too small for his eager, noncritical faith to consider important? If, as must be expected, it should be impossible to align the observations and interpretations of parapsychology with either of the two great prevailing ways of explaining phenomena—physicalistic or supernaturalistic—the few who work in parapsychology must, on account of their isolation, be the more sure, the more cautious, and the more circumspect. It is already clear enough that what has been found and the ways of finding it do not fit either kind of prevailing orthodoxy. To both of these viewpoints the whole psi research development seems radical to the point of being revolutionary; and to the conventional habit of mind that easily conforms to such dogmas as physicalism or supernaturalism, the results of the psi investigations are bound to be upsetting. That would be only a normal reaction to them.

On this account there will be a pause now to examine the strength of the case for psi, in a chapter that those who already know something about the evidence may be surprised to see is still needed in such a book as this today. Why it is needed is one of the problems for the chapter. There would, of course, be little use in going on to the structure of relations and meanings that will be built on the foundations of the discovery of psi if there are any lingering unresolved doubts about the quality of the evidence.

Chapter **2**

CLAIMS, CHALLENGES,

AND CONFIRMATIONS

■ From this point on I shall assume that the world of psi is definitely new to science. But how strong is the claim that has been made for it? How sound is the foundation of fact which must support the structure of conclusions built upon it?

It may be helpful to consider first how such matters as the strength of a claim of this kind are decided. In general, the soundness of a case depends more upon the adequacy of the methods used to investigate it than upon anything else. Under methods I include all that goes into the research from the phrasing of the question to the formulation of conclusions. It can be seen that much depends upon whether the experimental procedure be so designed that the results obtained can be interpreted without qualification or ambiguity. A well-designed experiment is intended to eliminate, if possible, all but one possible answer to the question that is being investigated. In the present instance it is the hypothesis of the occurrence of psi that is to be tested. If results are obtained under conditions in which nothing but psi could operate, then and only then can the conclusion be reached that the hypothesis is sound. What constitutes a psi phenomenon was defined at the outset of the preceding chapter.

The over-all value or strength of a conclusion would, of course, depend also upon the *amount* of evidence supporting it. Any new conclusion requires confirmation. A new and revolutionary one needs still greater confirmation. Confirmation by *independent* investigators is especially important in cases in which the conclusion is one that is likely to encounter skepticism. This is necessary because in every field of inquiry it is possible that there may be certain uncontrollable factors involved. If any of these is overlooked by one experimenter, presumably it would be reliably dealt with by others if there is sufficient independent repetition. One example of this type of factor is the character or the competence of the experimenter himself. One investigator might be incompetent but the likelihood of incompetence decreases with numbers.

These necessary specifications for scientific inquiry are fairly general for all the sciences. The primary role of methods and the importance of independent confirmation apply to one science as well as to another. They apply to a new one as well as to an old one. The chief difference for the various branches of science lies in the specific techniques of observation required for the experimentation. It would seem, then, that all that would be necessary in order to appraise the situation in parapsychology would be to see whether the methods used met the general standards and whether sufficient evidence had been accumulated from independent sources to compare with that required in other branches of inquiry.

Before turning to see what the evidence is, a word is in order concerning some things *not* to be looked for—at least not yet. For instance, it is not necessary to explain psi in order to establish that it occurs. It need not be interpreted in any given way or be made to operate on demand or be brought under control or practical use. None of these, in fact, is needed—or even should be considered—in the first step of investigation. The first step is the problem of seeing whether the results obtained in any of the psi tests are beyond explanation by anything but psi. Whether or not they are depends on the test design and the conditions of the experiment.

How well has the research in parapsychology met the requirements as far as *amount* of evidence is concerned? The question can be answered at once. There has been during the last seventy-five years so much evidence of some form of psi capacity in terms of numbers of independent repetitions which have given significant results that the interminable retracing of the same course is in itself a phenomenon that calls for explanation. Why, one wonders, should there have been so many repetitions, extensions, and variations of these experiments when so much of the work reported indicates that a psi factor did operate?

There is, too, the counterpart of this question: Why does there remain any question as to the occurrence of psi after all this history of independently repeated tests proving the same thing? These repetitions have, in fact, been so numerous that there is no likelihood that any adequate appraisal of the total amount of the evidence of psi on record to date in different parts of the world will ever be made. Some idea of the difficulty of reaching an over-all evaluation of this evidence might be secured by attempting to appraise the work reported in one periodical alone, for example, *The Journal of Parapsychology* during the limited period (now about seventeen years) of its existence. Taking this one section of the history of parapsychology, there are somewhere between four and five thousand pages of scientific reports. These, for the most part, deal with experimental work. There is no way to combine into any over-all valuation all the various results, obtained with a range of methods and conditions, and dealing with a number of problems. For any useful or reliable sort of measure of the strength of the case, the magnitude of the work has long since got really out of hand.

No one, however, is ever going to make an appraisal of all this accumulation of fact establishing the occurrence of psi phenomena. Most students of the subject will be more concerned about the *quality* of the evidence and the adequacy of the methods on which it depends than on the quantity. They are likely to think that something must be wrong with the methods used in all these experiments, since general scientific recognition of them has not been achieved. It will, in fact, be manifest to anyone who goes very far into the subject that either there is something very much at fault, something wrong that runs through the whole large body of accumulated results, or else some other factor must be at work to cause rejection of the results of these investigations. At any rate, there is no need to consider further the actual extent of psi research on record.

The question of the quality of the evidence of psi, however, is crucial. For one thing, it is obviously important to find out whether or not the endeavor to accumulate more evidence of psi still continues because the work already done is of poor quality. It is essential to discover just what the nature of the resistance to the conclusions concerning psi really is; how much, if any of it, is the fault of the evidence, and if that should not be at fault, what other factors there are to explain the situation.

The first thing to do then is to inquire of those who reject the psi evidence just what fault they find with it. This means that attention must be given to the group that has been most critical. As should be expected, since psi belongs to the general field of psychology, the profession of psychologists has had most to do with the general rejection of the results of research in parapsychology.

It is not difficult to find out something factual about the general reaction of psychologists. There is now in publication the report of a recent survey of the reaction of the American psychologists to the ESP research, made in 1952 by Dr. Lucien Warner.[1] Dr. Warner sent a questionnaire to one third (515) of the Fellows of the American Psychological Association. The Fellows, of course, are the individuals who would naturally be the more established members of the profession. Of the 360 who responded, only about one in six (16.6 per cent) were willing to accept the occurrence of ESP as either established or even a likely possibility. If this survey is representative, a large majority of American psychologists, roughly five sixths, do not consider the case for ESP acceptable. It is not that they think the subject beyond the pale of science. Instead, 89 per cent of Dr. Warner's respondents considered the investigation of ESP a legitimate scientific undertaking and 78 per cent considered it to be within the province of academic psychology. There was, therefore, no rejection of the research as such; what was rejected were the results that indicated that ESP is a genuine occurrence.

One might suppose that a survey of the younger psychologists might give a somewhat different distribution of attitudes. Perhaps among these younger men a higher percentage might accept the conclusions concerning ESP. Or if comparisons were made with European psychologists a better degree of recognition of psi among them might be indicated; but as yet there are no figures on such comparisons and the facts of Warner's survey may as well be faced and an attempt made to see where the trouble lies. Is it in the evidence or is it in some factor of attitude or some group reaction or philosophy?

Warner's survey itself furnished something of a clue. According to this clue not many of these psychologists represented by the survey have ever considered the evidence. More than two thirds of them had not read an original report. That is a large section. I need hardly say that it is *only* from the original reports themselves, which give details as to conditions and procedures and methods of evaluation, that one scientist can appraise another's work. What is most illuminating, however, is that, of the five sixths who rejected the reality of psi, one in three stated that he made up his mind about ESP on a priori grounds; that is, without considering even secondhand reports or reviews of the evidence! In other words, over 30 per cent of these psychologists just knew without any evidence at all, any kind of evidence, that ESP does not occur. For them ESP is an impossibility; therefore, there could not be any such thing as an ESP test. They have some way of knowing about such matters other than that of experimentation, these Fellows of the American Psychological Association, these scientific psychologists.

This type of reaction is not entirely new; for one thing, Dr. Warner (with Dr. C. C. Clark) made a similar survey in 1938[2] and obtained very similar percentages.

Back through the years of controversy over the ESP work, too, there were indications that some factor other than the quality of the ESP evidence was the real basis for the reaction of some of the critics. That much is evident from their reactions when the criticisms were effectively answered by the experiments. Take for example the mathematics issue. Following the first report of the experiments in ESP at the Duke Laboratory in 1934, a number of critical papers were published by psychologists (though none by statisticians) attacking the statistical methods of evaluation that had been used.[3] The issue had become a heated one by 1937 and at its annual meeting in Indianapolis that year the American Institute of Mathematical Statistics issued its now well-known press release on the mathematics of the ESP work, flatly endorsing that aspect of the investigation. It was an independent statement from the most competent authority, prompted largely by the leadership of the late Professor Edward V. Huntington of Harvard University.

Now if the mathematics had been the real issue, those who had attacked the work in parapsychology on mathematical grounds should, in some instances at least, have withdrawn their opposition and shown an interest in other phases of the research. But as it turned out, those who had been critical of the mathematical method now turned their attention instead to a criticism of the experimental methods. No appreciable effect seemed to have resulted from the fact that the criticisms of the mathematics had been adequately answered. No conversions were registered from among those critics.

Again, in the succeeding year, the criticism of the experimental conditions in the ESP experiments had become so heated that at its annual meeting in 1938, in Columbus, Ohio, the American Psychological Association held a Round Table discussion on the methods of the ESP research.[4] One of the critical speakers took the position that there was inadequate provision to exclude sensory cues in the ESP tests. However, this psychologist, when faced by the facts, fairly and frankly conceded publicly that he could see nothing wrong with the experimental controls against sensory cues maintained in the most crucial experiments. Those crucial experiments were naturally the ones on which the conclusions had been based. One of these was the Pearce-Pratt experiment already described. But was that critic persuaded, when his criticism was met, to reappraise the evidence? He was silenced; that is something, of course. But he is still sending out reprints of the critical article he had written before the APA Round Table. It does not appear that it was the possibility that sensory cues could explain the results that was really in his way after all.

Another psychologist at the discussion in Columbus claimed that the hypothesis of recording errors could explain all the results obtained in the ESP experiments. His opponent in the debate, however, showed effectively that in such an experiment as, for example, that of Pearce and Pratt, there was no possible way in which errors could be made so as to favor the ESP hypothesis. In that experiment, be it recalled, the recording was done completely independently and even in duplicate. The critic was left helpless to suggest any grounds for disqualifying such a series. But did this straightening out in any way change his attitude toward ESP? Rather, on occasions when there is no parapsychologist on hand to reply, he still repeats his earlier criticism,[5] even though that criticism was so adequately met at Columbus that this particular speaker refused to allow his paper to be published along with the series.

These facts certainly indicate something wrong, and it is not the evidence. Could it possibly be in the critics themselves? That professional scientists could be anything but open-minded, unprejudiced seekers after truth is naturally a little hard for the idealistic student of science to believe. The lad who remarked on his first look at a giraffe: "There ain't no such animal," was from away back in the sticks. One would not expect the same reaction from a psychologist with a Ph.D. degree, long-experienced in research and teaching. And yet there actually is one who, when asked what he thought of the ESP research, replied: "If it were on any other problem, one-tenth of the evidence would satisfy me. As it is, ten times the amount would not be enough." This university professor of psychology knows something about the ESP work, too, from fairly close acquaintance with it. One of his students once gave him a successful demonstration of it, under the conditions laid down by the professor himself. When this man says, "There ain't no such animal," one must look for some explanation of his opinions other than the weakness of the evidence. There would be no use in presenting him with better evidence or still more confirmation of results.

And so it seems now that it is high time to analyze the psychologist himself. What is this hidden factor that cuts off the light, closes the shutter, and prevents any registration of facts when these facts involve something like psi? Or more to the point is the question: What is it about psi that operates such a "cutoff"? What is it that the psychologists are avoiding and are so determined to avoid that they, like some of Galileo's confreres who refused to look through his telescope, will not even consider the evidence?

In such an inquiry into motives it is better, perhaps, not to try to impute reasons or attitudes to these psychologists who seem to be irrationally and unalterably opposed to the psi hypothesis. Fortunately, it is possible to quote a self-analysis bearing precisely on this question and recently published by one of the better known of the younger psychologists on this side of the Atlantic. He would appear to be representative of a large element in the profession.

He asks the question: "Why do we not accept ESP as a psychological fact?" And here is his own answer: "Rhine has offered enough evidence to have convinced us on almost any other issue where one could make some guess as to the mechanics of the disputed process. Some of his evidence has been explained away, but as far as I can find out, not all of it. Until a complete rebuttal is provided or until we accept ESP, let us not talk about enlarging our notions of neurology to meet the psychological 'facts' with no external criterion of what those facts are. *We are still trying to find our way out of the magic wood of animism* (italics mine), where psychology began historically, and we cannot give up the talisman of a knowledge of material processes. Personally, I do not accept ESP for a moment, because it does not make sense. My external criteria, both of physics and of physiology, say that ESP is not a fact despite the behavioral evidence that has been reported. I cannot see what other basis my colleagues have for rejecting it; and if they are using my basis, *they and I are allowing psychological evidence to be passed on by physical and physiological censors* (italics mine). Rhine may still turn out to be right, improbable as I think that is, and my own rejection of his views is—in a literal sense—prejudice."[6]

This honest analysis of the situation discloses what it is that is unacceptable about the psi evidence: *The phenomena do not submit to physical explanation.* A psychologist who is trying to find his way out of the "wood of animism," fighting what he suspects is only a disguised supernaturalism, fears that the admission of the psi findings to the field of psychology would cost that branch of learning its hard-earned status as a natural science. It would force upon psychology a philosophical dualism and throw it back into the classification with the occult, a classification from which it has long been fighting hard to escape.

The psychologist quoted can be, I think, considered a representative one; representative, that is, of all those who have an anti-psi bias. In his analysis he fairly represents not only the attitude of the majority of psychologists but a large number of scientists in general. In this straight-forward, plain-spoken account of his difficulties in accepting the ESP evidence he has told parapsychologists what they have long been needing to know. Now they should understand why they are making such slow headway with the psychology profession. They might wait a long time for a more honest look behind the rejection of the psi evidence than that provided by this quotation.

What makes this representative psychologist's statement especially significant is the fact that he does not allow himself merely to concoct some flimsy complaint about the evidence for psi. He concedes that it is not a question of the evidence; it is the fact, rather, that ESP is not physically explainable that creates the difficulty. As the tendency is with all of us who have been educated in the sciences in the Western world, the only grist his mill will grind is physical fact. It would seem a great pity that nature has overlooked this requirement and in psi phenomena produced something that is not physical, something that operates in such a manner as to produce *psychological* evidence. But at least one can see how hard it would be for a thoroughgoing devotee of materialism to accept a factor in man characterized by its nonphysical properties. It would *not* make sense.

The above candid quotation may, however, actually alter the situation by itself. It so completely lets the philosophical cat out of the psychologists' bag where it has been hiding all the time!

The hidden factor is now out in the open where at least it can be seen. Perhaps this very exposure and the clarification of this hitherto unrecognized element of prejudice is all that is needed to secure a fair hearing for the results at issue. For one thing, the statement of the representative psychologist may in itself carry some weight with those who feel as he does. After all, psychologists *may* go on rejecting psychological evidence even when it is beyond criticism, as he concedes he is doing, because it does not make physical sense; they *may* continue to make it impossible thus to find out if a nonphysical order of psychological process exists; they *may* go on sawing off the limb on which they are sitting; but it would seem that they should be less likely to do so once they recognize what they are doing.

This recognition by both psychologist and parapsychologist of the metaphysical factor in the bias against psi could in itself well be a turning point in the struggle to get fair recognition for whatever is new in the field of parapsychology. This clear formulation of the bias against which the research has had to struggle could easily become a classic event for parapsychology. At any rate, the illuminating words of the representative psychologist can never be withdrawn; it takes only one word to break a silence, one link to break a chain of resistance, one example to expose a fallacy. Any psychologist who has read those words will in the future at least be less likely to attempt to rationalize his philosophical bias into a hasty, ill-informed criticism of the psi experiments.

We, ourselves, in parapsychology can see our own position better the more we understand the viewpoint of the anti-psi bias of our representative psychologist. We should have known better than to expect to win that professional group with mere *psychological* evidence; not, at least, until the psychologists have found their way out of the philosophical wood they are in.

At this point we can profitably indulge in a bit of self-criticism and recognize that the beam has not been only in the eye of the psychologist but that something suspiciously like it is discernible in the parapsychologist's own eye. For now we can understand better the reason for the repetitive accumulation of independent confirmatory experiments in parapsychology that have been carried out through the decades. Each newcomer to this field has brought with him something of the same philosophical bias against anything in nature that is unexplainable by physical law and, accordingly, the evidence produced by *his* predecessors has seemed almost as incredible to him as it has to the representative psychologist. Perhaps the only way in which those who have eventually become parapsychologists differ from those who repudiate this field of research is their willingness to look, plus a certain grasp of the significance of the problems. The point is that this physicalistic prejudice is in everyone. For some, this negative prejudgment of the psi problem is set aside as the experimental facts come into view. With others, apparently with the large majority, that further scientific step of allowing the facts to correct presupposition has still to come.

After the above reflections it is now possible to see with greater detachment the whole controversy over ESP of the last fifteen years. One can understand the passionate extremes to which some of the antagonists of psi carried their activities in the heat of the battle. The mood of righteous indignation that some of the psychologists felt led them to do things they would not otherwise have done had they not evidently felt that they were defending their professional field from a menace that threatened to undermine its hard-earned scientific status. There is no need or desire to expose here, now that it is all over, the more intemperate efforts that were made to block the development of the psi researches and the publication of the reports. It should not have been surprising (though it was) that attempts were made by these critics to achieve their purpose in some instances through personal attacks upon the parapsychological workers, attacks that were not even confined to the open. In some cases pressure was brought to bear upon the departments to which these parapsychologists were attached and even upon the university administrations concerned. The editors of psychological journals and program committees for the professional scientific meetings felt, and in some cases responded to, this pressure to restrain what probably seemed a wild excursion into the hinterlands of the occult, a hinterland from which psychology had rescued itself.

Altogether, this period of outspoken criticism, with its undercurrent of hostility of many forms, is not one of which anyone will ever be proud. But, as the representative psychologist would interpret it, these psychologist critics did not see any sense in psi evidence because it could not be interpreted physically. To them it was all unsound, phony; it had to be; yet here it was capturing the imagination and attention of a large public and even a fair number of professional people as well. As one psychologist put it in one of his critical articles: "The public is being misled, the energies of young men and women in their most vital years of professional training are being diverted into a side-issue, and funds expended that might instead support research in problems of real importance for human welfare. This has gone so far that a new *Journal of Parapsychology* has been founded."[7] He plaintively hoped that "it might seem unnecessary to prick the bubble as the truth eventually will out and the craze subside." Referring, of course, to the public interest in ESP.

The bubble, however, refused to be pricked; or, rather, it seems to have turned out to be a porcupine; and the "craze" has developed into a serious, intelligent interest on the part of the general public, both here and abroad. Not only that, but this interest has, in turn, sustained the researches (even if on slender margin) in the universities and has helped it to spread to all the continents where research is carried on. Gloomy as the picture of reaction among psychologists is as given by the Warner surveys, those surveys nevertheless show that even amongst the most established section of the psychologists themselves during the period between the two surveys, the percentage of psychologists recognizing ESP as an established fact or a likely possibility rose from 8.8 per cent in 1938 to 16.6 per cent in 1952. Slow as it is, this is at least evidence of progress in an area where, as one now can see, it might least have been expected.

By this time tempers have cooled and better judgment is possible. More than ever it should be clear that the methods of natural science should provide the basis for a decision, not only about psi itself, but even about this underlying issue that has been blocking the attention of psychologists to the evidence. The question whether or not there is anything genuine in that evidence is one that psychology will have to deal with on the level of empirical science. It dare not leave it to speculation or assumption or faith to decide whether or not there is any reality in personality beyond what has been discovered by means of the physical sciences.

The entire difficulty with the psychologists, then, boils down to something that can be settled by experiment. Better still, the experimentation has already been done. The answer to the representative psychologist's rejection of ESP because it doesn't make sense in physical terms is that it is now experimental fact anyhow. The metaphysical assumption that requires all evidence of natural law to be physical is itself in error. The assumptions of science have to give way in the face of contradicting facts, or science would not fit the realities of nature: they would not work or apply. The odds are good that the representative psychologist sees this point himself, and those whom he represents will gradually see it, too. Then they will know that it was just a working assumption that said all nature had to be physical, and one that has too long been overworked.

At this point some will ask how extraphysical operations can be investigated by physical means, as would appear to be necessary. That question, however, need not trouble the parapsychologist. In many of the sciences the research is done almost entirely by indirect methods, relying upon converted, secondary effects to investigate principles that are not directly observable. A radio wave furnishes a familiar example; it cannot be sensed at all, and to be detected has to be converted to another form of energetic effect. Similarly, if it is to be observed and recorded, a psi operation has to be changed over to an effect the senses can deal with, in ESP the subject's overt response, and in PK the way the dice have fallen. Most of the world of science depends on the translation of one effect into another for record, psychology as much as any other branch. Subjective states can only be observed in another person as behavior, and that is a conversion of psychical to physical effects.

Thus far this chapter has dealt mainly with the opening of the lock of metaphysical prejudice which has been barring the way to scientific progress into a new area of inquiry. This rusty mechanism deeply overlaid by confused thinking about the nature of man is an anachronism that ought now to be laid away in the museum of the history of ideas. It belongs on the shelf beside the fifteenth century concept of the flatness of the earth. That idea held back the explorers and geographers from new worlds just as the materialistic dogma about human nature is doing to the psychologists, among other groups of scientists, in the twentieth century. This disproved notion belongs now with that long series of discarded concepts that at one time or another have confined human thought: geocentrism, special creation, animal magnetism, Newtonian mechanics, the evil-spirit theory of epidemics, and the like.

If a sufficiently large number of the students of the psychological sciences today should come to see this mechanistic concept of man as a museum piece, then certainly more and more of the psychologists for whom our representative psychologist speaks will come to recognize that the proper study of psychology is, after all, psychology; not physics, not even physiology. Naturally physics and physiology are involved in problems of psychology, but these fields have their own principles, and psychology should have its own as well.

I said earlier that no comprehensive review of the total evidence for psi is possible. What is possible, and may be helpful, is to review the advancing lines of evidence as they fan out from the shores of this new world into which the researches have progressed. A few representative experiments along the various lines can be spotlighted but many students will want more than these and will also wish to base their final judgments upon at least some of the original reports. To do so is necessary if they are to make up their own minds in the soundest possible fashion concerning this evidence. The justification for outlining the evidence here is partly in the fact that panoramas, too, and larger perspectives, have their value. Just now one is needed for preparation for what is to follow in this book. Such a perspective may even be useful to some extent in guiding the research student to the localized area into which he may desire to go more exhaustively.

The first line of evidence of psi is composed of the results of the tests carried out specifically for the purpose of finding out if psi occurs. The goal in these experiments was to see if results above chance could still be obtained when safeguards were set up against all counterhypotheses that have been suggested. One of the most striking of these is the Pratt-Woodruff series of ESP tests carried out at Duke in 1939.[8] This experiment was designed for the express purpose of meeting all the criticisms that came up during the years of controversy. In the entire history of psychology no experiment has ever been carried out with such elaborate controls against all possible error. Five pages were required for a full account of these precautions in the report, but I shall take the space here only to review the main outlines of precaution taken.

The experiment was built around the success which Dr. J. L. Woodruff, now of the College of the City of New York, but then a graduate student in psychology at Duke, had had in getting results in ESP tests from unselected subjects. Dr. Pratt was in charge of the experiment. His function was to insure that all the precautions outlined were in full force throughout.

The test was designed to control against error, both conscious and unconscious. Experimenter JLW held a shuffled pack of ESP cards (the target cards that were to be identified) face down behind an opaque screen. The subject on the opposite side of the screen had five key cards, on each of which was printed a different one of five symbols, hung up on his side of the screen so that JLW could not see their order. This order was a random one and was arranged by the second experimenter, JGP, who, although he, of course, knew the order of the key cards, did not handle the target cards. In the operation of the test the subject pointed underneath the card he thought matched the top card in the target pack which JLW held in his hand. The pointer was visible to JLW through an opening in the screen (which gave one-way visibility only). At that point the experimenter laid the top card (in his hand) in the designated position on his side of the screen, still keeping it face down. At no time did he look at the cards during the test, the point being that he, not knowing the card in his hand or the symbol represented by the subject's pointer, could not, either by error or by fraud, place the card to fit the target. The subject continued pointing to key cards and the experimenter continued laying down cards until the pack was finished. Then

JLW turned the cards over and recorded their position before learning the order of the key cards. Experimenter JGP recorded the position of the key cards, before knowing the order in which the cards had been laid. Each man deposited a copy of his record in a locked box and only then, after removing the screen, did they check the target cards against the five key cards for number of successes. Thus the location of the experimenters and the entire arrangement of the test were such that neither experimenter alone could willingly or unwittingly produce any sort of error that could bring about extrachance results. Neither could the subject. At the time of publication the research report was reviewed by a number of critical psychologists (whose comments were also published[9]) and has been in print for about fourteen years. There has thus far been no reasonable criticism made of this experiment and no call for a further improvement on its controls.

What were the results? In 2,400 runs through the pack there were 489 hits above the number to be expected from chance alone. This result can be evaluated in terms of a critical ratio which, for this amount, is approximately 5.00. Now the likelihood that a critical ratio as large as that would occur by chance alone is something like one in a million. The results, therefore, were not due to chance. No explanation has been proposed that will account for them except that of extrasensory perception. Such perception of unknown objects would be clairvoyance.

This experimental series, as stated above, was made in order to see what results could be obtained when the conditions met all the criticisms, reasonable and unreasonable, that had been leveled at the work previously done. To be sure, it would not make any difference how many locked boxes there were or how many experimenters were watching each other or how many tiers of precautions were heaped upon a test procedure such as this if those who were passing judgment on it were not sufficiently detached to consider the results on their merits. A strong enough bias can, of course, keep the best evidence from being given a fair hearing. But it would appear that if the Pratt-Woodruff results are considered fairly, the proper question would be that of why any further experiments are needed to confirm the hypothesis of ESP.

Incidentally, not a few psychologists would be interested to learn that the highest scoring rate achieved by any of the Pratt-Woodruff subjects participating in this series was that of a psychologist who frankly says he finds it extremely unpleasant to be forced to the conclusion that it seems there is this thing called ESP. He had responded to Woodruff's request for subjects for the tests primarily because the latter was doing other research work under him.

Another strong position in the main line of ESP evidence is represented by the work of the two British investigators, Soal and Goldney,[10] which has already been mentioned. Dr. Soal, a mathematician of Queen Mary College, London, set out to repeat the Duke experiments, although, as it happened, he was quite skeptical about them. For more than two years of investigation he had been unable to get extrachance scores in his tests and was finally about to report his failure to confirm the American results. However, a British psychologist, Whately Carington, who had also been experimenting on the problem of ESP, called Soal's attention to an effect he himself had found in his own results and had called "displacement." He had noted the tendency of a subject to hit the next target (either forward or backward in the series) to the one at which he was aiming. Carington urged Soal to look for this effect in his own data. Soal did so. It was present to a marked degree in the records produced by two of the subjects he had tested. Thereupon he and Mrs. K. M. Goldney, an officer of the Society for Psychical Research, set to work to see if this displacement effect would continue. With one of the former subjects they carried out a new series of experiments under very strict conditions.

They found that the displacement did continue. After two and a half years of work and card tests consisting of 11,378 trials, they obtained results that, when all corrections are made, left them the remarkably high critical ratio of 13.6 and a corresponding probability that would require 35 digits to express. Soal's forthcoming book[11] will include a full report of this work.

It is difficult to do justice to so extensive an experiment as this. Only those who have labored for years under the strain of equally complex precautions can come anywhere near appreciating the evidential quality of these results. Such a person surely is entitled to wonder why anyone asks for further evidence. After all, what more could further evidence add to the assurance that under certain conditions ESP does occur?

There may be those who would feel an added assurance that results in this area are reliable if more recording and counting machinery had been used. In the glorification of the machine that seems to characterize the present age, there are many who tend to think that if a machine is used in obtaining a result, that makes it really authoritative. Now actually some of the confidence in gadgetry is well deserved, but some of it is poppycock to the experienced research worker. In every case of the use of machines in testing psi someone has had to check and double-check on the accuracy of the machine. A human observer has had to see that the machine was performing properly. Thus complete duplication by nonmechanical methods was required anyway. Then, too, in the use of machines, there are always judgments of exceptional instances, interpretations of doubtful cases, or readings and computations of some sort in all of which the human factor is involved.

The first requirement of a sound procedure is, of course, complete objectivity of recording and computing. When and if this can be accomplished more efficiently by machine than by human beings, well and good. It should be *done* that way. But, as any qualified experimenter knows, it can also be achieved without machines and without risk to the research. A research can be so carried out that no errors can be made to favor any theory or mislead anyone. All such safeguards should be included in the design of the experiment. As already demonstrated, in the Pearce-Pratt and the Pratt-Woodruff series the experiment was so set up that these precautions were included. Similar provisions were made against error in the Soal and Goldney experiments. It has now become a more or less standard procedure in the psi work on which any major conclusions are to be based that all precautions against error are included in the experimental design. For example, the person who makes out one record or who checks one record is by design kept ignorant of the other record. Any errors made under that condition could not produce evidence of psi; they could only favor the chance hypothesis. At the most they could only dilute any evidential value the results might have. And by the time the data are checked and rechecked, errors in checking or computation are reduced to the vanishing point.

An example of a mechanical method of handling ESP test data has recently been reported.[12] It occurs in a series of experiments carried out at Harvard University by a student, S. David Kahn, assisted by another student, Ulric Neisser, and with some collaboration from the Psychology Department. The tests were so set up that the record sheets could be scored by the International Test Scoring Machine, manufactured by the International Business Machine Corporation. A target sheet was made out and turned over by arrangement, to be filed in a locked cabinet of the Department of Psychology, while the record sheets were distributed to the subjects, who were instructed to try to fill them out so as to match the positions filled out in the target record. Kahn reported that from the total call trials registered numbering 43,278 he obtained an excess of hits of 271 and that the odds against getting so large a deviation in such a series by chance alone are in the neighborhood of one in a thousand.

Another example of mechanical aid in testing can be drawn from one of the PK investigations. This work comes from the Department of Physics of the University of Pittsburgh and was done by Dr. Robert A. McConnell and his associates using a machine constructed at the Duke Parapsychology Laboratory. The machine was designed to throw dice automatically in a long, slender, transparent box that rotates and to photograph them when they had fallen. The subject, of course, had no physical contact with the machine; he was asked to try to influence the fall of the dice by direct mental action. While this work is still awaiting publication, it has been briefly announced in print as having given significantly positive results, adding further to the evidence of PK.[13]

The second line of research results consists of evidence within the evidence. It consists of traces unwittingly and incidentally left along the main course of development.

One of the most common examples of this type of evidence

is the effect associated with the position of a trial in a series. The most familiar of the position effects is the decline of scoring rate within a run (or in some other unit of the experiment) of card calls, dice throws, or other serial trials. Far back among the earliest psi investigations it was noticed that the scoring rate of subjects tended to fall off if they were kept at the task through a long run of trials. Professor Charles Richet, the French physiologist, pointed this out in his book, *Thirty Years of Psychical Research*. Dr. G. H. Estabrooks noted a similar decline in a run of only twenty trials in his ESP tests at Harvard,[14] as did also Miss Ina Jephson,[15] a British investigator, even in a short five-trial run. Declines became so apparent early in the investigations at the Duke Laboratory that they have come to be recognized as an almost characteristic feature of ESP, at least with a certain type of test.

The point here is that these declines in scoring are in themselves good evidence of psi, and, if possible, more difficult of explanation in terms other than psi than the results of high scoring. Take, for example, the Estabrooks test at Harvard. Estabrooks had subjects in one room attempting to identify playing cards at which he was looking in an adjoining room. The connecting door was closed. His results were significantly above chance. Critics could (and did) say with at least a grain of reason that perhaps there was some sensory cue that could be heard through the closed door. But it turned out that Estabrooks' subjects dropped so greatly in scoring rate from the first half of the run to the second that the difference between the two halves was in itself an extrachance phenomenon. No one then could say that that difference could be attributed to sensory cues. If there had been any sensory basis for the results it should have worked at least as well in the last as in the first part of the run. Also, when Estabrooks removed the subject to a more distant room, and the average score fell to a point nearer than expected from chance, the decline continued, nevertheless, and even became more pronounced. There can be no reasonable explanation for the decline based on sensory cues, and this work of Estabrooks is a much better confirmation of the ESP hypothesis than even Estabrooks himself knew it was at the time.

The already described Pratt-Woodruff series of ESP tests offers still another example of evidence within evidence. In this series different sizes of symbols were used. They varied from large, heavy symbols to very, very small ones. The objective had been to get some idea as to the importance of the size of the target. Now it was found that as long as these symbols, any one type of them, were new to the experiment, the subjects made higher average scores with them than they did later when a given size of symbol had been used for some time. When the first half of the tests made with any given size of symbol was set off against the second half, the whole Pratt-Woodruff series showed a difference so great that it would not be expected by chance once in a thousand experiments of this size. Here, then, was a secondary effect within the psi test data which was not discovered until, months later, it was caught in the course of the routine, independently checked analyses. There was no possible change of conditions that could have brought about this comparatively regular decline.

Even by this time the reader may well be more than satiated with evidence of the occurrence of psi. Nothing short of an extravagantly built-up conception that it was necessary to have better and better evidence and to avoid even the most highly speculative possibility of error could ever have led to the long-drawn-out and endlessly patient search that was involved in following up these position effects for more evidence from within the evidence.

For the parapsychologist, of course, all this now means something more than simply evidence for ESP. He has long been curious to know the cause of the declines. He is now more interested in such facts as that the size of the symbols meant nothing in itself, that its novelty did make a difference, and that the novelty did apparently wear off and produce a decline of scoring rate. He is now looking for possible explanations.

There literally are volumes of this evidence from these internal differences, mostly in the form of declines. In some researches the subject knew when the end of the run was coming. In such cases his scores would rise at the very end of the run so that over the last few calls he would score almost as highly as he had at the beginning. Such primacy and terminal effects were so general that they came to be characterized as "salience" and were recognized as characteristic of psi performance under certain test conditions.

All these secondary effects, evidence within evidence, are, of course, unconsciously produced. The subject does not know that his scores are declining. It is safe to say that, if he knew how he was getting his psi effects, then he could tell introspectively how and when declines were taking place and this decrease in scoring rate would not be allowed to occur. But psi is unconscious and it *does* occur. This fact has to be faced, and it is to be expected that still further consequences of the unconscious character of the psi process will be encountered.

Another of these buttressing types of evidence is the displacement effect. I have already mentioned this as the factor that saved Soal from writing off his work as a failure when displacement was called to his attention by Carington. Actually, the first displacement results ever reported had been noticed by the American astrophysicist, Dr. C. G. Abbot,[16] then Executive Secretary of the Smithsonian Institution. He found in a series of ESP tests with himself as subject that under certain conditions of fatigue he tended to miss the target and hit the neighboring card. But the most significant and extensive work giving evidence of displacement came from the English workers, first Whately Carington and, following his suggestion, S. G. Soal. In all these cases, however, the evidence came to light after the work had been completed and, in Soal's case, as mentioned, even as he was about to dismiss all his results as explainable by chance.

The strongest evidence of psi that has yet been encountered on this secondary line occurs in the research on PK. It is the result of what is called the QD or quarter-distribution analyses of the position of the data on the record sheet. It will be recalled from the preceding chapter that in these analyses the record sheets from all the dice-throwing tests available were quartered for a comparison of the frequency of the hits falling in different sections of the record page. The greatest clustering of hits occurred in the upper left quarter and the lowest percentage in the lower right. This made a diagonal decline across the page that was a combination of a top-bottom decline and a left-right decline. This effect has prevailed in a general way through a large number of experimental series. Since all the data that could be combined in this way had been pooled when these analyses were made, these QD analyses were carried out many years after the original research had been completed. It was not until then that the idea of looking for such internal evidence had occurred. The results of the analyses of position effects, since they supported the direct evidence, seemed to be definitive against any sort of hypothesis of error yet proposed.

Even so, when Dr. Humphrey and I had finished with this comprehensive QD analysis, in order to guard still further against any possibility that we had somehow fooled ourselves in the conviction to which this internal data was driving us anew, we called in Dr. Pratt. As it happened, he had spent the summer several hundred miles from us and so had nothing to do with our analyses. Neither had he participated in the original work on which it was based. He was asked to go over the whole thing independently with a view to showing us for our own information just what an inquiring committee would find if it went over the analyses we had made. Dr. Pratt's recheck[17] showed that we had made remarkably few errors—on the whole none serious enough to make a noticeable change in the results. His totals effectively confirmed our own and assured us that the case is one that will stand up under the most objective analysis.

The recent McConnell work, previously mentioned, in which an automatic film-recording device was used, showed this same type of decline. In that work also the decline produced a resulting difference that is mathematically significant of an extrachance factor. This is the best type of evidence of the occurrence of PK.

There is a further line of evidence for the reality of psi: the third. It concerns the studies of personality in relation to psi capacities. A great deal of effort has now been made to see whether ESP or PK correlate with any personality type or trait or condition. The results constitute a solid body of quite independent evidence of itself. One of the most interesting features of this kind of evidence is that it has in great part come from test series that did not produce scores of extrachance significance and therefore would otherwise have been passed over as explainable by pure chance.

Take, for example, the extensive studies of Dr. Gertrude Schmeidler,[18] a psychologist at the College of the City of New York. Dr. Schmeidler, working in conjunction with Dr. Gardner Murphy, found that when she gave ESP tests to her students in the classroom after first getting records of their attitudes toward the possibility of ESP (favorable or unfavorable), she could, on the basis of this attitude alone, divide the group into two score levels. The sheep, as the "favorable" subjects were called, tended to score above the chance average of five hits per twenty-five, and the goats, as the "unfavorable" subjects were called, tended to average below. Over the last decade Dr. Schmeidler has accumulated a vast amount of such data, and the same relationship has held to a remarkably consistent degree. If all the differences she found between the two groups are combined, they make a strong case against a chance theory. The odds are at least a million to one against the occurrence of so large a combined difference by chance alone.

It would take a long time to go thoroughly into this sheep-goat research of Dr. Schmeidler's, for the glimpse I have given is only the beginning; in fact, Dr. Schmeidler's book on the subject of her work, now in preparation, should be consulted by anyone desiring an adequate account of it. Using the Rorschach test and later still others, she went on into the study of the personality traits of her subjects. By means of these tests she was able to effect still further and clearer separations of those who tended to score above from those who tended to score below chance average.[19]

As a matter of fact, if one should have amnesia for all the earlier psi data when tackling the Schmeidler work and should start all over again, forgetting the earlier evidence I have presented, one would still be driven after the Schmeidler study to a conviction that only extrasensory perception could explain these results. Dr. Schmeidler and Dr. Murphy have not, of course, been working all these years just to pile up more evidence of ESP, but the evidence secured as to the relationship of psi and personality quite effectively serves this purpose too.

There are other sectors on this personality line of evidence representing different kinds of personality studies and different kinds of psi tests that might be mentioned. For instance, the late

Dr. Charles E. Stuart of the Parapsychology Laboratory at Duke found that he could successfully separate high and low scorers in ESP tests on the basis of certain psychological ratings.[20] One of these which he developed was an interest test—a test in which the subject indicated his likes and dislikes down a long list of pertinent topics. With the addition of certain improvements[21] which Dr. Betty M. Humphrey added after Dr. Stuart's death, this interest test has proved successful to a significant degree in affording a basis of separating high and low scorers in the large number of series to which it has been applied.

Dr. Humphrey developed still another method of separating the high and low scorers in ESP tests.[22] Her separation test consisted of rating certain features of the drawings which the subject made as a part of a clairvoyance ESP test. The subject was presented with a picture enclosed in an opaque envelope. He was asked to make a drawing of what he thought it might be. These drawings had been accumulated by Dr. Stuart, with whom Miss Humphrey, then a graduate student in psychology, was working in this research. The latter then rated the resulting drawings as to certain form qualities, such as the tendency to an inordinate expansiveness or, on the other hand, to undue compressiveness (criteria taken from the Elkisch method of appraising drawings in a test of maladjustment in children). She found it possible thereby to separate high and low scorers in the ESP test. More than that, she found that there were characteristic differences in the scoring between the expansives and compressives in clairvoyance and telepathy tests. The expansives scored positively in clairvoyance and negatively in telepathy while the compressives did the reverse.

I must observe that each of these paragraphs in which I so briefly describe a piece of research represents years of work. For full appraisal and appreciation it would be necessary to consult a number of different scientific reports. Again, amnesia for all but the personality studies would show that that line of evidence alone would also inescapably indicate the operation of the factor we have called psi.

There is, however, at least one more clearly discernible line of evidence even further out, and I should mention it. In a way it is the most technical one yet. At any rate its description is the most difficult of all to abbreviate, and yet for any honest intellectual critic who still has a residue of doubt in his mind it is perhaps the most inescapable. This is the line in which the most refined and sifted and superanalyzed sort of evidence is to be found. It has been refined by a sort of redistillation of the distillates of the evidence that was developed through the other methods of analysis.

One or two examples will suffice. Let me take the reinforcement effect discovered by Soal in the work which he did with Mrs. Goldney. He and Dr. Pratt,[23] after a long series of studies, extracted and firmly established the existence of this effect which is double displacement. In the displacement which Soal and Goldney found originally it will be recalled that the subject, in working with one particular sender, tended to go forward *or* backward to the card adjacent in sequence to the target. Soal and Pratt found that when the same symbol occurred on the card just before and on the card just after the target (say, the cards are star, circle, star when the subject calls star opposite the circle), it looked as if the combination of both forward and backward displacement gave the subject not merely double the amount of ESP success but something like five or six times as much. The results are very significant, very far from a chance effect. The odds against getting so marked an effect by pure chance are of the order of thousands to one. Indeed, it is one of the most striking effects yet encountered in this field of unusual effects, and it challenges further inquiry accordingly. It especially presents psychological problems: Why did this one subject give this effect with this one sender? And how, one would especially like to know, did he do it?

Such analyses as these require careful and expert handling of the delicate instruments of statistical analysis, but the work in parapsychology has been particularly blest in one respect, and for this we are most grateful. It has appealed to a large number of the most able statisticians, particularly in this country and Great Britain. These experts have been almost literally looking over our shoulders as we have worked on these problems through the years. There can be no doubt that a great share of the dependability of the results is due to this generous collaboration.

The reinforcement effect is just one example. It would take too much space to tell about all the odd effects that have been found on this line in the course of the deep-dredging statistical analyses that have been made. But I shall mention some of the "subterranean" psychological effects that are emerging from the more advanced analyses. I will take, for example, the consistent missing effect discovered by Dr. Remi Cadoret in work he did with Dr. Pratt.[24] Examining old data, Cadoret at first suspected and then, from analysis, established that certain subjects, in their ESP calls, form peculiar associations between symbols. Certain individual subjects, for instance, may persistently call a star a circle. But he may not necessarily reverse the wrong association and call a circle a star, and he may not make any regular mistakes with any other symbols. Of course, we suspect that there is some deep-laid psychological reason for such a tie-up; we now know, in any case, that it does occur in some cases significantly enough that there is very little question of the effect being a real extrachance result.

Next in this inspection of evidence comes a most peculiar variety. It consists of a type of data that tends to cancel the ordinary evidence instead of add to it. It is an effect that has done much to frustrate the experimenter's effort to produce high score totals in psi tests. The phenomenon referred to is known as psi-missing;[25] it shows up in the test results in the form of a significant negative deviation produced by a scoring rate *below* the average which chance alone would give. It is as if the subject were trying to miss the cards, though we know fairly well by this time that this is not the explanation. It is more like the case of a rifleman who unwittingly gets his sights out of line and thereafter the better he aims the more consistently he misses the target. The Cadoret type of consistent missing mentioned above is just one example of general psi-missing. In that case a wrong connection is consistently made between two different symbols.

Psi-missing fooled everyone badly, indeed, for a long time before it was recognized. But now that it has been found out, it turns evidence of special value. This is the way it goes: A subject may be trying his utmost to obtain *high* scores and the experimenter, too, is interested in the same objective. Something, however, throws the subject off a little in some subtle way of which he is unaware and he, therefore, consistently scores so far below the chance average that the mathematician says that it is not reasonably to be called a chance performance. If this happens again and again, as it has, it represents something meaningful in addition to the evidence of ESP itself. It is, of course, as valuable and definite evidence of ESP as an equally large *positive* deviation would be. The significance of the negative deviation is the same as the positive. There is, however, an added fact about ESP and the conditions under which it can occur in this psi-missing effect. This further connection will come up again later. For the moment it is enough to note that in the psi-missing results we have evidence of psi that was not known of at the time of the experiment, either by the subject or by the experimenter. This unwitting, unexpected, involuntary, backhanded kind of support of the case is as indisputable as the best fingerprint evidence.

And, finally, there is still one further type of evidence of psi. Should there be any remaining interest in the kinds of support the case for psi has received it should be directed to what amounts to a fifth line of evidence—a sort of hilltop position that commands a more general range of observation and outlook. The review already given has shown that any piecemeal or section by section appraisal of so large a body of evidence can give no adequate over-all picture. There is too much to comprehend in any local scene. A better perspective can be gained by examining the interrelations of the major researches and attempting to arrive at a general rationale as to the strength, consistency, and reliability of the general case.

It is noteworthy first that ESP and PK together make up a functional unit, a unit that makes sense. It is not only that they are analogous to the parallel sensorimotor system which functions through known physical interrelation between organism and environment. It is more than that. The concept of *reaction* is an integral part of the more basic idea of causation. Until there is some reason to do otherwise, one will naturally continue trying to think about psi phenomena in terms of causation (even while we respect Dr. C. G. Jung's suggestion that in psi operations his hypothesis of synchronicity may supplant causation[26]). From whichever end of the subject-object relation one starts out, he theoretically must trace an action that calls for a counterpart re-action. The psychophysical interoperation in either ESP or PK is, I think, to be regarded as a reversible one. The simplest opera-tion of PK seems to require the occurrence of ESP to make the process rationally comprehensible. The subject's action on the object has to be cognitively guided. For that sensory perception is insufficient.

Conversely, it has often been pointed out that if ESP occurs, then something like PK would have to result in accordance with the Law of Reaction. (For every action there is a reaction.) The idea is that some reaction must occur to the object end of the subject-object action involved in ESP, and the subject would have to leave some effect on the object itself when in a perceptual ex-perience it acts psychophysically on the subject. It would, of course, require a PK reaction.

There is another of these larger relationships that makes sense. It is the fact that, as far as the investigations have gone, ESP is found to be independent of both space *and* time. Certainly it would not make sense if it were found to be dependent upon one of the two and not upon the other, any more than it would to have obtained evidence of either ESP *or* PK but not of both. In either case one would be infinitely more puzzled to fit these fragmentary findings into the natural order of things than is the case as it is.

There is a third point, too, in this appeal to reason. It is the fact that telepathy and clairvoyance seem to combine well under a single comprehensive heading, extrasensory perception. Al-though no one yet knows what the final investigation of telepathy is going to yield, it would be reasonable to expect that a psi func-tion that operates independently of space and time might show a comparable freedom from limitations as to *what* it could perceive as target or stimulus. The evidence of telepathy and clairvoy-ance together indicates a wide diversity of stimulus range. In other words, even with present limited understanding, there is a certain rational consistency in this independence of space and time on the one hand and this independence of specific target limitation found in the telepathy and clairvoyance studies on the other hand.

There is one point on which it is safe to be emphatic: The discovery that psi functions at an unconscious level advanced the rational understanding of psi more than any other psychological observation that has been made about it. Once it was realized that the subject in a psi test has no reliable knowledge of when his experience occurs and whether or not it is correct, many of the most curious and confusing effects that had turned up made sense at once. The most baffling of all these was the psi-missing effect with its negative score deviation. The list of the other consequences of this handicap of unconsciousness is a long one, including declines, displacements, reinforcement, consistent missing, salience, and the like. With the recognition of the unconsciousness of psi the elusiveness of the phenomena could be understood and the mystery was removed from many a frustrating failure. For it had been shown that good intent on a conscious level is not sufficient. Psi operates in a deeper stratum and the conditions there are important also.

There is one further essential point in the psi rationale: Psi effects are lawful in their way, and quite as much so as any other occurrence in nature. Not only do normal people have them, but the same mathematics may be applied to them as to memory tests. Psi may be motivated by the same sort of purposive effort and interfered with by the same types of distraction or inhibitions. In a word, psi is not unlawful, unnatural, supernatural, or anything of the kind. It operates with sufficient similarity to other mental functions to indicate that it belongs to the domain of personality. The distinctive feature is that it clearly is not physical, no matter what else there may be about a person that is. The characteristic rationality of this lawful integration of psi with the personality as a whole is the answer to a lot of anxious doubts about its reality.

Here, too, is a natural happening that is not physical itself, yet is still capable of interacting with the physical world. That is what one sees occurring in these very tests. It has to be that. A psi effect could never be discovered if the psi part of the operation did not register eventually upon some physical aspect of nature which can be apprehended by the senses. It is much the same as the case of cosmic radiation; the sensory endings cannot intercept it, and it would be entirely unknown if there were not instruments through which it is converted to something that does register on human organs of reception. One might say that a human being is so constructed that within himself he contains some kind of conversion mechanism for turning psi effects into sensorially perceptible effects or sensory equivalents in experience (hallucinations, dreams, etc.). Man has his own "Geiger counter" for that energy-converting job.

But to try to tie a metaphysical dualism to the psi process just because it has been found to be a nonphysical element in nature is only making unnecessary difficulties. From the facts on record about this new world of psi operations it is absurd to force such a connection. There is obvious interaction between subject and object if there is anything at all. And if interaction is to make any sense, some common basis for it must exist in the two interacting systems. That logical necessity is enough to rule out the possibility of any absolute dualism. Just now the emphasis upon unification and the basis of interaction is the more important, since the distinction between what is physical and what is nonphysical has been established.

This latter relationship can be called a *relative* dualism (as it could a relative monism). There are many such relative dualisms in nature and they need not be upsetting. If there were any absolute dualisms no one would ever know it. It takes interaction to convey evidence, and the slightest interaction itself would refute the absoluteness. It is time for less nonsense over imputed dualisms and more emphasis upon ways of finding out what it is that bridges the gap they represent and how deep they go.

There are definite limits, of course, and the main goals of research are still far from attainment. The science of parapsychology has now advanced beyond the stage of a haphazard conglomeration of patchy incoordinated results that characterizes every area of exploration at its beginning. Even so, neither a basic insight into the nature of psi nor a usable mastery over its operation has been achieved. As to basic understanding, however, the new field is no worse off than the whole of general psychology; that older science is itself still far from understanding even the nature of understanding.

On the other problem, that of gaining control over the exercise of psi capacity, the handicap is very great. The stage of nicely repeatable experiments that would allow the demonstration of psi effects on any or all occasions has not yet been reached. At the present point of progress such a question is not yet even in order. From this survey it should be plain that the occurrence of psi is still largely spontaneous. There are so many uncontrolled variables in its functioning over which the experimenter cannot count on keeping reliable mastery that he must at this stage still work with considerable uncertainty. He must be sure, however —and he can be—that when he does get results they will be due to psi and nothing else but psi. That is the criterion, the level, of the present period of the psi research. It will be a different one later, of course, when and if the psi explorer learns to produce psi itself on demand.

In the meantime, let no one be allowed to say unchallenged that because there is still much to learn about a phenomenon, therefore nothing is known; that because an effect cannot be produced on demand, it has never been produced. Once one understands adequately what the known results indicate, and along with that something of the vast amount that still remains to be found out, he will not expect of a pioneer research that complete mastery and control be immediately achieved before the subject is mentioned.

Not inconceivably the intellectual task of readjustment to the psi findings will, for a sizable percentage of professional men, be too great a shift to make in a lifetime; but for those who care to make the effort, those to whom the intellectual challenge seems worth taking up, the rest of this book is dedicated. It seems fair to proceed now in these pages, as is being done in the research, on the assumption that there is a firm basis of experimental facts to confirm some, at least, of the hypotheses suggested by the spontaneous psychic experiences.

It is time now to raise the horizons a little and to include in the perspective the relation of these facts to the neighboring areas of science. It was necessary, as already explained, before going on to this larger effort to show that the foothold the research results have given on the shores of the new world is a thor-

oughly secure one. And now that that has been done, there is
one more introductory step. Preparatory to reaching out to this
larger perspective of relations, I shall first consider in the chapter
that follows what is known about this new world and especially
its internal relationships. Just such a review of the facts will be
basic to the later discussion chapters.

Chapter 3

THE PRESENT RESEARCH FRONTIERS

■ What do the first-drawn charts reveal of the outlines of this new world? Now that the evidence for psi has been surveyed, the question that most demands attention concerns the basic types of psi phenomena: What are they and how fundamentally distinguishable are they? These questions merge with the problem of the scope and character of the psi function itself, and beyond these arises the question of the place of psi in the total personality of man and in the general setting of nature.

There has been some difficulty in distinguishing between types of psi. As discussed earlier, there is still a need for experiments to discriminate more conclusively between telepathy and clairvoyance. Some people are not satisfied that experiments in precognition and psychokinesis have been so conducted as to make their explanations mutually exclusive. A few years ago there was something of a good-humored controversy within the field of parapsychology itself over these issues, although, as of this writing, it appears to have pretty well subsided.

It has been common practice to divide all psi, and that means all psychic phenomena, into those that result in physical effects (psychokinesis) and those that result in a form of experience (extrasensory perception). It seems logical to think, however, that these two broad types of psi represent mere arbitrarily selected aspects of the same basic psychophysical (subject-object) interaction, and that these are only end products. The effect measured in the PK test is one made upon the object; in ESP it is upon the subject. (Probably there are combinations of ESP and PK in natural occurrences of psi, and even other modifications or intermediate forms.) Thus the purpose and design of the experiment determines which end of subject-object relation is to be stressed. The fact that in the individual this fundamental ESP-PK relationship parallels the sensorimotor relationship between subject and object gives plausibility to the concept of a basic unity of these psi operations. It must be remembered, however, that the support of this concept of unity is still largely a matter of logic rather than experiment.

A more serious classification problem is presented by precognition. The practice has grown up of speaking of ESP of future events as something deserving a name of its own, while ESP of events far distant in space is still unqualified ESP. This usage probably is a reflection of the thought patterns of the time rather than a fundamental distinction relating to differences in the processes. It is impossible with present-day concepts to understand the operation by which a subject could perceive an objective event of the future, one that has not yet occurred. It is easier to imagine that a subject could perceive an object distant only in a geographic dimension. But mere imaginability has proved to mean little or nothing even in the study of the physical world. Something, however, has had to be conceded to convenience at the expense of consistency in many a science older than parapsychology. For the same reason it is likely that simply as a practical measure the use of the term, precognition, as designating a separate psi category will continue.

A more fundamental difficulty arises in the attempt to distinguish between telepathy and clairvoyance; in fact, the effort to find a thoroughgoing distinction between the two seems to be getting nowhere. On the surface the problem does not appear difficult. It would seem to be only a question as to what is the range of stimulus or target which ESP can handle. Early pioneer workers properly enough named the phenomena on the basis of what seemed to be taking place. If the target was the thought or experience of another subject, the test was called one of telepathy. If the target was an object not being experienced by another subject at the time, it was called clairvoyance. Now that it is known, however, that ESP operates equally well in tests with objective and with subjective types of target, it looks as if the original classification may have no relevance to the actual process involved. Starting out afresh with what is known today, probably no one would think of saying that there are two kinds of ESP. He would surmise, rather, that just as ESP covers in its range of target material the exceedingly near and far, the small and large, the visible and invisible, and the present and future, so it may include the subjective and objective.

But, still, convenience and familiarity have their measure of importance. On that account the terms clairvoyance and telepathy and precognition will likely continue to be used just as if they really all meant something fundamentally different. All three of these subdivisions of ESP, however, probably should be thought of as just chalk lines that have been drawn on the surface for convenience of usage. Fundamentally, this question of types involves relationships between psi, the subject, and the rest of the universe. Whether there is any fundamental difference between telepathy and clairvoyance as forms of ESP is impossible to settle until something more is known of what the subjective (if it *is* subjective) target in the telepathy tests really is. In other words, the answer to the questions depends on the nature of thought. Until some experimental distinction between the subject's experience and the neurophysiological accompaniments of his experience can be found, there is no way of knowing what sort of basic reality is represented in the "mind" dealt with in the test situation.

Even on the surface, these type distinctions give plenty of trouble as, for example, in the matter of test methods. As mentioned in the first chapter, the telepathy experiments have already progressed to the point at which the sender's thinking has been shown to be a sufficient stimulus for successful telepathic perception. No objective target of any known kind is needed. This leaves the problem in an impasse because the nature of the telepathic target is not known. To date researchers are frankly at a loss to suggest a way further to clear the target "thought" of all objective associations. The task of isolating telepathy and establishing it as a nonclairvoyant type of ESP is, therefore, at least for the time being, at a standstill.

The status of the case for clairvoyance is, however, clearer than that for telepathy. In certain quarters in parapsychology there has been a philosophical bias against admitting the possibility of clairvoyance and in favor of trying to explain all the evidence by telepathy. The result has been that vigorous efforts have been made to account for the earlier results of clairvoyant experiments in terms of precognitive telepathy. This is the counterpart of the hypothesis discussed earlier that used precognitive clairvoyance to explain telepathy. The proponents of this counterhypothesis of precognitive telepathy argued that when the subject in a clairvoyance card-calling test succeeded in identifying the card order he could be doing it by going forward telepathically to the time when the experimenter would look at the cards to record them. Nothing beyond telepathy was needed if telepathy were conceded the possibility of also being precognitive. Such an explanation could apply to most of the evidence for clairvoyance.

However, there has not yet been a completely satisfactory experimental case made for the actual occurrence of precognitive telepathy.[1] One technically weak point about the only controlled study of precognitive telepathy yet done (Soal and Goldney)[2] is that (to consider one alternative) the results *could* have been produced by a sort of reversal of the process of precognitive telepathy. In these tests the subject, B.S., identified the card a few seconds before the experimenter picked out (of a large number of them) the colored chip that would decide what the target was to be. This looked like precognitive telepathy, but the experimenter could have been influenced in his supposedly random choice of chip by ESP of what the subject had already said was to be the target. There is no way to be certain in which direction psi operated here. To make an adequate test for precognitive telepathy would require a condition that would limit the transfer to one direction only. Such a condition should be possible to arrange, but it would involve all the added difficulties of the telepathy problem itself. On the other hand, precognitive telepathy is not an unreasonable possibility, if one assumes that the occurrence of both telepathy and precognition has been established. The hypothesis is certainly sufficiently reasonable to justify experimental consideration as a counterhypothesis to clairvoyance.

Fortunately, however, this particular alternative to clairvoyance had, in a quite incidental way, already been met at the time the question arose. Some of the clairvoyance experiments that had already been done when this issue first came up adequately meet the requirements for the establishment of clairvoyance on terms that precognitive telepathy could not explain. One of the clairvoyance tests that did so has already been mentioned. It is the ordinary matching test. Again, the already familiar Pratt-Woodruff test series will do to illustrate. In that test, it will be recalled, the experimenter laid the target cards in the place and order indicated by the subject. The latter indicated his choice by pointing to the position of the key card which he thought the target card would match. Now, if the subject were to try to use precognitive telepathy in going ahead to the time at which the card would be observed by the experimenter, he (the subject) would be up against the fact that his response would by that time already have been made. In other words, he could only go ahead to the *consequence* of his own *response* and, therefore, would have had to commit himself before he could put precognitive telepathy to work. Hence, precognitive telepathy is effectively ruled out of this test on logical grounds.

As it happened, various other experiments, too, had incidentally been so designed that they automatically excluded the possibility of precognitive telepathy. There are several other types of clairvoyance tests that, in a similar way, seem quite effectively to bar the possibility of precognitive telepathy. Clairvoyance, therefore, as far as critical examination has gone to date, seems to be a well-established aspect of the psi function.

Telepathy, it is true, is for the time being in a waiting category.

But while it is awaiting the genius of a freshly designed approach, it may be well to bear in mind that the question that has been raised here by experimental advances in the telepathy research is a most important one, indeed, for all the sciences of man. It is the question of the nature of man's subjective experience in its relation to his physical brain—the question that needs a sound scientific answer before any of the sciences that deal chiefly with human personality can be sure of their basic principles.

Next comes the challenging problem of precognition. And it is just the type of phenomenon that would naturally be expected to raise the most controversy of all. In fact, the precognition hypothesis is likely to be one of the great battlegrounds of science. Nothing in all the history of human thought—heliocentrism, evolution, relativity—has been more truly revolutionary or radically contradictory to contemporary thought than the results of the investigation of precognitive psi. Even some of those who have followed the psi investigations up to a certain point without having intellectual convulsions have, on learning of the findings on precognition, reacted with violent skepticism. Even within the field of parapsychology itself there have been from the beginning vigorous efforts to explain the results of the precognition tests in terms of a more rationally acceptable alternative. The fact that few of the psi workers themselves have tackled this problem is partly due, perhaps, to the inherent incredibility of the idea.

The most plausible alternative explanation of the earlier results suggesting precognition was that the significant scoring rate they showed could have been produced by the operation of clairvoyant ESP. This might conceivably have been possible in cases in which the cards were shuffled by hand by the experimenter. A collateral research on what came to be called the "psychic shuffle" had shown that ESP could be used so to place the cards in the process of shuffling them that they would match another pack of cards to a degree that ruled out chance as an explanation.

After discovering this surprising fact, hand shuffling was discontinued and machines were substituted to get around the psychic shuffle effect. The alternative of explaining the results as due to clairvoyance was thereby eliminated.

Next the PK hypothesis was advanced as an explanation to counter that of precognition. So long as the shuffling was done mechanically, there was still, as was early recognized, the possibility that the cards might be influenced by PK to fall so as to match the order of prediction. That is, either the subject or the experimenter perhaps could have psychokinetically influenced the card order. Accordingly, in the procedure that was then adopted the deck of cards, after being shuffled, was cut in a way that excluded the PK hypothesis as a reasonable explanation. This cut was made on the basis of the temperature readings printed in a specified newspaper for a designated future date. But even then there were still a few individuals who held out for the possibility that PK might have been a sufficient explanation of the significant results obtained.

I will digress on this alternative for a moment, for any who want to take it seriously. It may be recalled that the results which Dr. Humphrey and I had obtained in the precognition tests with children were from experiments in which the temperature cuts were used. We recognized, of course, the seemingly fantastic alternative that the experimenters, or someone aiding them, might conceivably influence the actual temperature or the instrument recording it or the persons observing it, in such a way that the cards would be cut so as to produce more than a chance number of coincidences between them and the distribution of symbols on the large number of record sheets that had been accumulated. However, this complicated hypothetical operation appeared fantastic enough to be ignored at this stage. Very commonly, the ascent of science in solving a complex problem takes on a staircase character. The full achievement, like Heaven, "is not gained by a single bound."

In science there are no absolutely final settlements anyhow. The best policy in sharpening the experimental focus on the question of precognition is just to go on increasing the difficulties for the alternative explanation by PK. Those who are dissatisfied are, of course, free to go on further with the issue and its solution. Experiments have been carried out in recent years with an addition to the device of the weather cut of the cards. This added feature is a sort of intellectual roadblock aimed at preventing any form of psi except precognition from producing results in the test. It works as follows: When the temperature readings are taken they are not simply applied to the cutting of the target pack of cards. Instead, they are used as the basis for complicated mathematical operations which have to be produced by a computing machine. This operation itself is hedged by fixed rules so that there is no choice on the part of the experimenter regarding what he will do on the machine. Of course, the machine itself does not exercise any choice nor is it subject to influence by PK. Therefore, when it finally comes out with its answer, and this answer is used, then, as the basis for cutting the pack of cards, something has occurred between the temperature reading and the cutting of the cards which is so far beyond the intellectual powers of anyone concerned as to exclude any possible use of PK in making the cards turn out to match the predictions.

While this method has not yet been described in publication, the results obtained with it thus far, even in the limited tests to which it has been applied, are strongly suggestive. The scoring *rate* has not been altered by the added precautionary device, but as yet sufficient work for a conclusion has not been completed.

There has also been a converse argument to this precognition-psychokinesis issue. Precognition has been a counterhypothesis to PK too. There are those, well represented by the zoologist, Dr. C. B. Nash, who have maintained that precognition is a possible explanation for the results of the psychokinesis tests.[3] To many readers this will seem to be farther fetching the already farfetched; but it should always be remembered that at one time or another nearly everything now accepted in science appeared to some professional group too farfetched for credence.

The argument of the precognitionist (as we might call him for the moment) is that in the PK test either the subject or experimenter may have precognitive awareness of all the dice as they will fall in the test to be conducted and on the basis of such awareness can judge which would be the most advantageous target face to choose. If one were to grant the possibility that the subject could get such a helpful precognitive impression and grant also that he would be allowed to choose the target face or the order in which the target faces were to be used, it is conceivable that he could, even in a purely chance series, pick out a favorable order of target faces or combination of faces and thereby produce a significant deviation without benefit of PK. In some of the PK experiments it is true the subject was allowed to choose the target order because the exercise of this choice increased his interest.

The psychokineticist's side of the argument might run as follows: To use precognition successfully the subject would have to foresee and mentally add up the results of thousands of different die throws. It would involve a mammoth order of mental computation that, to begin with, would necessitate the assumption of an order of precognition such as no tests have ever yet demonstrated. The job of mental arithmetic involved, and especially within the time allowable, certainly would be beyond anyone's normal powers. But the precognitionist could reply: "How do we know the limits of the unconscious in matters of this kind? And, after all, psychokinesis is a pretty big order to take; we can't explain it either."

The best experiment yet for excluding precognition in a psychokinesis test is that of the psychologist, Dr. R. H. Thouless, of Cambridge University.[4] In a PK experiment in which he tested himself, he used a standard method known as the Latin Square technique to insure that a random order of the targets would be followed. The significant results he obtained could not reasonably be attributed to any kind of precognition hypothesis yet suggested. At least this carries the argument a long way toward the PK side of the issue.

There have been a number of other PK experiments in which the experimenter followed a fixed target order determined by some rational consideration, and others in which the target was selected by the throw of a die. Another type of experiment also bears on the issue. It may be illustrated by the Pegram high-dice and low-dice tests in which the subject threw two dice and willed them to fall with either a high or a low combination of faces uppermost.[5] In this series of tests the number of successes above the average expected from chance was significant. Such a result would be claimed by the precognitionist as having been produced by precognition which guided the subject in deciding whether to make high dice or low dice the target for a given session. But in the analyses performed years later on these Pegram data something was found that gives the precognition theory a lot of difficulty. These analyses showed that the tests for both high dice and low dice gave a remarkably lawful and similar hit distribution on the record sheet. The data had been recorded in sets of three columns per sheet. The first column in the set, both in the high dice and the low dice tests, had by far the largest number of hits. A decline in rate of scoring over the second and third columns followed. This meaningful and statistically significant distribution in itself was evidence sufficient to warrant the conclusion that PK was operating in producing the results. Now, if the subject had been choosing her target (either high dice or low dice) on the basis of precognition, her task was to pick the combination that would give not only total scores above "chance" but also such a distribution of hits over the set that these striking declines to be found years later would result.

But even that is not the end. The subject would also have had to do her precognizing in such a way that she would get another equally marked distribution of hits, for when the hits *in the column* were analyzed, it was found that, both in the high-dice and in the low-dice tests, there was a very marked decline in scoring rate as the subject proceeded down the column, and there was a rise in rate of scoring at the end of the column. And, again, this distribution would, all by itself, sustain the conclusion that PK was present in the experimental data.

Still more could be added in kind to this discussion; but perhaps I have gone far enough to show that to use precognition to produce the results in this Pegram research would be a task far beyond the human intellect as we know it; that is, precognition could have aided the subject to choose the better target combinations only if, throughout the months of testing, she had made these precognitive surveys of the large numbers of die faces as they were to fall. The results of such surveys would need to be summarized and analyzed mentally, both for total deviation and for distribution of hits, and the distribution of hits would have to be analyzed for its distribution in the set as well as in the column.

To continue still further, it so happens that these same distribution curves are rather typical of PK test results (and even bear great similarity to the curves of the ESP data). The similarity even extends beyond the field of psi investigation to other psychological test data. In a word, something general and lawful was occurring in the trial to trial progress of the subject. It cannot be explained by supposing that the precognitive choice of target is causing it. That choice would hardly produce the various distribution curves *within* the set or column and the total deviation at the same time.

I have, no doubt, seemed to overlabor this point. Thouless's results were enough, surely, in themselves to settle the issue for most people. But research people have to plod almost endlessly over these worrisome ramifications of alternative interpretations, and listen patiently to countless counterclaims, lest important points be overlooked. What is pictured here illustrates some of the difficult terrain that must be traversed to cover the debatable frontiers of a problem area like this. It is a sample of what goes on in the zone of rational analysis. Eventually, however, the issue graduates from the rational to an experimental test such as that of Thouless.

The main types of psi phenomena have now been examined. How do they stand, in a summary of the present stage of things, with respect to each other? Altogether, the evidence as distinguished by the gross experimental operations themselves brings out fairly clear cases for clairvoyance, precognition, and psychokinesis.

Whether or not these abilities are the same thing at some basic level is another question. I suspect they are. And whether telepathy is, indeed, the ESP of something other than objective states in the brain or a psychokinetic effect initiated by the sender and exerted upon the nervous system of the receiver, we will not be able to say for some time to come. Since the wave of argumentation over the distinction has passed, it is not likely to arise again until new issues are drawn.

One thing needs emphasis concerning these types of distinction. The general case for psi is in no way strengthened or weakened by the success or failure of these efforts at a crucial separation of the psi types. The value of the data on the basic problem of the occurrence of psi is not affected, no matter how the question of distinguishing psi types is eventually answered.

Psi is by definition a very broad concept, but the two main subdivisions, ESP and PK, would seem to cover all the possibilities conceivable. The familiar types of manifestation of ESP, however, with which the research has been concerned need not be regarded as the only possible ones. We suspect there are other forms of psi response or variants that may come as close to deserving separate headings as these we already "know by name." These further possibilities are part of the recognized unfinished business of parapsychology that await the day when the research facilities and personnel can reach them.

What, for instance, about the question of retrocognition? This is one of the things belonging in this context about which almost nothing is known. Whether ESP can reach into the traceless past as well as into the nonexistent future is still an unanswered question. It will be necessary first for a method for investigating this possibility to be devised. One must be found in which a target that is set up for the retrocognition test can then be eliminated without, at the same time, destroying all possibility of checking up on the test response. One method of doing this is to use exposed but undeveloped photographic film on which would be the record to be used for the checkup. This method has already been used to a limited extent with results far from discouraging. But the puzzle is one of how to get around the alternative that precognition could operate in such a test. It would be a precognitive perception of the situation when the film is developed. Besides, it would be necessary to know in this connection whether or not clairvoyant ESP could operate with invisible chemical patterns as targets, for that is the sort of target represented by an exposed but undeveloped photographic film.

There stands out, too, the question of whether the precognitive perception of one's own future experiences is a possibility. Precognitive sensory perception would be just one type. There is nothing known to exclude the possibility of this experiencing of one's sensations in advance. Some of the spontaneous cases even suggest it. But, again, no design yet proposed permits its investigation under adequate control against such a known alternative as, for example, precognitive clairvoyance. But it is conceivable that, with a free range in devising mechanical apparatus and ingenious experimental design, this hypothesis may be reducible to effective testability and final solution. This and many other good questions will, however, have to wait until more research resources, time, and personnel are available for this area of problems.

Some people think "psychometry" is a special kind of psi. This absurdly named effect—for there is nothing metric about it—seems to be nothing more than clairvoyant "free association" in connection with a token object. The object is given to the subject for the purpose of stimulating him to draw from its contact information associated with its history or that of persons to whom it belonged. The information sought has, of course, to be attributable to extrarational and extrasensory sources in order to meet the requirements for "psychometry." It is apparently a sort of loose and unappraisable token-object test of ESP. But we now know that controls and measurements could be applied to such tests if there were good reason for doing this type of test in preference to others.

The claims for dowsing, too, present a problem that already has a name attached. The turning of a rod in the dowser's hands as he tries to locate underground water for the purpose of digging a well is a familiar effect. Barrett and Besterman[6] are correct in saying that the rod is turned by unconscious muscular action, and that if reliable location of water is effected without sensory rational guidance, the cognitive principle would have to be clairvoyant ESP. Nothing else would be needed. The degree to which this practice is reliable and successful is a question which, for lack of sufficient systematic research effort, is still unsettled. The dowsing art, however, is not waiting for scientific validation. The practice has taken over new applications and is no longer confined mainly to water finding. Oil and ores are being sought with the aid of the rods or with various substitutes therefor. The newest specialization of the general dowsing art is in finding the forgotten location of pipes, conduits, cables, and the like in industrial and urban areas. Dowsing is going to town! Dozens of public utility companies equip workmen with rods designed to swing

easily, as the dowsing rod must do in the service of an automa-
tism. Metal appropriately supplants the green witch hazel. All
this utilitarian interest may force (and even finance!) an adequate
research on the problem of dowsing, perhaps one that will extend
to the whole big psi branch of inquiry of which it seems to be a
twig.

There is another problem awaiting research attention that may
be a touchy one. It is the question of whether telepathic intrusion or coercive thought transference is possible and, if so, under
what range of conditions. Can a sender influence a receiver with
whom he has had no preparatory contact? If he can, what is the
effect (if any) of common experience, acquaintance, friendship,
love, linguistic barriers, doubt, and many other states and factors?
The problem is one that has considerable significance for many
fields and it especially concerns the field of mental health. It is
one into which parapsychologists have not as yet been ready to
plunge. However, the problem cannot be put off indefinitely.
The mentally ill individual can be assured that telepathy has never
yet been found to have been used reliably by anyone to persecute
or harm another person. But many psychiatrists have suggested
that there are constructive and beneficial possibilities that need
to be explored in the interest of psychotherapy and mental hygiene.

It is in order next to consider the place of psi in the personality. One good question to ask at the start is whether psi is a
part of the normal personality or whether it is some sort of aber-
ration. The answer to this is already fairly clear and adequate.
Psi is not a symptom for the psychiatrist or the clinical psychologist. Certainly as far as the psi investigations have progressed to
date, nothing has been encountered to link psychic functions
with mental illness or with abnormal deviations of any kind. It
is interesting to note, too, that no general theory of psi phenomena or of mental illness has ever linked the two together.

This is not to say, of course, that there are no interconnections.
As a normal function of the individual, psi may operate in con-
nection with abnormal processes just as any other ability may.
Nor do I wish to imply that, because psi is not a pathological symp-

tom, it is of no interest to the practitioner. Indeed, its significance for psychology and psychiatry makes headings for later chapters of this book.

Psi phenomena, it is true, are often confused with the abnormal. The surface resemblance between the two is often striking, as in this case reported by a medical friend . . . ⟨About the time of the ending of World War II, a woman in Florida awakened one night crying out between sobs that she had seen her soldier son go down in a burning plane. Her husband could not convince her that it was just a foolish nightmare, even when he reminded her that the war was over and that their son was not even in the Air Force. The physician was called in to give the woman a sedative. The next day a cheerful letter arrived from the son, and the woman was able to gain control of herself. Five nights later, however, the same nightmare occurred to her, and this time the conviction was uncontrollable, the sedative ineffective, and she was taken to the psychopathic ward of the hospital for rest and treatment on the assumption that, since she was entirely wrong about her son, her behavior was irrational. So far as I have learned she did nothing that would not have been considered rational if she had actually witnessed her son's death, but was unable to make anyone share her terrible knowledge. A telegram came the day after her second nightmare and confirmed the dream. Her son, who had been stationed in the Far East, had been sent home on an airplane which had caught fire and gone down on the night of the mother's first experience.

This clairvoyant dream of the tragedy took a form which is common enough among abnormal experiences. The unstable personality torturing itself with an unresolved conflict may break out in something like the same type of nightmare as the woman had in this veridical experience of her son's death. The two experiences might very well look the same from a superficial account of them. Where no checkup is possible, a genuine spontaneous experience of ESP could, for a time at least, well be taken as a symptom of mental disorder.

What further complicates the matter is the fact that in certain pathological states, especially those associated with delusions of persecution, a person often uses a belief in some form of psi process as a mechanism or device to make the delusion rationally acceptable. Perhaps the most common of these delusory beliefs about psi is that in which the sufferer believes himself to be the victim of someone who is influencing him telepathically, planting evil thoughts in his mind or doing him harm by a kind of PK action. So far as the record goes there has never been found any basis at all for any of these claims of persecutory psi; and besides there usually are also present certain characteristic symptoms of paranoid reactions to support the diagnosis of delusion. We definitely need a better educational preparation in order, on the one hand, to deal with the abnormalities and, on the other, to understand psi experiences themselves as normal, spontaneous occurrences in the life of the individual. Certainly there is no need to be afraid of them or to consider them unhealthy in themselves.

The ESP research workers have already taken their tests into the mental hospital, both in this country and in Europe,[7] and sufficient testing of patients has been performed to give a fair basis for judgment. It can at least be said that there is no special reason to look among the mentally ill for exceptional psi performance. In them evidence of ESP capacity has been found at approximately the same general scoring level as that shown by groups of the general unselected normal population. Some experimenters have found marked differences in the ESP scoring rates between the different classifications of mental disorder, but such differences could be due to the degree of cooperativeness or other personality states associated with the type of illness. They do not indicate any tie-up of ESP capacity with any psychopathic type or trait thus far studied.

This conclusion is supported by the impression gained from the more general studies as well. Amongst the normal population that has been both tested for psi capacity and given some form of personality inventory or test dealing with mental health, the indications are, rather, that the better adjusted the individual, the more likely he is to score well in the psi tests (e.g., in Schmeidler's work with the Rorschach method).[8] But here, again, no one should consider that this association is one directly tied up with the amount of psi capacity; rather, it is more likely that the better the individual's adjustment, the better he is able to adapt to the necessarily artificial situation of the test.

Subnormality, like abnormality, seems not to be significantly related to psi capacity. In fact, in relation to subnormal intelligence and ESP, something of the same judgment can be rendered as in the case of abnormality of personality. The results are not extensive enough as yet for any final sweeping conclusions, but there is sufficient acceptable evidence to keep us from claiming either that ESP is a gift only of the normally intelligent or that it is any special gift of the subnormal.[9] Some fairly clear indications of ESP have been obtained well down the intelligence scale into the subnormal. The best tentative judgment now would be that intelligence has proved to be mainly a help in adjustment to the test, but if the experimenter exercises a sufficiently superior intelligence to make up in that regard for the deficit on the part of the subnormal subject, the latter may score above the chance level.

Psi, then, is normal. That conclusion helps to place it in the general psychological framework. But the most significant and revealing characteristic of psi is the fact that its operation is entirely unconscious. So far as is known, the subject is never conscious of the occurrence of psi. That fact alone tells more about where psi belongs, what to expect from it, and, above all, what not to expect than any other one thing. As a matter of fact, once this fact is firmly fixed in mind, a great deal of the mystery is taken out of psi. In a word, psi activity is natural enough when understood as an unconscious function of the personality.

Let me emphasize, too, that psi is profoundly unconscious. It is not merely one of those transiently subconscious processes that go on practically all the time in everyone, mental activities that can be consciously recovered if one tries and knows how to do so. It is not even one of those more hidden kinds which the psychiatrist can bring to the surface if, because of an unhealthy attitude, control over them has been lost. Neither is the psi experience similar to the dissociated or submerged section of consciousness which can be allowed to operate by itself during sleep, as in dreams; rather, psi is simply not capable of being

dragged into consciousness unconverted and direct. Such seems
to be the case as it stands today. There are not even any good
leads to conscious control in sight.

Consider the experimental findings themselves. They are consistent on this point, that the subject simply does not know reliably when the act takes place in an ESP test or whether the
response he makes is right or wrong. Riess's[10] famous ESP subject felt just the same when in the short second series she was
getting only chance results as she did when in her main series
she was averaging over eighteen hits per twenty-five cards. Only
on very rare occasions does the subject in ESP tests experience a
flash of conviction or certainty that he is correct when he is.

In the spontaneous cases, however, there is one big difference,
as Louisa E. Rhine has already reported.[11] She examined 1,600
such cases on just this point of whether the person who had the
experience was convinced of the truth of the impression he received. More than half of those reported to her showed definite
conviction, and of those who did, a large portion were so strongly
convinced that they did something resolute and radical as a consequence, such, for example as calling off a pleasure trip, or getting
up in the middle of the night and taking a train home, or putting
through a long distance call at some unreasonable hour.

On this point the spontaneous cases are calling attention to
something the experimental studies tend to miss. An experiment
is, by its very nature, circumscribing and restrictive; yet even in
these spontaneous cases, this feeling of certainty that comes into
consciousness along with the picture or meaning or message still
does not give the subject any true introspective awareness of
how he got the message, nor does it identify its port of reception
into his mental world.

No, the basis of the subject's conviction is unconscious, too.
What happens—and I get this, too, from the study of cases just
mentioned—is that however the unconscious psi operation begins,
it has to get across the frontier into consciousness by utilizing
one of the conscious devices or mechanisms or functions. If the
subject is awake, the barest essential meaning may filter through,
either partially or completely, without elaboration. It is just a simple impulse: "I must go home"; or an elemental fear: "Something

terrible has happened"; or a telegraphically brief thought: "Dan won't be back." This type of experience is familiar as *intuition*.

Or, again, perhaps depending upon the personality of the individual, there will be a more vivid, dramatic experience and the percipient will project the content of the message into some form he can seem to sense. He will see an apparition that symbolizes the significant fact or meaning, or he will hear a voice warning him, or, if a painful injury is concerned, he will experience the very same sensation felt by a loved one who is suffering pain at the moment. At any rate, something is thrown onto the screen of sensory hallucination. It seems like a way of "tossing the message across the boundary line" into consciousness. Perhaps this method may be used because it is an avenue that is most open for the individual concerned, but it will take a psychological study of these individuals to confirm such a suggestion. It is a sufficient first step merely to discover the devices of entry of which the psi function takes advantage. This second type of waking psi experience, then, depends on the device of *hallucination*.

If the percipient is asleep and, therefore, one may suspect, less likely to be guarding his mental frontiers against invasion from the unconscious sources, he may project on the screen of his dream consciousness a well-worked-out elaboration of the essential psi message, full of dramatization, rich in symbolism and fantasy. Then, when he awakens (and it appears that often the significance of the message is sufficient to make the drama too stirring for sleep), he has the task of interpretation. When a genuine psi experience clothes itself in the fantasy of dramatization and elaborate symbolization and masquerades across the threshold, we have called it an *unrealistic dream* type.

But different dreamers, again doubtless due to differences in personality, do not dramatize or symbolize their psi experiences but merely see the distant or future scene in an uncolored, matter-of-fact way, as if a photograph had been taken or a moving picture made. Later the unfolding dream picture is re-experienced in the waking state, literally as it occurred in the dream. When the dreamer awakens, he can direct the search party to the place where the body lies; or he may, as he turns the next corner, come upon the scene; or it may be the next day or the next year. This photographic psi experience, known as the *realistic dream* type, although occurring most often in sleep, is experienced even when one is more or less awake or thinks he is.

In all these four main categories of spontaneous psi experience, there is the basic problem of getting an idea across into the area of the personality where conscious recognition can take place. It is no wonder, then, that when the experimenter undertakes to pin down psi functions in the laboratory, he runs into many difficulties and quite a few peculiar effects.

But these effects are less peculiar when one keeps in mind that the essential psi function operates completely in the darkness of unconsciousness. The subject has none of the introspective awareness such as he commonly experiences in connection with his sensory world every minute of his waking life. One easily localizes most of his waking sensations. He is aware when they begin and end. They are, within their range, almost completely at the service of what is called attention, introspection, and the conscious volition of the individual. There is, in fact, such close connection between the sensory functions and the whole of conscious experience that efforts have been made to build a concept of mental structure out of these sensory elements and their derivatives. Without joining this Sensationist School of Psychology in all its extreme views, one may, at least, raise the question of whether the state of consciousness itself may not be the exercise either of sensory processes or of derivative processes that were originally sensorial. This is, I repeat, a question, one that is raised by the fact that *extra*sensory perception is *un*conscious.

Allow now that these psi operations are subject to all the factors that normally influence the individual's mental life. They are, to some definite degree, guided by his will. If they were not, then such directed testing (involving subject motivation) as that by which the main bulk of the evidence for psi has been secured would have yielded nothing. In one type of experiment the subject tries to identify a given card in a particular pack of cards at a specific time. In another he tries to influence the fall of a particular set of dice at a particular time and toward a particular objective. Probably in terms of volition there is no difference between psi activity in these tests and the use of the sensory functions.

The difference in the results must be found in other characteristics. In a word, psi is an unconscious but by no means a completely involuntary function.

Spontaneous psi experiences often do seem to be involuntary so far as the individual percipient is concerned. He appears to play merely a passive role, to receive an impression with no sign of effort on his part. The degree of purposiveness in such cases, however, is quite similar to that in sensory perception. The volitional aspect is often not manifest, but it seems safe to infer that in some rudimentary sense it is always there. Perception is by nature purposive, always involves drive or directed action to some degree, and all of these are volitional concepts. In spontaneous ESP the experience occurs to a particular individual because it concerns him and there is, presumably, some sort of readiness or receptivity on his part that would not be expected of just anyone. The fact that the message conveyed to him arrives in some way of which he is unconscious means only that there has been no conscious volition on his part.

Unconscious volition is, of course, a familiar concept. Everything that has been learned from the depth psychologists about the operations of unconscious mental life gives it a character as truly volitional and purposive as that of conscious mental operations.

The experimental results reflect in many ways the unconscious level on which psi operates. The most disconcerting of these effects of the unconsciousness of the psi process is, beyond question, the *psi-missing* effect already mentioned. It has, in fact, been the very devil of the psi research, and one who has been paid dearly! Before its effects were discovered, it worked havoc in many researches and defeated the purpose of the experiments. In some of the earliest of the Duke experiments in ESP, it was found that under certain conditions the subject would consistently score below the chance average. When showing such a trend he would go about as far below "chance" as he had normally gone above. Since this negative trend canceled the positive margin, the experimenters naturally, if they recognized the effect in time, tried to avoid getting the subject into the state that produced this psi-missing tendency.

Some of the states that usually produce psi-missing are known. The strain (or other effects) of excessively long runs, the condition of being put on the spot to demonstrate ability under conditions of social stress, or intellectual conflict over the question of whether psi is possible—these are some of the conditions in which the subject has swung over from the positive to the negative side of the chance average in his scoring.

This effect, however, is not the same as that produced by conscious volition. Subjects could, of course, produce low scores if they consciously tried. It was interesting to see that when subjects were asked deliberately to try to avoid making hits the negative deviation from "chance" thus produced was approximately equal to that obtained by the same subject when trying to score positively. This threw some incidental light on the kind of process that was involved in ESP hitting, as I shall discuss a little later. But it also furnished an idea of what was going on in psi-missing; in general, a consistent *negative* deviation of number of hits could be taken as evidence of the same amount of psi ability as a positive one of the same magnitude, even though there was a 1-in-5 chance of hitting and a 4-in-5 chance of missing. (The scoring needs to be kept on the same basis; that is, number of *hits*, not *misses*, in making such a comparison.)

At first it was thought that this psi-missing was all due to unconscious negativism. It seemed most reasonable to suppose that the subjects who were actually missing the targets to an extrachance degree were unconsciously negative toward either the test, the experimenter, or ESP, even though consciously they might all have wanted to achieve high scores. There had been experimental series in which it seemed especially plausible to suppose that there was unconscious negativism. An example of this is given by the research of Dr. Schmeidler, already referred to, in which she found that the favorably oriented subjects, the sheep, tended to score positively, while the goats were on the negative side of the chance mean. Some of the goats, it might be supposed, may even consciously have wanted to score low in order to bear out their point of view. It was easy to suppose that they were unconsciously negative.

As the evidence of psi missing accumulated, however, this

explanation that it was caused by simple negativism came to look increasingly inadequate. First, there was a great deal of evidence in which it simply did not make sense. Take, for instance, the different series in which one part of the run, usually the first part, is above the mean and another part below, the deviations or the differences being large enough to be significant. In such cases one could not suppose that the subject shifted his motivation appreciably between the beginning of the run and the end, changing from a sheep to a goat and then shifting back at the start of the next run.

Rather, it now seems that most psi-missing is a kind of psi illusion. The subject consistently follows some wrong system or device in his attempts to make high scores. In this blindness he unwittingly but persistently misuses the very process by which he could achieve success and, since he is unconscious of what he is doing, he adheres to the error. We have evidence of many such devices, but there is one that has been already demonstrated to occur that would tend to produce a psi-missing effect (though I doubt if this particular one *is* widely applicable). This is the "consistent missing" effect noted by Cadoret and already mentioned. In this the subject forms some kind of fixation of an illusory character on a given type of symbol so that when he tries to identify that symbol, let us say a "square," he persistently responds with another kind, say "waves."

Another queer effect of the fact that psi is unconscious is that of "displacement," the hitting of a symbol in another position in the series than the target intended. Most of the displacement found has been merely shifted to the adjacent card in the run, the one just forward or the one just backward of the regular target; but displacement has also sometimes been found to extend forward or backward to the next run. So far this scatter effect has been greatest in long-distance experiments that extended over a long period of time and involved general ESP and a free range of target material.[12] This suggested relation deserves to be explored further than as yet it has been.

In the card-calling tests, however, the displacement is pretty closely limited to the first or second card forward or backward from the central target. The most striking examples of this in the card tests was the work of Soal and, later, that of Soal and Gold-ney. As I have already said, this displacement was not only un-known to the subjects in Soal's first ESP card tests, but it was unknown to Soal himself until his attention was directed to the possibility of such an effect and he was led to investigate.

One might suppose that, as Soal and Goldney continued with one of the two subjects (B.S.) whom Soal found to have pro-duced significant displacement effects, the subject, knowing as he did of the earlier finding, would have been more or less con-sciously trying to keep up the high order of displacement which had distinguished his work, and that this new attitude would have altered the effect or even abolished it. However, the dis-placement did continue to operate in later experiments with this subject, although with the other of Soal's leading subjects (Mrs. S.) it discontinued. Unconscious reactions are, indeed, hard to interpret.

We shall likely be a long time in recognizing and evaluating all of the consequences of the unconsciousness of psi. The psi-missing and displacement effects are only the more conspicuous of the consequences. I will describe a few of the other types and in doing so will draw again upon the work of Soal and his asso-ciates, since the background has already been given.

One such effect was found by Soal and Pratt in the reaction of Soal's subject, Mrs. S., to "doubles." Doubles are cases of two successive target cards of the same symbol. Whereas 20 per cent is expected from chance alone, Mrs. S. got 28 per cent right on "singles" and only about 17 per cent on doubles. Now, of course, there must be a "reason," a psychological one, for this differential scoring. The results are not explainable by chance, but as yet the experimenters have not been able to discover what the reason is. It is fairly certain, however, that the unconsciousness of ESP was a factor. No one thinks for a moment that Mrs. S. was conscious of what she was doing or that she would have scored as she did if she had been.

One of the most challenging psi effects yet discovered is that of reinforcement, already mentioned. This phenomenon was dis-covered by Soal in the results of his subject, B.S., and has since been confirmed through the further analyses jointly conducted by Pratt[13] and Dr. T. N. E. Greville.[14] In this effect, as I have already explained, the subject displaced his hits sometimes forward and sometimes backward to the cards adjacent to the nominal target. When the same symbol appeared in both of the two adjacent positions (for example, circle, square, circle), the subject tended to give a response (circle) that made a double hit on displacement and the scoring rate rose to the highest level reached anywhere in the whole series.

The mystery is still a puzzling one as to why in such cases the scoring rate should go up to something like five to six times as high in its deviation from a chance average as it had been on the ordinary target sequence. At most, something short of a doubling of the rate by the addition of the two displacement effects might have been expected. The solution to that mystery may be the only clue needed to lead on to the control and use of psi ability. But the investigation of this problem, like the psi operation itself, is subject to the limitations of the state of unconsciousness—and of such unconsciousness as prevents any satisfactory exploration by any of the techniques developed thus far in the whole range of depth psychology. Depth psychology is not instrumented yet for *such* depths.

What does this unconsciousness indicate about psi? Perhaps the most important thing, aside from the practical difficulties it has placed in the research worker's way, is this: To be as deeply unconscious as the phenomena are, the process might have to be an extremely primitive one—or perhaps I should say, one that is fundamentally close to the basic life processes, one that emerged very early in the evolutionary scheme. One wonders, then, if it may not have predated the origin, not merely of language and of reason, but even that of the sensory functions themselves. Could it be associated, one is inclined to ask, with the basic organizing forces of life, with those energies that direct the structuring of the cell and the form and growth pattern of the complex organism throughout the whole realm of living nature?

Frankly, the answer to these questions is unknown as yet. Simply putting together two unknown problem areas because they seem to be contiguous can serve at least to raise questions. To be sure, if psi were moved back to the preconscious stage in the evolution of mind, it would be putting it far back, indeed! But it would also be making it rather basic, identifying it (hypothetically) with the long-range directive system of life processes so effectively described by Dr. Edmund W. Sinnott in his book, *Cell and Psyche*.

Consciousness does seem to be associated only with sensory experience; perhaps all conscious mental life—even the most imageless of thought and feeling—is compounded of derivatives of what were originally sensations. As I have said, no one knows pro or con. At any rate, some such view led Aristotle to say: "Nothing enters the mind except through the channels of sense." Today, recognizing that psi is unconscious, one can better understand how Aristotle, approaching the nature of the mind as he did introspectively, overlooked psi completely. For ESP to enter consciousness where Aristotle would have recognized it would have required that it persist through to conscious experience in some characteristic form or feature. Actually, as is now known, it has to be converted first to a sensory derivative in consciousness, a hallucination, a dream fantasy, or such, if it is to reach the stage of awareness at all. The psi process itself leaves no identifying trace in the subject's mind to make it known as a psi experience. It enters the stream of consciousness only in disguised or converted form.

But suppose that the psi function *is* rather primordial in its nature, perhaps primitive in its evolutionary origins. Assume that it *has* been overlaid and its operation inhibited, or at least modified, by the evolution of elaborate cerebral structures associated with the higher intellectual powers of man. One could hope to understand the function only by rationally putting it in its proper place and trying with this evolutionary origin and organizational level in mind to discover its relationship to the rest of the personality. I shall try out this approach (if only for lack of a better) and see how logically the research results fit into the concept of psi as a function submerged and overlaid by the development of the association network deriving from the sensory functions on which consciousness depends.

One can recognize in the sensorimotor system the means by which the organism maintains its interrelations with the physical world most effectively and familiarly, the world of space, time, mass, substance, motion, and all the various sensible energies. In the psi function it may tentatively be considered that a world of causality new to science is necessarily involved. Its operations, though imperceptible to the senses, are nonetheless energetically real, since results that are discoverable are produced. This world of psi, of course, as I have said before, must produce effects that can be converted to equivalents directly or indirectly appreciable by some form of conscious experience, or its presence could not be detected.

This entire area has remained hidden from the prevailing sciences, not because they could not have investigated it, but because they have naturally erected their structures of knowledge out of the products of the senses and have a sensory orientation that would never lead to a discovery of extrasensory effects. The senses, of course, can directly give knowledge only of the physical world. Thus the limitations of human cognitive equipment might well have continued indefinitely to confine all thinking to this physical world had it not been for the challenge of these spontaneous psi experiences and had there not been a few unorthodox inquirers prepared to study them and to question the dogma that the senses are the only gateways to knowledge.

Let me return now to the research. The hypothesis that the psi function is of primitive and neurologically submerged character will, I think, help to interpret the next block of findings, that dealing with the position effects. As will be recalled, the term refers to the effect produced on the scoring rate by the specific location of the trial in the run, on the record page or in the session or series. As I have pointed out, the position effects that have been noted consist for the most part of declines in scoring rate within the given block or unit of test-trials (runs, page, session, etc.) taken for the analysis.

The declines, which have already been mentioned, are, in fact, the most common manifestation of psi in the test data. Only a few experimental series of any length have failed to show some kind of decline in scoring rate as the test progressed. This downhill trend of scoring has, unfortunately, had much to do with making uphill work of the psi research. The decline represents an interference with the optimum operation of the psi function and cuts down the total number of successes upon which the evidence is generally based. However, the decline effects early became so well established as almost to be a characteristic of psi in the test situation, and it became routine to measure the extent of the decline as a test of the significance or extrachance character of the results.

It would be too much of an undertaking to review here all the various types of decline and other position effects represented in specific researches. A few examples have already been presented in other connections in the preceding chapters and others will be referred to from time to time as we go on. The reader will readily recall the decline of scoring rate that appeared in the Pratt-Woodruff series as the novelty of the target symbols (of different sizes) wore off following the introduction of each new type of target material. Likewise, there is the outstanding case of decline in the quarter distribution of hits in the PK researches, a decline to the right across the page and from top to bottom in the column. The diagonal decline from upper left to lower right was made the basis of the evaluation for the PK research data.

What is producing this peculiar distribution of scoring? What makes it high in one place and low in another with sufficient consistency in so many wholly independent series as to make a lawful and significant case? What known parallel effects are there to help point the way to an explanation?

In looking for similar manifestations it is always best to turn first to the familiar. These decline curves most resemble the performance curves found in tests of memory and learning. Psychologists have found, for example, that there are curves of success in the recall of items in a long list of nonsense syllables to which the subject has been exposed.[15] In terms of number of exposures required, the subject will show the greatest success (in this case require the smallest number of repetitions) on the first item and the success will decline (number of repetitions increasing) with the second, and so on through the list. In the recall test toward the end of the list there is an increase in rate of success. Such terminal salience often appears, too, in the distribution of hits in the psi test if the subject knows that he is approaching the end of the run.

The curve is similar in maze-learning experiments in which a long series of equivalent units are learned. Whether rats or men are the subjects, the first trial crossroad is the easiest to master, the second more difficult, and so on, but with the same salience at the end. These salience effects (primacy and finality effects) in psychological sequences, in which the ends of the run stand out, are much the same as in the psi tests. One finds there the same general tendency to declines. They suggest at least that some common principles are involved.

Yet I doubt that memory and learning tests can help very much to explain what is going on in a series of psi tests, even though at first glance they look as if they should. The cases are different, at least in one important respect. In both the memory and learning tests the subject has a primary mental task of keeping the items disentangled, distinguished from one another by some kind of mental structuring of his own which becomes more complex as the list lengthens. But in the ESP and PK tests each trial can be for the subject a distinctly separate unit. When he releases the dice in a given trial he does not have to concern himself with the other trials at all. Each trial can be an independent act. There is supposedly no need to attempt to distinguish it from the rest of the trials of the run—that is, to organize the whole run—as is the case in the tests of recall and learning.

Why, then, isn't each psi trial just as separate and distinct for him as the first one or the last one? The curves indicate it is not. If a learning experiment or a memory test were conducted on the same basis as the ESP test, that is, allowing for the same individualization of the trial, I think there would not be the gradients and curves that the memory and learning experiments have yielded. So I think in the psi tests it is necessary to look for something else than the mere obscuring that goes with location in the interior of the run or list as in the memory or learning tests. We all know that in sensory perception the end points do stand out in any sort of structured field because of the effect of the crowding of the inner items in the series. In the psi tests I am now convinced it is not that, although I once thought it was.

I now think, rather, that it is the progressively complicated conscious activity going on in the subject as the number of trials are extended that clouds over and interferes with the psi function to a serious degree, even at times effectively blocking it. In some instances it distorts the psi process so that psi-missing or the avoidance of the target takes place. In general, the subject's first trial in the run in his first experiment is the most nearly spontaneous of all he may make. There may, of course, for given individuals be special inhibiting conditions, perhaps created by their own approach, that will make even the first one far from a truly spontaneous response on their part. But suppose that the subject is well-prepared and well-adjusted and has some psi capacity. The second trial, then, is likely to have a factor of association in which his habits of thought come to the fore and interfere with his spontaneity. The further he progresses the more he will bring into operation the habit system associated with his cognitive judgment in selecting symbols to put on the record sheet. He will almost certainly take some cognizance of the symbol just called. He may ask himself if he should repeat it or consider whether the next one to come to mind does so from mere association in his thought. If so, he will consider rejecting it, and so on. Some subjects will be more successful than others in avoiding the overburdening accumulation of these habit patterns. The most reliable subject, the one who avoids serious decline, is the one who can maintain throughout the run something of the original spontaneity of the first trial.

One of the best indications that there is something to deal with here that is different from the memory and learning curves is the fact that in a large number of these decline cases the subject goes right on down to a significant *negative* deviation before he gets through with the column or the series or whatever the unit is within which the decline occurs. This shows that there is a factor involved that is not of the nature of crowding (e.g., poor distinguishability of targets), because that would produce only chance scores. This effect is one, rather, that actually alters the mode of judgment and consistently distorts the results into a psi-missing effect.

As I have said earlier, this missing effect cannot reasonably be considered a shift of motivation from a positive one at the beginning of the run to a negative one at the end. It looks, rather, as if the accumulation of associative patterns of thought that snowball as the test run continues presses the subject into some *alteration of his psi operation*—unconsciously of course—until he is systematically using his psi ability to reject the target. Toward the end of the run for the last trial or two, possibly three, he may be able, knowing it to be the end, to give himself a spontaneous anticipatory leap ahead into the clear and thereby give the ending the virtue and advantage of a beginning, thus producing the terminal salience effect.

Looking at psi as a submerged process that must find its way through whatever overlying cross fire and complication of conscious activity the subject is indulging in, one can understand that this condition would normally become more pronounced as the series progresses. In going from one session to another or even from one run to another, there is a certain upturn from the end point of the preceding unit, a beginning over again above the level at which the previous unit left off. Associations develop and become more complex from the contributions of memory. It is understandable, then, that although turning to a fresh run or a fresh record page or a new session would have some novelty, no later unit could be the same as the first one, unless the subject were to be made to forget completely everything he had earlier done and thought.

This concept of the cause of the position effects may lead to a clearer understanding of what is going on in the psi tests. If it is correct, it should give a better idea of the kind of persons to be sought as subjects, whether the attempt be to find them in the natural state or to develop them by one technique or another.

There is a further, final point about these declines. The psi investigator who has often to struggle with the philosophy, "Sweet are the uses of adversity," has managed to find a jewel in the head of the "ugly and venomous toad" of the decline effect. Let me explain first that the really *big* immediate objective in psi research at present is to learn how to get some control over the capacity, and any trace of what looks like control is a real nugget of encouragement to the explorer. Take, then, the fact that in these declines it appears that the conscious effort of the subject to choose carefully and to bring pressure to bear on the psi function is having a considerable effect, even though it is an adverse one. If it is true that conscious effort can interfere with scoring rate, at least in a negative direction, one has a right to expect that a better conscious control, a more enlightened effort, may succeed in producing positive deviations.

It is so often the case in science that an advance is achieved by the proper interpretation of a failure or a frustration. It may be that the very lawfulness and regularity of these declines promises a start on this important project of getting control. If so, it would, indeed, be turning adversity to account. The idea has only recently developed, and will take time to expand. It is by such ideas, however, that explorers are lured over their mountains.

The question of the kind of personality that is most closely associated with outstanding psi performance has been very much on the minds of investigators. Today, however, the ability appears to be so generally distributed that this fact itself now stands out as the most remarkable one. What had been most expected was that there should be some breed or strain or grouping, perhaps of fortunetellers or psychically gifted practitioners of some sort, or of some primitive folk, who would by this time have been shown to give consistently significant results in controlled tests. It is still too early to say that nothing of the kind *could* happen, and, of course, the search will go on. But sufficient time has now passed and sufficient field exploration has taken place to make it look very unlikely that there is anywhere in the human race any characterizable group of outstandingly gifted psi performers.

It cannot be claimed that all the evidence for this hypothesis has been derived from comparably standardized tests carried out under equally good conditions. But there again, if it is recognized that this judgment is necessarily tentative, it is at least safe to say that no class or race or nation seems especially to stand out in the records. The tests with American Indian children[16] have produced about the same order of results as those with the Caucasian; results with American Negroes have shown approximately the same level of performance as those with whites; results obtained in Australia on the aborigines[17] are similar to those obtained on the general populations of the United States and Western Europe. Pupils in a school for the blind[18] score about the same as do those in a similar school of seeing children in North Carolina. The better controlled test results obtained in India are, as well as can be judged, comparable to those obtained in the Occidental countries.

There are some general *conditions* related to psi performance; age of subject, for example. As I have stated earlier, children adapt more quickly and easily to the conditions of the test than do adults and a greater percentage of them are likely to make significant scores. However, this does not mean necessarily that they have any greater psi ability; it could be the result of better adaptability. There is, likewise, noticeably less inhibition in the average nonprofessional woman when it comes to participation in the tests than there is among men. This difference, too, is reflected in test performance to some extent; however, it is not likely a difference in ability. Rather, it probably is an aspect of the sheep-goat relationship, as already mentioned, found by Dr. Schmeidler. The adult as compared to the child, and the average professional man as compared to most adult women, are more inclined to be critical or hesitant in acceptance of the idea of the test; this "goat" attitude may depress the scoring rate in a psi test.

As stated, too, no significant correlation of psi ability with abnormality, subnormality, or any other deviation in personality has been found. Differences in degree of cooperation and other states associated with these abnormalities are, as should be expected, important. It would be a strange psychological test of any kind that would be entirely unaffected by such factors.

But, in general, there has yet to be found a group of people that does not show some sign of psi ability when considerately and adequately tested. Likewise, there has been found no classification of people of any sort that, by virtue of its class (either professional or cultural or ethnic or political) seems to give evidence of more psi capacity than others. It must be remembered, of course, that only a small part of all that is necessary to make these judgments valid on a generalized scale has as yet been done. All that can be said is that the statements are true so far, and there has not been the time or the resources to go far. This is the point: A sufficient range and amount of data *have* accumulated, however, that if there were anything very striking, either in the absence of, or the outstanding presence of, psi capacity, it would likely have been noted and investigated.

The scoring rate in psi has, it is true, been found to correlate with certain measures of personality traits, attitudes, and states of one kind or another. For the most part these correlations have had to do *not* with the amount of psi ability evidenced in the test results but with the very different question of whether or not the scoring is above or below the average score expected from chance alone. In other words, they are based upon whether psi-hitting or psi-missing occurs. For a convenient illustration let us go back first to the "sheep" and "goats" of Schmeidler's experiments. The scores of the sheep gave a positive deviation as a whole and that of the goats gave a negative one. The goats required as much ESP ability to produce their negative deviation as the sheep did for their positive one. In fact, there seemed to be considerable association between the attitude of the subject toward psi and the sign of his deviation.

The same is true for Humphrey's separation of ESP subjects. It will be remembered that in her case the separation was based on drawings made by the subjects in the tests. The drawings were judged on the basis of certain qualities of form referred to as expansiveness and compressiveness. Humphrey obtained quite significant differences between the two groups, the expansive subjects scoring positively in their clairvoyance tests and the compressive subjects negatively. The personality trait that was indicated by the type of drawing was associated, then, like the sheep-goat attitude in the Schmeidler experiments, not with the *amount* but with the sign of the deviation. In other words, mental state or trait may have determined whether psi-hitting or psi-missing would result.

Now there have been a number of these successful separations of high and low scorers, and there is a fair amount of consistency of correlation shown by the different groups. But thus far one cannot be sure that any of these discriminations made on the basis of personality differences are dealing with the extent of psi capacity, for they may be related only to the psi-missing tendency. Though that is important in itself, it is a different question than that of extent or amount of capacity. For example, when Schmeidler was able with the use of the Rorschach test to widen further the gap of score average between her sheep and goats, she may still have been only further pointing up the association between the subject's attitude and his psi-hitting or psi-missing tendency.

The late Dr. Stuart of this Laboratory succeeded in making significant separations of high and low scorers in ESP tests on the basis of his subjects' patterns and strength of interest. Humphrey obtained quite effective separation on the basis of the Bernreuter Personality Inventory using the extraversion and introversion scale; and there have been other separations by these and other workers in the field. Even a full-scale review of all this work, however, would not lead to any different generalization or any serious qualification to this one; namely, that no sure linkage has yet been found between a measurable characteristic of personality and the amount of psi capacity that an individual possesses.

To get this understanding of the relation between certain personality correlates and psi-missing has been a progressive step. With all the clarification in interpretation of results it has given, it may now be possible to make progress toward the original and more fundamental problem of correlating personality differences with the *amount* of potential psi capacity (quite apart from psi-missing, test conditions, and transient mental states that may affect performance); that is, if any such relationship exists.

There is, however, one valuable point on this search for personality correlates of psi that does not need to await further developments. The results just reviewed seem to indicate afresh that here is being dealt with something not localized, not recently acquired, not a surface feature, but something very basic, something springing from far down the stem of psychological origins. It should have been expected under the hypothesis of psi outlined above that there would be found just what these studies of the personality correlates of psi have revealed. Psi seems to involve a submerged order of activity overlaid by the later developments of evolutionary progress. From this situation one should not expect to find outstanding differences in performance attributable to the native ability itself. Such variations of success in test performance as are found might be expected to result from more superficial elements in personality affected by the test conditions. Also, one should not anticipate finding natural groupings within the human species that would have a "corner" on psi. Rather, the problem is opened up as to what the full biological background, origin, and basis of the psi process may be.

The next step to be taken is across the species line. Probably everyone is by this time ready to ask whether psi is an exclusively human function. It can now be fairly definitely stated that it is not, although one cannot yet point to great accumulations of evidence such as have been amassed indicating the occurrence of psi in human beings. In the past there were the all too isolated reports of Bechterev's telepathy experiments with dogs[19] and the reports by my wife (L.E.R.) and myself of our experiments with the horse, Lady, at Richmond, Virginia.[20] However, recently initiated investigation of psi in animals has already begun to bear experimental fruits. Dr. Karlis Osis[21] of the Duke Laboratory has reached the conclusion that some kind of psi relationship between cats and human beings has been demonstrated in his experiments. The actual nature of the psi involved therein is the subject of further experimentation.

In his experiments Osis, with all the animal's sensory factors controlled, undertook to influence by means of psi its choice of one of two food dishes. Though less dramatic than the prophet Daniel's experiment with the larger cats (likewise, trying to keep the cats from eating in the wrong place!), Osis's results are significant enough and sufficiently well controlled to constitute a fresh start on the study of psi in animals.

Almost as impressive at the moment is the result of a survey[22] that has been made of the unexplained natural behavior of animals that may be due to ESP. Consider a few illustrations: The long annual migratory flight of certain species of birds over thousands of miles of open water to the tiny mid-ocean island on which they breed; the homing records of hundreds of pet animals, chiefly dogs and cats, that have been transported, often in enclosed carriers such as railroad cars, to distances ranging up to thousands of miles; and even a few instances in which animals are reported to have followed their masters or playmates when they were left behind as the family moved into territory to which the animal was completely strange. ESP *could* be the explanation of all of these. At the present it cannot be said that it *is*. But the challenge to find the explanation is too strong and the accumulation of material too great now to allow these types of behavior to go on being neglected and not subjected to scientific inquiry.

One more of the outstanding challenges in the unexplained behavior of animals is the amazing exploits of the homing pigeon. That behavior is still without any acceptable physical hypothesis. The problem of pigeon homing[23] offers a most suitable point of attack, however, and it ought soon to be possible, after concentrated experimental study, to say whether or not, along with its sensory equipment, known and unknown, the homing pigeon also uses ESP.

The investigations of psi in the animal kingdom, though still preliminary, have already served to call attention to the large promise that it holds. It will be important to learn whether the animals show any relation between simplicity of nervous system and amount of psi ability. There is an interesting hypothesis that they will. Out of these comparative studies with the different species should come some basis for checking up on the evolutionary origin of the psi capacity. There might come, also, some important leads for an understanding of the neurological foundation of psi.

A comparative study of psi in animals should disclose what has been the effect on the psi function of the development of the association areas of the human brain. It also could give a checkup on the hypothesis that those areas have overgrown and inhibited the functioning of this ability, not eliminated it; that psi is hidden, but not vestigial. What an exploration it should be!

The difficulties can now be profitably re-examined. In the light of what is now known, it should be surprising, indeed, if psi were *not* elusive and *not* difficult to bring under control. Operating, as it does, on an unconscious level, obscured as a rule by the more dominant conscious thought processes, and difficult in the extreme to convert into expressive, recognizable form, the psi function should be expected rarely to be exercised effectively in human beings and still more rarely caught in action when it is exercised.

Moreover, since the facts about the phenomena of psi were such as to have prevented them from being included in the orthodox psychology of the time, it should not be expected that such phenomena would be easy to catch experimentally. If they had been, they would have been caught and accepted long ago. Accordingly, acceptance at so late a date must be expected to come hard, even when the facts are caught. Burdened with these handicaps, the remarkable thing is that the psi occurrences have been successfully brought into the laboratory at all.

But while all these difficulties have delayed both the research and the recognition of its contribution, the fact is that there has been progress. Most important of all there have been advances in understanding of the phenomena under investigation. If, for the present, at least, psi cannot be raised into consciousness from its deeply submerged status in the total scheme of personality, it can now, at any rate, be better comprehended. By the same token, experimenters now can know better how to face the many experimental and other practical problems that are associated with it. They can also better understand many of the experimental results that have long been puzzling.

It is true that no full-bodied, hypothetical concept of the nature of psi can as yet be formulated. Not much can be said even about the energetic foundations of psi; how a relationship is possible between subject and object under the conditions of a good psi experiment. (Although physics and physiology have furnished a fair amount of understanding of the objective end of sensory perception, general psychology has not gone far with the subjective end of the subject-object relation in perception by way of the senses.) Likewise, not much is known of the neurological and the general biological foundations of psi, although it is known that this capacity is so general, so nonsegregated, and so unspecialized as to appear to be something basic, something that is part of the general biological heritage of the organism, something that extends across the species line. It has yet to be decided whether the effects of narcotic drugs, as reported among the earlier researches,[24] are effects upon the primary psi function itself or are only the result of effects exerted on other mental processes essential to the test. When, as in the Duke ESP experiments with subjects given sodium amytal, a sharp drop in scoring ability resulted, it could well be, as it now seems, that the subject's *general* acuity of judgment was impaired. One should expect such impairment in a comparable task involving fine sensory discrimination. Now, almost any test involving psi that can be given a subject will depend on the operation of complex, delicate judgments. For example, they will be required in merely keeping all the targets equally available or in excluding disturbing counterinterests from the center of attention. It is an open question whether one can distinguish between a psi function proper and the whole complex judgmental operation of which it is a part. But comparable questions still perplex the general psychologist with regard to sensory perception. Parapsychology needs more time.

What, then, *can* be said about the nature of psi? In a general way, if physical considerations are omitted, the operation of psi is suggestive of the more familiar higher cognitive functions such as reasoning, humor, invention, and the like. (This resemblance may, however, be due to the fact that higher cognitive factors are closely involved in the psi test; psi may not be the variable producing this appearance of similarity. The psi studies with animals, among other evidence, offer a different concept of the level at which psi belongs. That poses a question for the future.) I have already mentioned that the drugs that have been tested seem to affect psi much as they would any delicate judgment. Then there are the experimental results suggesting that a number of conditions, such as distraction, boredom, monotony, and lowered motivation, work against the operation of the psi process. On the whole motivational side, reaction in a psi test seems to be much the same as it would be in any difficult mental task that involved repeated tests of a delicate nature. Reward and punishment have very much the same kind of effect, and the result of the excitement of strong interest on the part of the subject is the same in both psi and nonpsi test performances.

Perceptual judgment in psi tests follows, in a number of ways, principles that are well known in the field of sensory judgments. This is true not merely as to the condition necessary for successful judgment, as, for example, the protection of the subjects against external and internal disturbance, but in the operation of the judgment itself. I have mentioned the position effects, especially the tendency of end objects in a series to stand out, and also the likelihood of the rate of scoring declining through a long list or over a long experiment.

Psi, too, gives evidence of responding to wholes or patterns, seeming to follow configurational or Gestalt principles. The evidence on this point, however, is only incidental. For example, there is the pattern response represented by the reinforcement effect already mentioned a number of times in connection with the work of Dr. Soal. In matching tests, too, it has been known for a long time that a subject succeeds as well in trying to match two similar cards without actual identification as he does in trying to identify a single card.

Here, as in normal sense perception, it can be assumed that in the matching act a less complete perceptual judgment is required than in the naming of an individual card. This point was established when it was found that a given subject's ESP ability would produce about the same size of total deviation on the negative side, if the subject were instructed to try to avoid hits instead of making them, as it normally would on the positive. If he normally averaged six where five is "chance" and then swung over to an average of four when he tried to produce low scores, it would mean that to get the same deviation on the negative side he was showing a less accurate perceptual judgment of about four times as many cards on that side as he had been on the positive side.

In a word, then, the psi type of perception is graded or partial or relative as well as patterned, the same as is sensory perception.

As a matter of fact, there is nothing about psi to which one can point that is different fundamentally from the familiar psychological processes except, first, that it is always unconscious. Sensorimotor functions and other mental processes can operate below the level of consciousness, too, although they ordinarily do not. Second, of course, the basic difference is that psi does not relate to the space-time-mass properties of the physical energies with which the sensorimotor world is concerned. As I have said, I think these two points are closely related. Perhaps we have merely come upon a deeper lying unconscious stratum of mental life—a stratum that has had to wait for its discovery until a sufficient interest in the operations more peculiarly psychological (i.e., nonphysical) in man's personality have been awakened.

Above all other considerations at the moment it is necessary to re-examine the problems and difficulties of getting psi under some degree of control in order to facilitate as much as possible the work of the experimenter. A thorough utilization of all that is now known about psi, combined with the resulting viewpoints, should help psi investigators over the bar of much of their past frustration.

In the light of present knowledge one can *expect* now to find it difficult to arouse and maintain sufficient motivation to get the psi function to break through its overlying heritage of conscious processes. The mere recognition of this needed emphasis will make all the difference in the world on the method of tackling the problem of controlling psi. For one thing, it means that the business of getting psi on an experimentally productive basis is recognizedly still an art of human relations and not an easy one, either. It is an art that will call for the best skills of coaching and counseling. It means that in order to produce a suitable test situation for psi an order of interest must be sustained sufficiently high to compete successfully with the many other interests arising out of the subject's own personality and the test surroundings.

It is not possible, of course, to reproduce the highly motivated, often tragic, situations that, in spontaneous psi experiences, help psi to break through its barriers. It will not be easy even to find experimenters with a sufficient reservoir of enthusiasm for the objectives and the gift of personality traits essential to the communication of their own enthusiasm and challenge. Nor is it often possible to provide them with fortunate situations that fully liberate them from the many restraints that would normally interfere with success, and give them access to groups of willing, cooperative, responsive subjects with whom they can work sufficiently freely and long.

It is now clear that a psi test is probably not a psi test at all if the procedure is not sufficiently inspiring to the subject to free his psi function to rise above all the intellectual and motivational difficulties that stand in its way. There was a time when the attention of experimenters was entirely centered on controlling against sensory cues and such. Now we must think first, second, and third about controlling against apathy, unconscious (or conscious) resistance, distraction, misplaced efforts, a too rational approach —these and many other factors.

But motivation is not all. People will differ vastly and profoundly in the facility with which the psi function can emerge from its hiding place deep down in the cerebral system in the subject's unconsciousness. It would be easy to say that general psychology should be able to tell us how to get past these surface resistances and incrustations of habit. Maybe it will some day. For the present, however, the parapsychological explorer will have to grope his own way to his objective, and in doing so he might take either one of two general paths.

One of these is to try to find people whose personalities are by nature already so composed as to allow the psi function to operate with relative spontaneity. The discovery and selection of such individuals may be accomplished by working with those who have exceptional and frequent spontaneous experiences. This approach, however, needs a great deal more of careful circumspection than has been given it in the past. Such individuals cannot simply be seated at a research table and expected to deliver the goods in a psi test merely because they have had psychic experiences. The adjustment they have to make to the test is likely to be a big one for them—bigger than they themselves will realize.

Strong motivation itself can be misdirected and can even be bad. There is, for example, the experiment by J. M. Bevan,[25] in which he utilized a group of people in ESP tests who either had had psychic experiences themselves or were very favorable to the ESP hypothesis. They were compared with others who had had no such experiences. He found that those who had had the experiences tended to start off in reverse; in other words, they produced a negative deviation. However, in the later sessions, their scores were higher than those of the group with whom they were contrasted. Being put on the spot and given the feeling that,

"Now if you think you are psychic, here is a test that will show it," is, I am quite sure, one of the ways to bring out the perverse personality trait responsible for psi-missing (and perhaps responsible for a lot of other effects).

The indications are that people who have had psi experiences of the spontaneous sort may need the most careful handling of all. Many of them are sensitive about these experiences, especially about the way other people have reacted to them. Also, the tests are just as new to them as to anyone else, and they haven't the slightest idea how their spontaneous experiences really occurred. If they think they have, they are almost certainly mistaken. However, with careful handling, they may be expected to produce results of value, perhaps because they have a less tightly woven barrier of conscious intellectual habits which psi would have to penetrate than have those who have not experienced spontaneous flashes of psi. Also, they are likely to have a more sustained interest because of the strong conviction about psi derived from their own experience. They are genuine sheep and are not likely to turn into goats over a low score or two and strike a vein of psi-missing.

Something can now be done, too, about psi-missing (the tendency to miss the target and produce negative deviations). It should be possible to go on with the study of personality correlates to the point of learning what mental states are conducive to it and, better, what traits or conditions prevent it. In time, a "psi-misser" may be identifiable and screened out in advance. Even with what is now known, however, a great deal of control can be exercised over this disturbing element in the psi test; a considerable number of indications have been given of the mental states connected with psi-missing. They can all be included in the development of a working procedure aimed at providing ideal conditions for maximal psi performance.

For the time being some experimenters may still be able to make more headway with the following up of the individuals who more or less naturally manifest a facility for psi performance, giving them the benefit of such conditions for the test as have been associated with high yield of results in the past.

But the second route has its possibilities, too. In many ways it is

more challenging and inviting. This is the general method of trying to *make* an individual into a good subject. It has, of course,
already been followed to some extent, as has the other route. I
am thinking of all the efforts expended in trying to make an individual into a good psi performer with the aid of hypnosis.
Along with this could go most of the exploratory efforts on the
use of drugs. One easily tends to think that there ought to be
some drug that would do just what is wanted in this particular
situation, handicap the operation of the association areas of the
cerebrum and yet not disturb the brain areas of older evolutionary origin, thus allowing the more primitive function of psi to
come into freer operation. It is clear, of course, that the very tests
are so set up as to involve delicate judgments, and the whole design of the experiment, as the subject sees it, involves a certain
amount of intellectual appreciation. It is probably asking too
much at this stage to attempt to discriminate by pharmacological
methods between the psi-test judgment and the general association areas that may inhibit psi.

Psychological methods, in addition to hypnosis, have, of course,
been tried and doubtless will be tried and tried again; but new
ideas are coming in that ought to be included in the fresh approaches that will be made. Trances and other self-induced subjective states (which, incidentally, ought to be experimented with
only under professional supervision, preferably in the laboratory
itself) may yet develop into a method for the release of latent psi
ability. As to the use of hypnosis in improving psi performance, all
that can be said is: still promising; not yet very convincingly productive. On all these psychological methods of helping an individual to greater self-liberation there is need for more skillful procedures and a better understanding of the inhibiting mental
integuments that must be penetrated.

In research one easily defeats himself by a too strict adherence
to a single, oversimplified, half-good way of solving his problems.
On the other hand, there is danger, too, of overextending efforts
and energies that are so limited to begin with, but it is safer to
maintain a fairly inclusive approach for getting psi onto a basis of
more dependable performance and perhaps above all to encourage

a variety of approaches by different explorers. Furthermore, since Nature gives herself away to the discerning observer if he gets a sufficiently inclusive view of the natural occurrences, it will pay to study all the spontaneous case material available (and all that our readers can send us) for the suggestions that may emerge on how best to permit psi to come into fuller operation.

A return to this approach in studies at the Laboratory has already been made. It is safe to predict that the parapsychological research of the next decade will be guided very considerably by the studies coming out of these vast thousands of classified human experiences of psi. Then, with all that can be done to select promising subjects by all the selective devices that are profitable to use, the aim should be to apply what is learned from experiments and experiences together in helping these screened subjects to achieve their utmost under controlled test conditions. It may be possible to develop a course of educational preparation for subjects in psi tests with a view to getting the best combination of attitudes and orientation towards the research. It may be feasible, also, to retrieve by a program of re-education some of the outstanding subjects of the past. These objectives at least seem eminently reasonable in the light of what is known.

If such a program is based on the working concept that a subject should be well motivated and should be given the best possible test and tester and surroundings to help him catch and recapture the spontaneity that for him liberates psi capacity, and if then the fact be faced that probably only a few people are likely to qualify as capable experimenters in psi tests, and, finally, if it be remembered that psychologically no test *is* a psi test until it has the psychological conditions now known to be necessary for the liberation of this deeply overlaid, unconscious, and easily thwarted function, it may in the foreseeable future be possible to break out of this ring of difficulties.

It is a program with a challenge for this decade. But more than that, it is an undertaking to which the weary worker may look forward with immense relief; for it is now clear that the main difficulties are at least partly inherent in the nature of psi and its relation to life and personality. The reason progress has been so slow and difficult has not been entirely the fault of the research worker; and in so far as it has been, his role has been made more comprehensible. The effort now can be better directed toward the elements that are remediable.

Part **II**

RELATION TO OTHER WORLDS

OF NATURAL SCIENCE

■ The science of psi is not an island. New though it may be to the explorer, it has connections with the mainland; it is really only one section of a vastly larger order that has many and varied parts. In fact, much of the work of discovery of this new world of the mind lies in tracing the relationships between parapsychology and the adjacent parts of the national domain to which they belong.

The three chapters to follow deal with the field of parapsychology in relation to the main sciences with which it has close connections: physics, biology, and psychology. In these chapters is developed something of a concept of parapsychology as a natural science. It is not, of course, that these three branches make up the whole of natural science, but rather that they are the ones closest to parapsychology. Any light on the relationship of parapsychology to them will help to place it more accurately in the scheme of knowledge and make it more understandable.

The relationship of psi to fields of practice and application will be left for discussion in Part III; such relationships have to do mainly with the *fruits* of parapsychology. For the present, attention will be given to the *roots*.

Chapter 4

NONPHYSICAL REALITY IN NATURE

■ It is the unique relationship of parapsychology to the science of physics that helps to identify it. As I have already indicated, its significance, too, resides largely in the relation its phenomena are found to have to the physical universe. But since this relationship is the very one that makes parapsychology a controversial subject to all those to whom the physical world comprises the one and only reality, a special chapter seems needed in which to assemble and appraise what has been learned about the relationship (and the lack of it) between parapsychology and physics.

For one thing, the general formulation of the concept of psi as a nonphysical process is comparatively new; and being new, it needs careful examination. As a matter of history, it is only in relatively recent years that the field of parapsychology has been expressly defined with respect to physics, or, for that matter, in any general terms. Earlier it had been identified only by its specific problems. These problems were called psychic, metapsychic, or parapsychological, but during the first fifty years of existence of the psychical research societies the meaning of those terms was not distinctly defined. When, as late as the thirties, attempts were made to distinguish and characterize the parapsychological area, it was realized that the problems are, in some aspects, first of all psychological. All relate to phenomena that seem to be associated with some sort of personal agency, living or dead, visible or invisible, human or animal. Second, they are phenomena that do not lend themselves to explanation by any of the known and accepted natural laws.

Within still more recent years a yet sharper line of definition has been suggested. It is now fairly clear that psi phenomena are identified by the fact that they defy physical explanation and require a psychological one. They always happen to people (or animals) or involve some associated or at least suspected personal agency or experience; but at the same time they do not follow conventional physical principles.

Now, so far as physics is concerned, this definition is merely a negative one. The *positive* character of the processes included in the field of parapsychology resides in the fact that they are personal or psychological. They are separated from the rest of the field of psychology (the science that deals with persons and their behavior) by the fact that they definitely appear to challenge explanation by physical principles.

How much of the functioning of personality—aside from psi—*is* nonphysical? It is a good question, but no one knows the answer; even the way to find the answer is a problem in itself. Certainly in psychology there has been almost no progress toward discovering whether or not the most common mental operations belong entirely, partly, or not at all within the domain of physics. For one thing, metaphysical prejudices against anything remotely suggesting dualism have kept the psychologist from taking seriously anything that even looks nonphysical.

The cardinal fact is that the more familiar mental processes do not lend themselves to quantitative study with relation to physics, by any means yet known to science. Each of those processes is shrouded in an ambiguity on this point from which psi stands clear. (That is what makes it psi.) Memory, for instance, is comparatively easy to experiment with. But by what method could the question of whether or not it operates on a strictly physical principle be answered? Select what mental processes you will, learning, emotion, imagination, reasoning, volition—none is any more easily tested than memory as to its relation to physical processes. In sensory perception the subject, of course, reacts *to* the physical environment. The strength of the sensory experience has long been known to vary with a certain lawfulness of relationship to the amount of energy of physical stimulation (e.g., the Weber-Fechner Law). But a century of experimental psychology, much of it highly concentrated on this problem area, has failed to bridge with purely physical principles the psychophysical gap from the stimulus and the nerve excitation to the subjective experience. Likewise, it has failed to show that the conversion of stimulus energy to perceptual experience is one of transition to a *non*-physical effect.

The explanation of psi as a nonphysical phenomenon will, of course, have to be very convincing and well founded, for much depends upon it. The very status of parapsychology as a distinct research field depends upon it; a new concept of psychology derives from it; and as will develop later, its significance reaches much farther still. Accordingly, some conception of the evidence should be given at this point, if only such as can be gained from a brief review. (An earlier review will be found in *Extrasensory Perception after Sixty Years.*[1]) Only the main types of evidence and some later developments will be covered here.

Three main types of evidence bear on the question of ESP and physics. There is, first, the nature and range of the targets or stimulus objects or the variety of things psi can include and the range of target conditions under which it can operate. There is, second, the question of spatial relations between the subject and the target object. And, third, there is the problem of the relation of time to ESP success (that is, whether psi can penetrate the future). The same range of questions can be raised about the physics of PK. Thus far, however, most of the research in PK has involved the comparison of physical properties of the target objects.

In general, the results of tests made on the range of target objects used with success in ESP experiments not only does not lead to any hypothesis that the subject-object relationship is a physical one; it does not *allow* the application of such an hypothesis. Consider the two main types of ESP, telepathy and clairvoyance, from the viewpoint of a possible physical hypothesis. It is true, we still do not know what the nature of the target object is in the case of pure telepathy, but even if one takes the conservative view that a pure telepathy operation is only clairvoyant perception of the cerebration of the sender, there is still the problem of constructing an hypothesis to account for the range of stimuli on which ESP has been demonstrated to function. What physical theory is there that could cover the entire range of objective target material that has been used in clairvoyance tests (symbols, colors, lights, etc.) and still include the delicate and complex brain activities of the telepathic sender?

The second type of evidence concerns the results from the comparison of different distances. Even ESP tests made before 1940 presented a fairly good case against any reliable relationship of distance to success. Since that time a number of long distance experiments have been conducted, and they have given more striking results. They defy any application of the inverse square law of decline of effect with distance. The experiment of Soal and Bateman[2] with their subject, Mrs. Stewart, has already been referred to and the fact mentioned that the 200-mile distance between subject and experimenter in one phase of the experiment was accompanied by no lowering of the scoring rate.

Mr. Maurice Marsh[3] of the Department of Psychology at Rhodes University in Grahamstown, South Africa, has conducted an experiment in ESP using drawing tests in which the distance between senders and receivers was approximately five hundred miles. Though not easy to evaluate in terms of familiar figures, partly because he worked with drawings, his results were sufficiently beyond "chance" to demonstrate that ESP took place.

There is the still longer distance involved in the tests carried out between Zagreb, Jugoslavia, and the Parapsychology Laboratory at Duke University in Durham, North Carolina.[4] In this experiment the principal subject was Dr. Carlo Marchesi in Zagreb, who attempted to identify cards set up as targets at the Duke Laboratory some four thousand miles from him. This long series of tests also yielded results with a deviation from the mean expectation of chance so large as to be expected by chance only once in 500 such series. But later when Dr. Marchesi visited Duke University and attempted to identify cards a few feet away in an adjoining room, his results did not exceed the expected chance average. Certainly, Dr. Marchesi's psychological set when he came to Duke, where he must to some extent have felt himself "on the spot," was in contrast to what he felt when he was in Zagreb and first attempted to demonstrate his ESP capacity. This illustrates the general observation that (at least within the limits we have tested) the psychological rather than the physical conditions of the test determine the rate at which a subject will score.

If the type of target and the distance between it and the subject do not affect success, what about barriers? Thus far no barrier has been found that can exclude the operation of psi. It is true, there has not been any exhaustive and thoroughgoing test of all the types of barriers that could be invented, but to penetrate a formidable barrier of four thousand miles of atmosphere alone would place a heavy requirement upon whatever kind of energy it is that is active in psi operations. Or, if one considers the ranges of mountains, and even the earth itself, that have incidentally been part of the intervening terrain between sender and receiver in some of the experiments that have been conducted in the past, he can scarcely think of anything that could be interposed that would serve as a more effective physical barrier to the hypothetical wave length that might be transmitting card symbols. Anything which conceivably could penetrate such barriers as hundreds or thousands of miles of atmosphere and ranges of mountains would still have to be the sort of physical energy that could convey an impression of the sender's delicate brain state in telepathy or the wide ranges of types of objects that can be used as targets in clairvoyance.

The task of explanation on physical lines is made much more difficult by the fact that, along with long distances and barriers, there is the added circumstance that in most of the experiments the targets are very close together in space. For example, in the Zagreb experiment, as in many other clairvoyance tests, the cards set up at Duke University were in such close juxtaposition (approximately twenty-five cards to the quarter inch) that to separate the impressions gained from the individual cards would seem to be impossible on any kind of accepted physical theory. Surely the resultant effect of radiation from such a pack of cards would be a general confused blur.

In some experiments, however, the cards have been used when lying with the edges toward the subject. Perception of these cards from the edgewise point of view would give only straight line impressions of all the symbols if the basis was one of radiant energy differentially absorbed by the cards or emanating from them.

Summing up, there simply is no explanation based on physical principle that will do. It is proper to consider only present day physics, just as it is to deal only with the parapsychology of today. A few people who are interested in the facts about psi persistently anticipate an ultimate explanation within the general framework of current physical theory. But that is hardly more than an affirmation of a faith, since no hypothesis which could explain psi phenomena as a whole on a physical basis has been offered as yet by anyone. From time to time someone suggests an explanation of one or another aspect of the psi capacity, more commonly telepathy, but when all other psi phenomena and all the conditions that need to be taken into account are considered, the most devoted physicalist finds himself in the sloughs of insuperable intellectual difficulty.

The toughest aspect of the problem of explaining psi by physics is the time relation. No one has ever produced a plausible explanation of precognition based on established physical theory. This has not been done even for the short-term precognition covering a few seconds of time that might be involved in the forward displacement results obtained by Soal and Goldney with their subject, B.S. It will be recalled that in this forward displacement the subject kept identifying, not the card at which he was consciously focusing, but the one that was coming next, even when a randomizing method of selecting the cards was followed, and the next card was selected *after* the subject's response was given.

As the evidence for precognition has accumulated, most of those who have followed it have given up all expectation of an hypothesis that could explain it adequately on a physical basis. There are a few who insist that the evidence for precognition is not yet sufficiently extensive or the conditions eliminating the various alternatives have not yet been made completely logic-tight, and thus they avoid facing the issue. In reaction to precognition data there are various kinds of personal attitudes, but no one has been able to offer any suggestion of a physical theory that could explain the facts we now have.

So far the discussion of psi and physics has been confined entirely to ESP. But the PK experiments, too, offer a test of the hypothesis of physical explanation. There are several ways in which the test can be set up to bring out whether or not PK follows the laws of mechanics. There can be comparisons of dice of different weights and sizes to see whether the mass of the used objects affect success in PK tests; or comparison can be made of the distance between subject and object or of different degrees of rounding of the dice corners. Of course, there has not as yet been nearly so much research carried out on PK as on ESP. But so far as comparative tests that involve the hypothesis of physical causation have been made on PK, they agree fully with the ESP findings: Physical laws do not hold.

Only a few experiments have been carried out to compare the effect of different distances between the subject and the object to be influenced in PK tests, and those have involved only short distances of not more than thirty feet. Dr. C. B. Nash's experiment[5] is the best one on this point. He found that subjects thirty feet away from the dice succeeded as well as when located within three feet of them, giving significant results in both conditions. In the PK researches comparisons have been made of various physical conditions of characteristics of the objects used, such as the number of dice per throw, their size or density or shape. Sufficient research has been conducted involving different numbers of dice per throw[6] to give the strong impression that the success obtained does not decline with the increase in the number of dice thrown at a time. One die is not regularly more successful than two dice per throw or two more effectively influenced than six at a time. In fact, no reliable quantitative relation has been found.

Further, in comparative tests of different sizes and weights, there is no reliable indication that results are better with the smaller or the lighter dice.[7] On this point the evidence is moderately good and extensive. And, finally, although this last point needs confirmatory study, there is indication that the rounding of the corners of the dice so as to make rolling easier does not improve the scoring rate.[8]

Altogether, the differences that are obtained in all these comparisons are more plausibly accounted for by psychological than by physical principles. The dice which the subject finds most interesting or challenging or otherwise to his liking are the ones with which he is likely to score the highest. The experimental work has not progressed as yet to the point where it is possible to say what the limits of these mental factors are. It should not be assumed that they are unlimited or that the range of PK is limited only by the beliefs of the subject. It will remain for the researches of the future to find out how far PK can range and where the physical conditions do become effective. Unfortunately, there are now available only the researches of a few scattered, hampered workers—isolated eccentrics, they must seem—who think it important to find out whether or not the human mind can directly influence the movement of material objects.

To repeat, then, we can say only that so far as research has gone PK shows as much independence of mass as ESP has shown of the limitations of space and time. But to stress this difference now is not to ignore the questions it raises and it is not to generalize beyond the facts on hand. It will be enough for the present to say that within the now fairly extensive area covered by the psi investigations there is such definite lack of any regular relationship of the psi function and physical criteria that one can only conclude that they are two very different areas of causal principles. And parapsychology, whatever one may say about the rest of psychology, is a problem area in which the laws of physics, at least the physics of space, time, and mass (Is there any other?) has not been found applicable.

I might conclude this section with the curious but interesting fact that, for the most part, those who have made the strongest protest against the conclusion that psi transcends physical explanation are not the physical scientists but the psychologists.

There have been plenty of physicists who have agreed that the psi-test results cannot be explained by physics. They are, it is true, only affirming the research facts themselves. This failure of psi to conform to the space-time relations of physical processes is a confirmed experimental result, but it is often hard to see and hard to say a new fact. Comparatively speaking, physicists have approached the facts of the psi research with comparative open-mindedness.

The relationship should be considered, too, from the viewpoint of physics. That branch of science is expanding rapidly and the conceptual boundaries of the field have been considerably altered by advancing discovery. There are some major disagreements—even schools of theory—among physicists, and it would be hard to say how much of current physical theory is sufficiently settled for acceptance. The task of drawing a boundary line for the field of physics that would satisfy everyone would be difficult if not impossible.

But whatever uncertainty may prevail on the frontiers of current physical theory, there is thus far no sweeping abandonment of the criteria of time-space-mass relationships which are the ones involved in the interpretation of the psi experiments. No reason has ever yet been suggested why these criteria cannot be followed with reliance in dealing with the problems of psi so long as they continue to be fundamental to the description of the physical operation of the universe.

The person who most often expresses reluctance to agree to the specified boundary line between parapsychology and physics is the speculative enthusiast who is already looking ahead to the physics of tomorrow. Intoxicated a bit, no doubt, by the magnificent advances of this branch of science in which the problems have been so successfully mastered by mathematical methods, he will argue against calling anything nonphysical until the whole domain of physics has been mapped. In the extreme, this attitude can be reduced to the absurdity of saying, "Let us not do anything until everything is done, so that we will know just what to do." One cannot wait, of course, for further advances in physics or in parapsychology or any other branch of inquiry. It is necessary to take present knowledge, put it together as best one can, use the best working concepts available, and settle for whatever hypothesis can most soundly and simply explain the phenomena. The present conclusion, then, is that there is something in the psi-test results that calls for a type or order of reality beyond that which is physical—an *extra*physical one. Let the future of physics, like the future of parapsychology, take care of itself!

In any case, it is the fact of the difference between psi processes and physical operations, not the words used to describe it, that is important. It would make no difference in its significance if we called the area of psi problems "Unknown Physics," or just "X-Physics." As later discussions will show, the same consequences would follow and the only difference would be that the meaning of the word "physics" would have to be so far extended to cover this outside area that it would have hardly any useful meaning.

In every field of research one must be prepared to add or substitute improved criteria and improved working concepts when and as they are found. No one can say that the present conception of psi and the boundaries of parapsychology are permanent. Such judgments cannot be passed even in older fields than ours. It will admittedly be a vast research program, though a necessary one, that will go on to determine the extent to which the operations of psi are free from physical limitation and thereby to clarify the nature of the boundary.

Obviously, however, the *division* between parapsychology and physics is only half of the relationship. Equally important now, and eventually much more important, are their underlying inter-operations that transcend this boundary between psi and the physical world. However convenient and philosophically significant it is, this division into physical and nonphysical is relative and is an artificial one so far as the natural operations are concerned. It is reasonable to assume there is a continuity of causation* in all subject-object interactions, whether they are sensorimotor or

---

* C. G. Jung presents his synchronicity hypothesis in his recent book, *Natur-erklärung und Psyche* (with W. Pauli as co-author. Zürich: Rascher Verlag, 1952). This modification of psychophysical parallelism is a substitute for causation in certain areas of action, but as it challenges so entrenched a concept, it must naturally bear the burden of proof.

parapsychological. The subject-object distinction is itself only a relative one.

It will be the task of biophysics and psychophysics to find out if there are unknown, imperceptible, extraphysical influences in nature that function in life and mind, influences which can interact with detectable physical processes and thus convert energy to effects that can be scientifically recorded. This common psychophysical frontier is as much a physical as a parapsychological one, and it could be as great a discovery for one field as for the other to find this inferred basis of interaction between psi and physical processes. While it has been necessary first to recognize the distinctive character of the psi function, it will be just as urgent in due time to stress the fact that the distinction is not absolute, and that without integrative interaction between subject and object we should never know of the psi process itself; without some sort of subject-object interaction involving thought and the brain we should, in fact, never know anything.

Thus the kind of absolute dualism that earlier drove psychology into the arms of physics is, in the first place, not logically defensible; and, in the second, it has never had empirical proof. One cannot even conceive the possibility of two completely different systems interacting and, yet, at the same time, constituting so manifestly unified a whole as the personality of man—without having something fundamental in common. It seems logical instead to expect that any dualism within a universe would have to be a *relative* one. One can perfectly well see new divisions and diversifications within the personality of man without going to any such extravagant Cartesian bifurcation of him that would not allow the parts to be on speaking terms with each other. Those who are excessively worried about the integrity of the universe when parapsychology is mentioned might, I repeat, join in the work of tracing the causal connections of psi phenomena back to whatever basis of unification there is.

Certainly if psi phenomena are to be explained the present concept of reality must be extended. It *has* been extended, of course, time and again and none should be so foolish as to say we are through extending it (even though people may react that way with each new claim that comes along). The fact is, both philosophers and theoretical physicists have repeatedly inferred various substrata of reality underlying the phenomena of physics themselves, although these are often speculatively assumed to be forever beyond the reach of observation and measurement. Such hypothetical substrata would, of course, lie beyond the sensory range of man; but that would not make them any less real. For that matter, most of what concerns modern physics is, likewise, beyond the senses.

If one clings, as I think one must at least try to do, to the traditional concept of causation, then the establishment of psi calls for the hypothesis of a special determining influence or force, one that is capable of producing the results obtained in the psi experiments. What is really needed is another energy. Whether the effect is registered directly or indirectly, it would still qualify as the "capacity to do work," the words by which energy is defined. Such a psi determinant or factor should be supposed to be convertible to one or another of the known and detectable energies, since only thus could its operation be discovered and its effects be measured. But it need not have much in common with the energies to which it is convertible for science to be able to establish its presence and discover its properties. Directly perceptible energy systems (meters, etc.) are constantly used to detect imperceptible ones. And, in a roughly analogous way, mental imagery of card symbols that is obviously derived from SP provides the form in which ESP effects are registered in the subject's consciousness. Designers of experiments regularly use rational inference from the data of one kind of operation to reach an intangible one. The reaching-rod of scientific analysis crosses the curricular boundary lines of the Nature found in the textbooks with almost magical facility. Yet the very success of such inference implies some common denominator of interconvertibility, some interchangeable basis of causation.

Back of psi, then, and of all the rest of nature must be some sort of common energetic reality. There must be such a source of the known physical energies, some of which affect the sense organs under certain conditions and which produce effects more or less limited by time-space-mass relations; it has to be if the concept of causality has any validity. Such a common stock must be at the same time the source of this psychic energy that, within the range of conditions investigated, does *not* affect the senses, does *not* produce effects directly related to time, space, and mass, and yet *does* produce results, results that are indirectly observable when converted into the forms of subjective or objective records that can be perceived or otherwise experienced.

One cannot, of course, assume that as the psi explorations continue *no* limitations will be found in their relation to time, space, and mass. For that matter, of course, it is not yet known to what extent physical operations themselves are exempt from one or another of the usual time, space, and mass limitations. Certain physical phenomena have been described as exceptions to the usual laws governing physical bodies. Under certain conditions a particle may have no mass; under another, a phenomenon may be timeless; and under certain conditions a function is spaceless. There is to our knowledge, however, nothing but a psi phenomenon that appears to defy all these criteria of physical operation and at the same time displays intelligent purpose in the process.

Since physics as well as parapsychology has yet to find its causal roots in the natural universe, and since its boundaries and criteria are more fluid than those of most fields of science, we may expect help from it in a search for the common ground of energy interchange within the personality which enables psychophysical interoperations to take place. It may profit physics as well as parapsychology to push the research on precognition further into the more difficult ranges of timing, for time is still a problem in physics as well as in psychology.

Here is a final and a venturesome reflection: It seems justifiable to expect to find underneath the surface of our somewhat arbitrary academic distinctions (physics, psychology, biology, etc.) a less definable but more basic reality than has been known hitherto in natural science. At some point of development into its different forms of manifestation a process may still be indeterminate and not be either definably psychical or physical but only nonspecifically psychophysical or biophysical or just undifferentiated, unconverted energy. How will scientists ever know if there be such an undeveloped nonspecific reality? Like all the hypotheses that have since become established theories, if this one becomes the subject of active speculation for a time someone may think of some sort of crucial experimental trap and catch whatever the reality may be. But that will never happen unless there is active speculation over what lies behind the observable effects and an attempt made to formulate a testable hypothesis concerning it.

Nature, however, did not begin her task of laying out the universe with a good modern textbook of science in hand, curricular divisions and all. The student attempting to discover her design is handicapped by having to begin with these distinctions deeply stamped upon his thought. They may not represent the truth and may mislead him. But if physicists and parapsychologists and others, in attempts to close in on the great common unknown —the basic nature of personality—keep the primary fact in mind that the manifestation being dealt with is a whole, functioning, integrated system, they can work back from their several points of departure to any such deeper lying, undifferentiated root reality as there may be. It should be the same reality no matter from which side it be approached. And it will most likely be the physicists whose picks the parapsychologist will strike first if the digging progresses and the tunnels converge as it would seem they should do.

Chapter 5

THE PLACE OF PSI

IN THE SCIENCE OF LIFE

■ To the field of biology the psi researches stand in a very different relation than they do to physics. Between parapsychology and the physical world a deep distinction must be drawn even though the two do interact, of course, and through some common basis of interaction yet unknown are integrated. But parapsychology, in a general way, *belongs* to biology. To physics the problem area of parapsychology is a coordinate one, while to general biology in its largest significance parapsychology is unquestionably subordinate. No one questions that, whatever psi phenomena are, they have to do with living beings in some way, shape, or form; and biology is, of course, the science of living beings. There is much about this relationship on which to disagree; much, too, on which we are all still too ignorant for a wise judgment to be made. But it can be taken for granted that parapsychology and general biology have a long common frontier, the boundary of a subdivision from the larger whole of which it is a part.

The present comparison, like that involving physics, is necessarily a very unequal one. So little is known as yet in this new branch, parapsychology; biology, on the other hand, is already a relatively old science and is enormously broad and ramifying. As the sciences go, it has been immensely useful and successful; but to balance the comparison, it is important to remember that, even so, most of the larger biological questions are not very well answered as yet. Not only is life itself still a mystery, but the whole field of biology is stumpy with basic problems yet unsolved. What, for example, are the forces organizing the substances that make up living organisms and creating the form they take? How did the characteristics of species originate and how are they actually preserved and carried along in potential through all the stages of reproduction? Many questions like these are still unanswered.

It is baffling even to explain the simplest processes such as the rise of sap in the tree, the production of a teardrop, the impulse in the nerve fiber, or the ultimate distinction between a living and a dead cell. The accumulated knowledge concerning these various things is vast and burdensome enough for the young scholar to master, but still it falls far short of the good working understanding of how living nature functions, so necessary if men are to live wisely and efficiently as a part of it all. For that the very *least* they ought to know is where man himself, as a person, comes in: what kind of role he plays.

Thus, on the side of the unknown the two fields are less unevenly balanced than on that of the known. In any event these unknowns of biology should be kept in mind in this comparison with parapsychology, if only because they lie closer to the borders of the psi field than do any of the more familiar and well-explored areas of biology. If, as must be the case, psi has to fit in somewhere in the complete schema of the life sciences, it will surely have to be in some part of the general field that still remains largely to be explored. It is just this point that should make the discoveries of parapsychology most significant to the larger field; namely, that they promise not merely to broaden the domain in extent, but to add a new quality to its principles.

Of course, the biologists themselves must be reckoned with in this matter. How do *they* look upon this newcomer, parapsychology, that leaves problems on its doorstep that must seem, to some of them at least, of doubtful legitimacy? Are they as inhospitable as the psychologists? Do they, too, fear the implications of psi for their philosophy? There are, on this line of thought, some interesting comparisons to be drawn.

Biology, like psychology, has had its growing stage of insecurity concerning its scientific respectability. But this stage in biology is at least half a century farther back, not, as with the younger science, a recent if not a currently active experience. With biology it was a fear of vitalism, the hypothesis of a special nonphysical life force, that was a close counterpart of psychology's reaction to psychophysical dualism. For the young American biologist during the first quarter of the century to have attempted to build a successful career on a vitalistic theory of life, one that held that there was a distinctive life factor over and above the forces and substances that belong to the world of matter, would have been professional suicide. Driesch's entelechy hypothesis, Bergson's *élan vital*, and McDougall's horme found no great favor, at least in biological circles in the Western hemisphere. Rather, the American scene in the biological sciences was dominated by the strictly mechanistic philosophy of the organism represented by the views of Jacques Loeb.

Biology, too, in its origins represented a break with supernaturalism and, as early biological pioneers first sought the shores of naturalistic explanation, the first accessible landing point they found was that of the physical sciences. They naturally found the physical aspects of nature most easily caught by instruments and measured by mathematics. As the more material sciences and technologies grew and prospered, the belief developed among scientists that nature and the physical universe were one and the same thing. As for living organisms, they were just more complex machines that, for complete understanding, only required further study along mechanistic lines. Accordingly, since biology rejected all sorts of spiritualistic (or nonphysicalistic) theories in becoming a science, it became an unwritten law that any turn of thought in that direction would be an unpardonable retrogression. Any hypothesis that dragged in the nonphysical—that is, any vitalistic hypothesis—would be downright subversive to the prevailing scientific philosophy.

The difference today, fifty years later, is that biology has now so completely established itself and matured that its large membership of secure and confident scientists is no longer nervous over the issue. There are no more Drieschs, Bergsons, and McDougalls pointedly threatening the security of the physicalistic philosophy of the organism. And the few voices raised in anti-materialistic protest are, therefore, better tolerated. Lacking a challenging experimental case, such voices do not disturb the biologist's peace of mind or upset his philosophical equilibrium.

Now comes parapsychology, and it *has* some experimental facts. They are hard facts, too, for they have had to stand tests that are more severe than any of the other facts biology has already accepted. It is too early yet to say how much headway the concept of this new nonphysical world is going to make with general biology, but the prospects are at least more encouraging than they have been with the profession of psychology. This may be only a matter of the relative ages and stages of those two scientific fields. There have been, at any rate, no excoriating attacks and denunciations from biologists great or small. Perhaps they do not feel sufficiently on the defensive, considering that the subject belongs more to psychology than biology, as it has at least in the past.

Instead, some interest in the work in parapsychology has been shown by a fair number of biologists today. Long before there was any similar inclination on the part of general psychology there were biologists both in this country and abroad who were ready to consider the psi hypothesis in attempting to explain the baffling problems of animal behavior. Several naturalists have seriously urged the consideration of an unknown sense, a "sixth sense" or a sense of direction not among the recognized sensory powers of the animal. This unknown sense approach is most common among students of bird migration. But there are others who propose an extrasensory mode of perception as necessary to explain the observed behavior.

Some examples may be of interest, if only to show the wide diversity represented. N. J. Berrill of McGill, in his highly readable volumes, *The Living Tide* and *Journey into Wonder*, takes seriously the possibility of telepathic factors in the puzzling migratory travels of such species as penguins and seals. A. C. Hardy[1] of Oxford is impressed by the need for taking telepathy into account as an evolutionary factor. Edmund W. Sinnott of Yale, in his books, *Cell and Psyche* and *Two Roads to Truth*, recognizes ESP as something to consider in trying to get at the unknown forces that guide organismic activity from the growth of the simplest cell to the most complex human behavior. G. V. T. Matthews[2] of Cambridge University, although an ardent pursuer of unknown sensory factors in the homing flight of the pigeon, concedes that parapsychological factors will now have to be considered. And C. A. Naether,[3] practical pigeon man, proposes in his book on the pigeon that telepathy is a possible factor in homing. Rudyerd Boulton, formerly Curator of Birds at the Chicago Museum of Natural History, has long been willing to entertain the ESP hypothesis as a factor in the orientation of migratory birds, especially in the flight of the golden plover. F. B. Sumner,[4] late of the Scripps Institution of Oceanography, stressed the need to consider the possibility of extrasensory factors in the migratory movement of salmon.

There are others who, less explicitly or in more remote connections, see biological significance in the psi investigations and who are sufficiently independent of the current philosophy of biology to allow themselves to take cognizance of the psi investigations. In this country G. E. Hutchinson of Yale has taken such a generalized interest, as has Julian Huxley of Britain, the physiologist Hans Schaefer of Heidelberg, Germany, and in Australia the neurologist J. C. Eccles (who incorporated a consideration of the psi findings in his Oxford University Waynflete Lectures of 1952 on the mind-brain problem). In Britain the Society of Experimental Biologists held a symposium in London in 1950 on the findings of parapsychology. One of the papers was read by the biologist J. B. S. Haldane of University College, London, and the list could be continued if there were need.[5]

So it looks as though there will be plenty of consideration from biologists. The "parapsychobiological" frontier can be kept comparatively open, and that ought to be to the advantage of all. What advantage? That depends, of course, on the point of view.

It will be more appropriate here to look at the question from the parapsychologist's viewpoint.

The need is now particularly great for parapsychologists to get down to fundamentals. Biology is, of course, necessarily basic for their inquiry; the psi function *has* to have a natural history, a biology. Somewhere in the organism there may even be what in some sense can be called a locus, a place more identified with psi than any other. This does not mean that there has to be a specific receptor or a localized brain area; in fact, localization may mean anything in the way of a reception center or conversion point, not necessarily a gross anatomical structure or set of specialized tissues. If there is any localizable port of entry, or if none can be found, the knowledge of the fact would be most important.

Also, there has to be some sort of hereditary basis. The mere fact that psi capacity is one that is preserved in some way and degree indicates that there must be a genetic foundation of some kind that carries it from one generation to the next. What alternative is there except the fantastic notion that the capacity originates *de novo* in each individual who demonstrates it?

Then, too, as soon as one thinks of heredity, the thought follows through to the question of the evolutionary origin of psi, and this in itself is a problem with many ramifications.

One of the best features of these questions is that something can be done about them. The beginning that has already been made on the general question of psi in animals has been mentioned in Chapter Three. That beginning is hardly more than a preliminary step to the larger problems just stated, and it has been only recently initiated. Such as it is, however, it is a step in an important direction.

First of all, in thinking about the localization of the psi function in the organism one logically inquires about the distribution of this ability among the various species of animals that possess widely different nervous and other anatomical systems. One might hope to get a good lead toward answering the question by ascertaining which species show psi ability and what correlation, if any, is found between anatomical structure and the ability. For example, if the ability extends to a species that has no great cerebral development, then one would not expect to find localization of psi capacity in the cerebrum of the species in which that organ is developed. At the same time, such a survey of the presence of psi in the animal kingdom should, if it could be adequately made, give some idea of its evolutionary origin.

It was pointed out in Chapter Three that the results of the psi researches on the human species suggest that the ability is an acquisition of early evolutionary origin. It will be recalled that this tentative concept of it grew out of a number of considerations. First, there was the fact that the subject has no consciousness of how and when psi operates. The inhibiting effect on psi of the more recently acquired intellectual powers also appeared to support the point. Add to this the failure to find any group of people that has a monopoly on psi capacity and the fact that to date no trait or type of personality has been found to correlate with *the amount of psi capacity* (as distinct from the sign of the deviation from chance average). All of this suggested that psi is an elementary mode of reaction of the organism, one that probably represents the beginning of orientation in the initial adaptation to environment. This attempt at a biological hypothesis of where and how psi comes into the order of living things is only a trial beginning. It may do to start with and help to draw attention to the need for a theory.

It has long been a question whether, on the other hand, psi may not be a newly evolving gift of man. At an earlier stage of inquiry I suggested (*Extrasensory Perception*, 1934) that ESP showed some of the features of higher thought processes. This judgment was based in great part on the effect of drugs on the ESP test performance. It is true that the administration of narcotic drugs such as sodium amytal has been found to interfere with the performance of subjects in psi tests. And, also, the score-depressing effect has been counteracted by the use of caffeine. Such results would be expected of the more highly evolved mental functions.

There is, however, this complicating thought. These drugs may, for all that is known, not be reaching the ESP process itself, directly, at all; they may be affecting only certain other processes on which the successful performance of the subject in the test depends.

Similarly, all the interference with high positive scoring in psi tests associated with other mental states such as skepticism, boredom, or distraction could be accounted for as effects upon elements in the test response other than psi itself. One cannot be certain that the true psi function itself has yet actually been touched in these comparative studies of conditions, mental or physical, affecting test performance. There is much information to suggest it has not. This fact helps to point up the hypothesis that, in its evolutionary origins, psi may be a very primitive function.

How can such an hypothesis be brought to test? The very first approach to a consideration of it has seemed to be the making of a complete and thoroughgoing survey of unexplained animal behavior, more especially that which could lend itself to conceivable interpretation as a possible psi effect. Such a survey has been undertaken and it already is revealing large areas of quite inexplicable behavior that range far over the animal kingdom. In most of these areas psi could be a sufficient explanatory hypothesis. Happily the matter can be brought to experimental test and if the experiment is properly and effectively managed, the question about psi can be settled.

Among these still unexplained phenomena, those that stand out most dramatically, perhaps, are long-distance migration and homing, which have already been mentioned. The very important first steps of assembling the main facts of observation are already being taken. Without these it is hardly likely that any experimental work to focus the issue involving the psi hypothesis would be undertaken or, if it were, that it would be undertaken on lines that would conform sufficiently to the phenomenon to be studied. But the second step of following through with experiments is entirely necessary before valid conclusions can be reached. The observations of spontaneous performance, even when reported by competent observers, cannot have the significance of experimental demonstration.

On the homing problem, for example, there is a large collection of records of very puzzling animal behavior. In a large portion of them, the animal returned home after it had been lost or released at some distant point under conditions that could not have given any recognizable guiding clues. It is obviously a good question how such behavior can be explained. Or must one say that no anecdote is of any value to science and confine all his observations to the laboratory, no matter what happens outside?

Take for a typical example the case of a cat belonging to an army sergeant from Kokomo, Indiana. When the sergeant was transferred to Augusta, Georgia, the cat was sent to him. It traveled in an express car from Indiana to Georgia. The animal was, according to the account, an easily identified, huge yellow tomcat with definite hunting and eating habits, well known in its neighborhood. When, soon after its arrival in Georgia, the cat left the sergeant and his wife in Augusta and made the 700-mile trip back to the farm at Kokomo (in about three weeks), it was recognized by family and neighbors as it fell into its old routine of coming for its daily ration of milk and then going off for hunting adventures. We have to suppose that the animal found its way home by some method of navigation not known to conventional biology. The easiest way out of the puzzle for biologists would be to find an excuse to dismiss the story. But such dismissal is much more difficult after one collects and reads hundreds of other similar stories and interviews many of the people concerned. Among the latter are certain to be personal acquaintances, colleagues, and other friends. In many cases one can see no conceivable way, within the bounds of reason and intellectual honesty, of dismissing the case.

Even though the scientist draws no conclusions from these case studies and realizes the danger of mistaken identity, of erroneous reporting, of hoax, sensation-seeking, and other alternatives, still when the number of unexplainable cases multiplies sufficiently the point is reached where something ought to be done about them. The time comes when scientific judgment and common sense together call for a thorough investigation, not only to verify the apparent homing ability itself but to determine the nature of the orienting principle. Logically, the next move is to experiment.

Let no one, scornful of the value of anecdotal material to science, say that these cases of animal behavior have already been properly examined and rejected by the professional biologist. There is no record that any large collection of representative cases of spontaneous homing behavior has ever been systematically analyzed and appraised. It is not that these cases have been overlooked because they are obscure and scattered and beyond scientific reach. Take for an outstanding example a homing story that had extremely wide circulation in press, magazines, and books in the mid-twenties. It concerned a collie named Bobbie, who made his way home to Silverton, Oregon, six months after having been lost in Indiana while on an automobile trip. According to evidence collected by the Oregon Humane Society, Bobbie did not return by the route over which he had been taken east but took instead a southerly one several hundred miles off the eastward trail. The family had returned via Mexico. The facts seem reasonably well established for the present purpose of merely raising questions. How did he "navigate" over such vast territory on a journey that would have been fully as big a feat for him as the voyage of Columbus was for that great explorer?

One zoologist has suggested to me that the dog may have had a capacity to determine his latitude and longitude from the sun, the same theory proposed by G. V. T. Matthews of Cambridge to explain the homing of pigeons. However, Bobbie did not get home for six months, and the correction for all the changes in the sun angles during that period becomes pretty complicated. Thus far there is no evidence that any animal can make a determination of his absolute geographic position from sun position. Yet however farfetched the hypothesis may be, it deserves the thorough testing Matthews and Gustav Kramer[6] of the Max Planck Institut of Wilhelmshaven are giving it. What would be inexcusable would be the continued ignoring of these accumulations of long unexplained animal achievement, already known to zoology before the time of Charles Darwin.

In the case of ESP, however, we have an hypothesis already soundly established for the human species; there is now, as I have already indicated, even some evidence that ESP is not confined to man. Only a powerful bias against an extrasensory mode of perception could have kept scientists for over a century from wondering and then investigating whether Bobbie and the Kokomo cat and the hundreds of other animals on record may not have used that capacity (along with their other abilities) to orient themselves in the homeward direction.

There have been a few experimental studies of homing. But thus far the results have only tended to deepen the mystery. That is to say that, since they leave the question open, they have made it more reasonable to keep an open mind toward ESP as a possible explanation. For example, experiments were carried out with cats by the zoologist F. H. Herrick[7] of Western Reserve University. First he took his own cat in a bag on a streetcar from his home to his office, a distance of nearly five miles across the City of Cleveland. It escaped and returned in one night. In that case no sun angle could have been involved; the distance was too short. And no one will suppose the cat smelled its way five miles across the city of Cleveland. Herrick was rightly puzzled. In a series of further tests he released that cat (and others) after transporting it in a closed container to distances of from one to three miles from home. He made the test under a variety of conditions at different points of the compass and without allowing himself to be visible; yet the cat found its way back each time until, after a final release at 16½ miles' distance, it did not return.

Bastian Schmid's[8] homing tests with dogs, carried out at the University of Munich, gave results that are still unexplained in the textbooks. Two out of three dogs tested found their way home twice under well recorded conditions when taken to points from three to five miles from home. They were released in locations which they were definitely known never to have visited before. Careful records were taken of the weather conditions such as direction of winds, overcast, and the like. The record of the route followed by the dog was taken by persons with whom the dog was not acquainted. Each of the two dogs was released a second time at the same spot and each took partially different return routes the second time from the courses followed on the first.

There is, however, nothing in the experimental study of homing to compare with the work that has been done on pigeons. It has, of course, long been known that the carrier pigeon will home reliably within the limits of its training. In pigeon races birds are released at distances up to 1,000 miles or more, though always in a direction from which they have been trained to return.

Interpreting the results of these homing experiments, however, is difficult and puzzling. And it is well to note that such difficulty was foreshadowed by a wealth of case reports of pigeons that had spontaneously returned home on escaping from lofts to which they had been shipped and by taking directions to which they had not been trained. Matthews has now shown in well-controlled experiments that pigeons may be taken to release points at distances from 70 to 100 miles from the loft in other directions than, even opposite or at right angles to, those in which they have been trained to return and still return in sufficient percentages for the results to be conclusive. Moreover, by observing the direction of departure of the pigeons on release, Matthews found a sufficiently marked tendency to orient homeward at the start to be considered a demonstration of homing ability, whether or not the birds actually returned. By various controls he was able to eliminate the different explanations that have been previously advanced for pigeon homing. He then offered the hypothesis I have already mentioned, that the pigeon has some physiological mechanism that enables it to respond to the angle of the sun with the vertical. Matthews supposes that even when permitted only a few minutes of observation the bird, even though circling in flight, can measure accurately the differences in this angle, due to the relative movement of the earth and sun. It is necessary to suppose that it can do so with such accuracy that it can effectively determine its geographic position. He recognizes that such judgment would require an accurate appreciation of the time of day and the effect of the seasonal variations on sun position. But the Matthews hypothesis is that, with the geographic position known by means of solar angle and time of day and with accurate memory of home position, the bird can determine also which way to turn at the start and can follow a correct homeward course.

Kramer had already shown by some exceedingly clever experiments that certain wild birds could orient themselves to find food by observation of the sun's position and that they could even correct for the time of day. He and Ursula von St. Paul,[9] like Matthews, also demonstrated that pigeons can home without having had training in the direction from which they are released. They successfully used pigeons that had not been trained to home in any special direction but had merely been acquainted with the finding of the home loft from short distances. Pratt, of the Duke Laboratory, has now found even these short distance training releases unnecessary.

Kramer went still further; and what he has found makes difficulties for the Matthews hypothesis, for he has discovered that birds can be released with only thirty seconds' experience of sunlight and, in sufficient numbers to be conclusive, take off immediately in the homeward direction. However, the earth-sun movement in thirty seconds would offer only a slight change of angle on which the birds' computation would have to be made. His results have led Kramer to consider it necessary to look for some explanation other than the Matthews hypothesis to explain the birds' ability to take the right direction on release. He recognizes the importance of the sun angle as an orienting factor in enabling the bird to *hold* to the direction taken. His own pioneer experiments on the effect of sun position on bird behavior support this aspect of the hypothesis. But he has reached the point where none of the proposed hypotheses satisfy him as accounting for the homeward turning of the pigeon on release—its ability to start in the proper direction.

All the hypotheses that have been tested experimentally are sensory in nature. And since they have all been found wanting, the explanation is to be found in terms either of an unrecognized sense or else of an extrasensory mode of perception. For the next move in such a situation there are two possible things to do. One is to attempt to design a test that is, for the species concerned, more positively and unambiguously a test of ESP. The other is to keep on eliminating, as far as possible, all the hypothetical sensory explanations. Both of these approaches are being followed. On the one hand, Kramer is going ahead to see whether a still more definite test of the sun-angle hypothesis of Matthews can be carried out. Matthews, on his part, is trying to see whether his hypothesis stands up under increasingly severe tests of it. Attempts will be made, of course, by others to repeat these experiments. Already Pratt has accumulated evidence confirming some of Kramer's results.[10]

Can a still more direct attack be made on the question of whether animals have ESP capacity? Would it be possible to devise a type of test in which the question of possible senses, even hyperesthesia, known or unknown, simply could not arise? There is, as a matter of fact, a type of behavior reported, and reported surprisingly frequently, around which it may be possible to build such an experimental project. The idea is at least big enough to be worth talking about, even if too big to handle just yet. Some discussion may, in fact, help to remove the difficulty.

There is a type of case tentatively called psi-trailing, a case in which the animal follows someone to whom it is attached into territory new to it, and does so under conditions that seem to require psi as the orienting ability. To begin with an example, take the case of Tony, the mongrel dog belonging to the Doolen family who moved from Aurora, Illinois, to Lansing, Michigan, a few years ago. The Doolens did not take Tony with them but gave him to friends in Aurora. Six weeks later Tony rushed up to Mr. Doolen on the street in Lansing. Incredulous at first, Mr. Doolen was convinced of Tony's identity upon examination of the dog's collar. He recognized it at once as one he had bought and cut down to size for the dog in Aurora. He recalled the extra hole which he had made in the collar by a right-angled cut. I, myself, visited the Doolens to see Tony. He is a sufficiently odd-looking dog that there could hardly be any problem of identification, even without the help of the collar. Not only did all four members of the family recognize Tony, but members of the family in Illinois who had originally given Tony to the Doolens made a special trip to Lansing to see the dog, and they have written me a letter assuring me there could be no mistake. They recognized the long, slender pencil-width white line from chest to chin. If Tony found his human companions 250 miles away, there would be *no* kind of sensory guidance to explain the phenomenon.

So many cases of this type of trailing have now been collected, most of them involving dogs and cats but with a few cases of pigeons and other pet birds, that this type of behavior, too, must be given serious attention. By this I do not mean that a conclusive case for the occurrence of trailing behavior has been established. There is, however, a more than sufficient probability that in one or more of these reported instances the animal did actually follow and find its human associates. It is enough to justify setting up experiments to see if something of the sort can be reliably demonstrated. The need for investigation has finally been recognized and that is something. The first step is often the hardest one to take.

There are other types of unexplained animal behavior reported frequently enough to justify *experimental* inquiry. It would be scientifically inexcusable to continue to ignore these reports because they cannot at once be converted into absolutely watertight evidence. Scientific investigation rightly begins with the raising of questions. What does it even matter *how* the question is raised? The carefully controlled experiment and the conclusion reached are a long way from the initial stage of questioning. When scientists are afraid even to listen to things they cannot prove up to the hilt right on the spot, they make a travesty of scientific method. They are armoring so heavily for defense as to render themselves powerless to advance. I do not apologize, therefore, for listening to any account of unexplained animal behavior.

There is another type of dog story that I find reported with surprising frequency and which I am now driven to consider well worth adding to our collection. These are cases in which the animal is said to give a queer, mournful howl at the time the human being to whom it is attached dies, even though the death may occur in some distant hospital. The cases of greatest interest are those in which no one present knew the time of the death and were led to inquire by reason of the dog's behavior. Naturally, one is not so much impressed by the first dozen cases as when the number mounts and the collection of cases grows in which there was ample distance between the dog and the person who died. It is not easy to devise an experiment to test this kind of behavior. One cannot start disposing of people to see whether their pet dogs will howl; but an idea may come as to how a more controlled study can be made as we go on collecting the case material. That is, if the problems are kept in view, if an alert open-minded attention is maintained, and if no pharisaical conventionality is allowed to keep the world satisfied with present orthodoxies.

There is still another type of puzzling animal behavior that does lend itself to ready experiment, and some preliminary tests have been started. That type is the anticipatory behavior of the dog or cat as his master is about to arrive home. The animal may go and sit by the window, go out to the gate or to the end of the lane, or in some other way show expectant behavior typical enough to be recorded. Then, with sufficient variation in time of return and with care to be certain of the impossibility of any sensory explanation, the makings of the experiment are provided.

Still other types of odd animal behavior are reported and should be studied. Even the tricks of performing animals need to be kept in perspective. While, generally speaking, these animals are trained to respond to sensory guidance, there have been a few instances in which the evidence indicates that ESP may have been a factor. The best known case on record is that of two circus dogs studied by a Russian neurophysiologist, W. Bechterev,[11] before World War I. The dogs had been trained by a famous animal trainer, Durow, to give the answers (by the number of barks) to simple arithmetical questions written down by members of an audience. Professor Bechterev, when consulted about the dogs' performance, carried out some experiments. In some the trainer was eliminated from the test and Bechterev directed the dog himself; he changed the task to one not depending on the number of barks. More complex questions or tasks were given the dog in the new tests. It was, for example, *silently* commanded (by a thought) to bring a book from the table—or bark at a stuffed animal—or pick up a piece of paper—or go to the next room and jump on a chair, and the like. By eliminating one hypothesis after another, Bechterev and his associates reached the conclusion (exploratory) that telepathy between man and dog had occurred.

A recurrence of publicity over Lady, the "educated" horse of Richmond, Virginia, in 1952–1953, recalls the tests for ESP capacity made on that animal twenty-five years earlier.[12] My wife and I, with the assistance and counsel of Professor William McDougall, subjected this three- to five-year-old filly to some tests in the years 1927–1929, in an attempt to discover by what means she responded in her public demonstrations. Her usual act was to spell out answers to questions from visitors by touching her nose to lettered blocks on the table in front of her. We went through the elimination of one possible source of guidance after another as we imposed controls on the horse and her owner, Mrs. C. D. Fonda, until, as far as we were able to judge, there was no reasonable hypothesis of guidance left alternative to that of telepathy. We were able to get the filly to respond well (i.e., touch the correct block) when the owner herself was completely ignorant of the one chosen, and when only Professor McDougall or I knew it. Our own eyes were screened from view and our bodies held as motionless as possible. Later, after long public performance in a daily routine, we found that the horse had developed habits of following the slight unguarded sway of Mrs. Fonda's body. At this later time we got no results that suggested telepathy. In the earlier stage (1927–1928), however, Lady would pass into a trancelike state after a period of reiterated commands, and it was only then that she gave the results we thought were telepathic. By 1929 she had lost that characteristic type of action.

At one period, then, the mare, like Bechterev's dog, performed in a way that suggested a theory of telepathy. I would not make too much of either study, standing alone. (Why do such studies *have* to stand so much alone?) If the conclusions were sound, there are probably other dogs and horses somewhere that, if properly tested, would confirm the fact. And they could be found if anybody were sufficiently interested to make the search. In any case, it is necessary for an animal psi (anpsi) research program to go on further to more varied and better controlled tests, under conditions in which still better controls are possible.

That is precisely what is now being attempted. It is, of course, a most difficult field, with new methods required, new areas of expertness to be acquired, and new safeguards to be developed. The safest way, the only safe way, is to take advantage of every natural lead or cue, to build every experimental project around a type of behavior that has already been noted. Such was the basis for the experimental work of Dr. Osis,[13] already presented in Chapter Three. His procedure of attempting, by means of a psi process, probably telepathy, to influence a cat in its choice of a cup containing food was built on the observation that much of the reported unexplained behavior suggesting psi involved a relationship between the animal and the person to whom it was attached. Osis began by trying to develop a close attachment between the animal and himself. He obtained, as stated, significant evidence of a psi relation of some kind. His conditions were well controlled against error, and the results justified continuance.

At the point of writing, the cat experiments are in a new phase. The new test in use would be called a clairvoyance test. The actual target is unknown even to the experimenter. Osis has now obtained, with the assistance of Mrs. Esther Foster, enough evidence to indicate that for short series their cats give extrachance results in clairvoyant ESP tests. Ordinary telepathy is excluded in these tests, as it had not been in the earlier ones. Precognitive telepathy is still a possible alternative but that question is for the moment largely an academic one. In any case, the present step comes first.

This ESP-cat project has left on the parapsychology doorstep a whole litter of new and special problems that are too engaging to be ignored. It helps to justify ESP inquiries into other species, raises hopes for a more ambitious study of psi in cats, justifies more interest in the spontaneous behavior of cats from which new problems have already arisen. The psi-in-animals or anpsi program as a whole has, in fact, already grown into an active and fruitful branch of parapsychology.

The discovery of psi in animals, even though on a slender evidential basis as yet, widens the frontier for parapsychology a great deal; or, rather, it contributes to it something like another dimension. The comparative and evolutionary perspectives that are suggested at once add a depth of significance rather than a mere extension. With this greatly increased perspective it should not be long until significant new insights and hypotheses are forthcoming as new thinkers and new ways of thinking come onto the scene.

One can fancy these, shall I say, less literate species furnishing a clue to the solution of many problems in parapsychology. If the young science has got itself caught in a Cyclopean cave with the one-eyed monster of materialism preventing its escape, it is conceivable that, with the help of a humbler species, as Ulysses and his men used the sheep, its enemy will be outmaneuvered.

It would be in keeping with the history of comparative biology to anticipate a range of new possibilities on the basis of finding psi in animal species. It should, in fact, be equivalent to the triumphant step in medical research of finding another animal species that is subject to a major disease still unconquered in man himself.

It is understandable, then, that even so diversified and independent a group of individuals as the parapsychologists have almost universally approved the recent excursion into the study of psi in animals. But the improvement of prospects and the widening of frontiers is not all that is involved in this feeling of satisfaction. There is, as I said in the beginning, a definite logical affiliation of the parapsychological researches with the broad area of the life sciences. There is, too, a reasonable anticipation of finding in this natural connection little of the antagonism that was met in psychology.

It may not be in vain to hope that parapsychology can yield something of significance to the biological sciences. They, too, have had their metaphysical subservience to materialism. A philosophical restraint that few dare break away from is an immeasurable handicap to any branch of inquiry. As biology has tightened up its physicalistic modes of looking at its domain, it has also, I think, receded a little from its farther frontiers, shortened its reach toward its greatest issues, and somewhat lowered its vision of its major problems. The larger problems have a way of eluding science when approached only from the more conservative side.

In parapsychology energetic operations have been uncovered that do not appear to conform to physical law. In biology, however, those who have tried to introduce the concept of nonphysical forces or influences have been rebuffed. But perhaps in no such past case was there a sound experimental basis adequate to support it. Meanwhile, life is still a mystery and such major phenomena as growth, adaptation, memory, secretion, nervous action, morphogenesis, and a long list of others await scientific explanation and understanding. Now these parapsychological laws reveal that there is a nonphysical element, at least in one species. Biology is far enough removed from supernaturalism now to be able to admit natural operations and energies that are nonphysical without loss of face or integrity. It can safely rely on scientific method to test any new ground it traverses. It need no longer pursue its problems only to the frontier of physics and there drop them unsolved because the nonphysical is traditionally out of bounds.

In its own history biology has run into sharp controversy and handicap over resistances due to entrenched philosophical bias; its battle over evolution is familiar to everyone. Most biologists may already realize, too, that the barriers put up by man himself are the most difficult to overcome, and that men tend to feel more certain and more emotional about their mistaken notions than they usually do over what they have come to know for well-established fact. A professional group thus seasoned would be expected to be prepared, better than most, to understand the difficulties in parapsychology and to consider discerningly the possible role the psi function may be playing in the life and activity of the organism.

It would be hard to gauge the potential significance of the implications of psi for a vast field like biology; perhaps there is no real need to try to do so. But if one were required to appraise the prospects by some arbitrary rule, the method of incongruency is perhaps as good as any. According to this measure, psi is as significant for biology as its findings are incongruent with the prevailing body of knowledge of that field; in a word, the less it fits and the more intellectual challenge it offers, the more important it must be. By intellectual challenge I do not mean the knockdown, dragout sort of contest some of the psychologists gave to parapsychology some years ago. I mean, rather, the clarifying exchange of ideas that brings to the point at issue the pertinent questions and the available facts until this scientific problem is solved to mutual satisfaction. Actually, the incongruency of psi with physicalistic biology appears very great indeed; as great as it is with mechanistic psychology. One may hope, then, that this small branch of biology can, by the measure of its contribution to the general field, justify its claim to membership in so fruitful a composite science.

Chapter 6

PSI, PSYCHE, AND PSYCHOLOGY

■ That the whole problem area of parapsychology belongs to psychology there can hardly be any question. The large majority of the psychologists questionnaired by Warner conceded that the investigation of ESP was a legitimate psychological inquiry. The real trouble with psychology arose, as I have shown, not over either the problem *or* the research; not even over the discovery of psi; but over the fact that it turned out to be an extraphysical operation instead of just a "sixth" or unrecognized sense that could be physically interpreted. The large majority of psychologists are evidently not prepared for this fact about psi— not yet.

But where *within* the domain of psychology does psi belong? This further question runs into a difficulty that will surprise a great many readers, namely, that too little is known yet about the field of psychology to make it possible to localize this new concept with any accuracy within that field. Consider first the way in which the subject of psychology is defined, if indeed there is one definition on which a majority of psychologists could agree. One's concept of the field would have a lot to do with his answer to the question of where psi comes in. And over this concept of what psychology is there is less agreement probably than over general definitions in any other leading branch of science.

Psychology was originally the science of the psyche or soul (that is, of the mind as a distinct reality), but after long wavering years of uncertainty, American psychology in the first quarter of the century shifted around to quite a contrary position, becoming, as the popular expression went, a science *without* a soul. The mind as a real entity (that is, one having distinct properties and powers not attributable to the physics of the brain) was either defined out of existence or ignored as scientifically unapproachable simply because it was not directly observable from the outside. For a decade or two behaviorism became the dominant school of psychology in this country and behavior became the exclusive subject matter of psychology. The concept of a *person* or subject or self that would be central to all this behavior receded into the background and all but disappeared from the science.

But objectively observable behavior has, of course, to consist of *physical* action only. Accordingly, by defining itself merely as the science of behavior, psychology aligned itself with the older and more established and successful sciences. The only fundamental principles dealt with in these sciences, of course, *are* physical.

More recently a number of psychologists have recognized that behaviorism "leaves Hamlet out of the play" and they are letting the concept of mind come back into consideration. They are willing to compromise and call psychology the science of behavior *and* experience, though some of them hasten to add that no real distinction is made between mind and matter; no dualism is intended. Very few are frankly dualistic.

The latest contribution to the prevailing uncertainty is also the greatest. Psychology is, at the moment, *not* the science of the soul or the mind or behavior or experience or any of these combined. It has retreated to an extreme point of noncommittal abstraction—the science of the relation between the organism and its environment. And that makes about as neutral a definition as one could get. (It is actually, also, the standard definition used for that branch of biology known as ecology—a far cry, indeed, from psychology.)

What, really, is psychology? It is at least a start on a definition, and a safe one, to say that it is what psychologists do. Obviously, psychologists work with living beings as people or individual persons (not as anatomical specimens, not their physiology, not their cultures as in sociology, etc.). The generalized object of their work and study is the behaving person or his personality. Even in the study of animal life it is the personalitylike properties or capacities of these organisms that are of main interest to the psychologist. It is not merely the person's behavior, not only his relation to environment, not simply his subjective experience, but himself as a personality distinct from impersonal or nonpersonal things and processes and relations that is the ultimate subject of interest. To be sure, behavior, experience and environment and their interrelations furnish the data, the raw material necessary in the study of people and in dealing with their problems. From all this there emerges a concept of psychology as the *study of persons as such*—or of their personalities, if one prefers.

Why has so obvious a definition not become accepted usage long ago? Probably because to speak of the person as the target of study is to raise the question: Just what is the person? Especially, what is the difference between a person and a nonpersonal thing? But that is too deep a question for psychology at this stage. A few of the great psychological leaders such as William McDougall and William Stern at least kept the question of this basic distinction alive during their lifetimes; but, in the main, psychology has not developed to the point of seriously attempting to answer it. Consequently, psychologists have never known just where personality itself belongs in the larger scheme of nature. Many, like the behaviorists, have humorlessly gone so far as to rule out of the court of reality the whole range of conscious experience, even though the mere operation of their own science—any science—is based upon conscious thought. They were *not* conscious, we may assume, of the fact that they were sawing off the limb on which they were sitting.

Here, then, is the first place to tie in psi with psychology. It is just on this point of what distinguishes a person from a thing that the psi investigations have made their main contribution to date. They provide, in the coinage of the natural sciences, something scientifically tangible, quantitatively appraisable, and capable of mathematical treatment that experimentally differentiates between a personal and a nonpersonal world, between living beings as personalities on the one hand and impersonal things on the other.

The psi researches have established the occurrence of a mode of reaction of a living being that is both personal and nonphysical. The result is to provide psychology with its first clear deed to a distinctively *mental* domain of reality. The experiments on the psi-function do this as nothing else ever has. No philosophical argument, no authoritarian pronouncement, and no mystical revelation can define for psychology this field of reality that is peculiarly its own. Rather, if such a reality exists, its title must be proved by the methods of natural science! I think that the discovery of psi has now given that proof to psychology.

What is the result for psychology? That field can, of course, be allowed to go on comparatively undefined, tagging along in the hope of becoming a sort of pseudo-physical science. But while behind the Iron Curtain this imitation of physics by psychologists could be managed by decree, such a method is not proving wholly satisfactory in the Western world. The effort to have psychology keep step with physics has kept psychologists confined to the mere fringes of their field, timidly working out a technology on the borders of physiology, neurology, and other more objective neighboring fields. In fact, most of the great needs of human life and human relations, for happiness, morality, mental health, peace, and the like, have been left by this unventuring science to social institutions whose guiding principles have been derived from authoritarian sources and traditions. If medicine and agriculture were depending today upon a biology no more fundamental to its problem area than psychology has been to the main fields of human relations, we should be back in the Middle Ages in those branches, as, indeed, I fear we are in much of our practice of human relations.

The discovery of a nonphysical psi factor, then, introduces psychology to a new area to be explored in search of the principles that make people do what they do; for powers and processes that are personal, not physical; for properties of living beings that are psychical, not material. This discovery is an invitation to psychologists to give up trying to make their field into a sort of second-rate practice of human engineering operating on the secondhand principles of mechanics and to take possession of this uniquely psychological new world as their own.

But, however nonphysical psi may be, parapsychology is definitely a field of natural science. The extension of psychology it denotes is no more *super-* or *preter-* or *sub-* or *extra-*natural than anything else that has ever been met in the sciences. Even the prefix *para* will be dropped as soon as the psychologists themselves get over being sensitive about psi. It has merely been a linguistic convenience for this early stage of development. No phenomenon encountered in the whole range of psi occurrences has in any way appeared to be any less natural than, for example, those that are met with in a beginning course in chemistry. The realities dealt with in psi are less obvious, more subtle, and, therefore, more difficult to capture and measure than chemical ones, but they are realities just the same. What I am saying is merely that it is nonsense for anyone to be afraid to study and try to integrate a psi phenomenon with the rest of what he knows about nature. It will become familiar and lawful enough as its full natural history is revealed by continued study.

Psi, then, is rather central to this larger concept of psychology, central to an area that is as yet largely to be explored, central to a world of functions and influences and forces and relations that will have to be investigated if man is to find out what he really is as a conscious, thinking, purposeful, and perceptive being. This area will have to be explored if he is to discover what it is that underlies his system of values, any system of values, and enables him to set it up and hold to it, what it is that makes life meaningful. Once liberated from their own self-imposed confinement, psychologists have this great region for exploration. Into that area the discovery of psi has made an opening. Whether it is a big or little one is less important than that it is a break-through.

Psi is closely related to another central question of psychology, the old but unsolved mind-body problem. Although the most fundamental problem of all, there has been no progress towards its solution in a century. Psychologists have helplessly left it to philosophy and religion. Few even mention it as a scientific project for psychology. The majority follow a sort of vague notion that the two systems, mind and body, are somehow fundamentally unified on some complex but wholly unknown physical basis. The combining of the two is supposed to occur somehow in the mysterious organization of the nervous system. The idea is that when the brain becomes sufficiently well understood the whole story of mental life will be found implicit in the physicochemical principles of neurology. This half-formulated materialism is taken for granted; it has not been subjected to experiment.

On the other side of the mind-body problem area there are eminent neurologists who admit with frankness and forthrightness that there is a complete gap in what is known of the relationship between thought and brain processes and that they have no idea how the one interacts with the other, no conception even of a productive line of inquiry by which the problem could be solved.

What, then, does parapsychology contribute on the mind-body problem that these older, more established, better organized sciences, with their thousands of research workers and their millions in research funds, cannot find out for themselves? It gives some new facts, some new methods, and even an approach that has not been tried before, either by students of the mind or by students of the body. Time and again in the history of science the introduction of novelty of method alone has changed the entire character of a scientific field. Sometimes a new concept can revolutionize the empirical approach.

The main thing, however, that the psi researches contribute on the mind-body problem is a vehicle by which it may be brought into science. To accomplish this would not, of course, take the problem out of the hands of philosophy, but it would end the era during which it has been left, without any attempt at fact-finding by scientific method, entirely to philosophy and religion. A new stage is introduced merely by showing that there are certain human events that do not lend themselves to physical explanation. It is now no longer merely a matter of speculative reasoning to maintain that mental operations have reality, causal efficacy, or objective existence—call it what you will. From now on he who wishes to solve the problem by the most reliable methods of inquiry can bypass a great collection of elaborate philosophical theories and formulate his question in a way that would permit *experimental* search for the answer. Such a step would be only a beginning, but never was even a beginning more needed.

Through the psi experiments certain relationships between subject and object have already been established in a way and degree that would never have been possible with any of the more familiar processes of mind-body interaction. It may be that a great part of what goes on in a person may have the same nonphysical characteristics as psi. However, the point is, psi activities can be tested with regard to their physical relationships, but so far as is known at present, such a test is not possible anywhere else along the whole vast range of non-psi behavior and experience.

Scientists are always dependent on their methods. The methods of parapsychology, even at this early stage of the science, not only do catch psi phenomena, elusive as they are, but also they make it possible to handle such effects quantitatively and thus bring out the fact of their lack of correlation with physical law.

Just to have obtained evidence of the odd phenomena of psi is not the crux of the contribution to psychology. Even to have found that psi effects can be measured crudely by the tedious intricacies of statistical method is still not the main point, essential though the steps both are. It is the fact that these psi operations between subject and object are the kind that can be contrasted quantitatively with those common, better known functions that *are* governed by the laws of the known energies that gives new light on the hitherto baffling problem of the nature of man with respect to the physical universe.

This, then, it would seem is the course over which the exploration of the nature of personality with respect to matter will have to go. At present, there is no alternative route to follow. Now it is known, at least, that there are demonstrable interactions between a subjective self or mind and an objective world. Furthermore, these are not merely interactions without the recognized sensorimotor machinery by which most contacts with the environment are made; they are contacts without any known physical intermediation to serve as stimuli or instrumentation. They are even operations that take place without any familiar kind of relationship to time and space and mass.

The relevant point here that has not been made earlier is that since the discovery of psi psychologists, in approaching the mind-body problem, have a starting point, a sound position based on a distinctively mental causality. From that starting point an experimental path has been cleared for an approach to the problem of a mind-matter relationship by the methods of science. In the chapter on physics it was indicated that psi operations are necessarily energetic in character even though no energy described in the physics textbooks of today be involved. The suggestion is that in psi processes some form of energy is active that is peculiarly psychological. All these considerations point up to this question: Is it not now reasonable to hope that the psychologist (either para- or plain), following the lead given by the mind-matter relation represented in the psi experiments, will be able to go on to discover in these more exceptional operations the principles that also underlie the basic thought-brain interchanges that have been inaccessible by direct approach?

It could be that the greatest consequences of the psi researches both for psychology and for humanity will be the light they throw on the long-lost problem of the freedom of the will. What a question that is to have been allowed to drop out of sight in the academic shuffle! It is the general common-sense belief of all men— and even of those "machines" who call themselves mechanists— that they are more or less free in their volitional life. They believe, of course, that they can freely will to do certain things according to their own purposes or desires. Such a concept of freedom derives much of its significance from the fact that it is basic to all the other freedoms by which men value their personal and social life. All this is commonly taken for granted.

Obviously, the question of the personal well-being and happiness of the individual is closely bound up with the various social and civic freedoms. There is no need at all to discuss the importance of a problem that is, as here assumed, so fundamental to it. The question of the freedom of the will has been so prominent as an issue in religious doctrine and philosophical dispute at different stages of human history that one would suppose it would have been a major topic in the world of modern science. But that it certainly is not. Rather, it has come to be utterly neglected, completely ignored. And to what truant field does the process of volition and its nature belong? Psychology, of course.

This is not, however, to accuse psychologists of not being interested in volitional freedom. It is only fair to say that they have not known anything to do about it—even how to approach it. The fact is, the question does not logically arise from the point of view of a physicalistic psychology any more than it comes up in a physics laboratory. A psychologist with a materialistic philosophy would not be much better prepared to deal with the problem of freedom than a mechanical engineer.

The discoveries of parapsychology, however, furnish a basis from which to go after an answer to the question and they open a research road to follow in further study.

The first point to consider is whether or not the question itself has been sharply defined. When one asks whether volitional judgment is free, what is meant? Free of what? We can at once eliminate many things that we do *not* mean when we ask if we are free, many from which we do not want freedom. We do not mean are we free of the wisdom, educational advantages, training, memories, and the valuable experience in general that we have acquired. We do not mean to ask whether we are free of the psychophysical system, the thought-brain unit by which our very thinking and living are carried out. The basic lawfulness of all these realms of operation is something, rather, upon which we wish to *rely* rather than from which we wish to be freed.

Is freedom, then, just a delusory sort of question? Is there nothing verifiably real about this will to be free in one's personal choice and action? Is this notion of voluntaristic action that has become fixed in our intellectual life as a requirement of the normal individual, the healthy personality, only a pointless fiction?

On the contrary, the question of freedom of the will is a real one and there *is* an answer at least worth considering. From what is it that we so much want freedom in our volitional action? Freedom of the will to the average man means some degree of independence of the great material order of nature to which his own body and environment belong; an order that he touches through his sensorimotor system and learns about in school as the world of physics. Man has always been to some extent pitting himself against the inexorable mechanism of his physical environment and by means of the inner forces of his mental life seeking to escape from or planning to conquer his environment. He recognizes in his subjective life a different type of lawful principle from those applying to the material world of his environment.

Now, it should be easily apparent that if one takes the view that the physics of a man's brain can, when elaborately understood, explain all his personal life, if all the universe, including all life, is physical, as we use the word today, this notion of freedom, like many other notions of our primitive past, will have to be discarded.

If, on the other hand, man has any true volitional choice, if his life is not an entirely determined sequence of events, then there has to be some differentiation within the personality in order to allow one division to operate to some degree independently of the other. Such differentiation would require a concept of personality as having laws of its own, causal powers of its own; yes, a unique mental energy. I hardly need say again that one does *not* have to suppose that the older concept of a dual universe necessarily goes with this. That concept is contradicted by the obvious facts of body-mind interaction and of the natural integration of all causal interoperations in the universe.

It can be seen, then, that psi gives man a charter to personal freedom; first, by making it clear that there are two comparatively distinct orders or types of lawfulness within him, that his mind, at least in the operations with which these researches deal, does not work on the mechanical principles of his environment. That is sufficient to defeat the case for determinism. It is enough to open up a causeway by which psychological investigation can enter into a new domain of inquiry. With the pressures of a deterministic ideology strong upon civilization today, it may be that some psychological explorers need only to have their attention directed to this pathway to research on the freedom of man. If there are cornerstones to human happiness, or perhaps one might even say keystones, it is not an exaggeration to say that the concept of freedom comes very close to deserving that characterization. Who could conceive of human happiness without an assumption of volitional freedom? Yet who can discover any hope for such freedom while adhering to a philosophy that physical principles alone can explain both man and his universe?

Psychiatry gave to psychology the concept of the unconscious. Psychologists have not as yet done much with it, but there it is, more or less taken for granted, after more than half a century of practical demonstration of its significance in the world of mental illness. However, the experimental tools by which to deal quantitatively with unconscious processes have been and are being developed through the psi investigations. The fact that psi is unconscious has already been characterized as being the most important psychological fact about it. It can be emphasized further that the operation of psi is *really* unconscious. It is unconscious in a different degree or way from experiences that are merely forgotten or repressed or left out of consciousness by the shift of attention or preoccupation with an object of concentrated interest. The operation of the psi function is, so far as the researches can indicate to date, irrecoverably unconscious.

As Louisa E. Rhine has pointed out,[1] spontaneous experiences have a large, even a preponderant accompaniment of conviction or feeling of certainty. The person who has the experience that in later perspective seems to be a genuine psi case has more often than not a strong feeling of conviction that the experience is meaningful, true, or genuine. That does not mean, however, that the experience has come to him in a manner that he can reliably describe, or that any amount of questioning can help him to recall just how it was that he received the impression of a faraway event at the time or, perhaps, before it happened. As a matter of fact, it is now clear that, as the case studies already mentioned have suggested, in the psi process something goes on in the subject on an unconscious level, and the result of that unconscious process is converted or translated into a conscious experience so that the meaning or a fragment thereof becomes available to him. The types of conscious experience utilized in the transfer are the familiar types of human experience: hallucination, intuition, dreams, an outburst of emotion, or a compulsion to act.

But the fact that has come out of recent studies of spontaneous ESP is that a great deal more than has been suspected must go on in this unconscious area of operations, including judgment, selection, and conversion of the ESP reaction into a conscious form. And all of that thus far has been beyond the reach of the research methods; it has even been outside the area of attention.

In the psi experiments many things have turned up as products of peculiar, unconscious influences. Some of these have been listed in Chapter Three, the outstanding one being the case of consistent avoidance of the target or psi-missing, but with displacement, reinforcement and various kinds of declines as others of the more common examples.

The parapsychology researches, then, by means of their experimental methods, have now penetrated the unconscious level of personality to a depth of unconsciousness beyond that on which the clinical explorations of psychiatry had already led the way. If this is true, it adds a new depth to the system with which psychology will ultimately have to deal. It would, of course, be foolish to suppose that psi is the only function that operates at this low level of consciousness. There might be a great deal more going on down there. And when one considers that much of this vast unconscious area of directive activities, the area which includes the forces of cell organization, organismic functioning, and general behavior in health and disease, is still largely unexplored, we can all agree that orthodox psychology would do well to take over this subbasement level and help to find what more there is in the deeper life of man of which these few glimpses have now been caught.

If it is plain that psychology really does have a claim on an experimental area of nature not primarily material, I would like to go a step further. Up to this point, progress in parapsychology has been made only over the rough, hard-going trails of experimental research. The experiments, nevertheless, are such that at their best they can confidently, even proudly, be laid for comparison alongside the best, the very best, experimental work ever done in the history of psychology. No concessions need be asked. The case is good, not only for the occurrence of psi, but for its occurrence under a range of conditions that defy physical explanation. Therefore, if one assures psychology that it need no longer fear to break out of its stockade of physicalism and boldly cultivate some land of its own without fear of losing its scalp, he can do so on the basis of discoveries made as a result of painstaking experiments and tested in the crucibles of heated controversy.

Now, however, I propose to make another sort of effort. One needs to look ahead and far beyond his reach, and see what lies farther out than his instruments or his travels have extended. This orienting perspective can affect his science as well as his life.

If, now, one sits back and looks at the universe with as much detachment as he can, the thing that stands out as important above all—at least to my judgment—is a reality or influence or factor that can best be understood by everyone as *the human spirit*. I am not a spiritist or a Spiritualist, in either sense of the word. Once again, I am not even a dualist. I am speaking as a natural scientist; but I am referring to the same thing that I learned in the U.S. Marine Corps to call *esprit de corps*, and every Marine knows that means something. It is a force that works wonders in a symphony orchestra or a football team, in a nation going through the horrors of war or the austerities of depression. It is the kind of factor the discerning physician tries to stir to help an invalid fight for his life. It is the kind of reality that can sustain a courageous individual through long strain and trial and discouragement.

One would suppose that it had been written clearly enough over the accomplishments of men through history and around the world for the sciences of man today to have sufficient ground for a working hypothesis to the effect that there is a real agent or force or determinant represented in this expression, *spirit*. One would suppose, moreover, that among the sciences concerned with mankind and its affairs, this would be one of the great objectives of research. One cannot miss the fact that this human spirit is something operating in nature. Probably most will agree that it is, at least from man's point of view, his principal constituent.

Very well, then. Suppose it is agreed that it exists, and that it is the most important factor. What should be made of the fact that there have been no studies or experimental researches made to find out what it really is? No scientific effort has been made to sustain it, to develop it, educate it, correct it or whatever ought to be done about it. In psychology the little peripheral things have all come first. Mice in a learning maze make better, easier thesis projects than do men in the maze of mind-matter possibilities. The pebbles and shells on the beach have distracted attention from the ocean.

Again, I suspect the answer is that men, educated the way they have been, have not known what to do about this matter. But now, a start, at least, has been made in the methods of parapsychology and they may be the very methods needed for this greater undertaking, too. In fact, it may be that, in a small, almost infinitesimal way, this power of the human spirit is actually being tested in the psi laboratory. If so, I suspect it is a very poor test. It is necessary, of course, to make a lot of poor tests in order to find out how to make the best possible ones. And if, as may appear to an ambitious newcomer unaware of the difficulties, the experiments of the past seem of an anthill order of magnitude, and if there are those who can do much more mountainous things, the field of exploration is wide open and even better prepared now for a larger order of achievement. It is conceivable, though admittedly visionary, to think that an awakening psychology may itself be captured by the spirit to discover the nature of the spirit—the natural determinant in men that drives and sustains them, and enables them to know and like and do things. And for this discovery they may then be induced to look into *men*, and not into the latest books on physics.

Part **III**

SIGNIFICANCE OF PSI

FOR HUMAN LIFE

■ It is time now to ask: How *important* are these psi researches; how important, that is, to mankind? What are they worth that can justify all the effort, the time, the cost? Do they live up to the claim that they have opened up a new world? Naturally, the workers in parapsychology have raised this question, at least in their own minds, at every stage in the investigations. Of course, each one has his own individual answer, but there are certain shared group valuations as well. That the psi explorer himself should take his work with great seriousness is more or less to be expected. Nothing less could sustain him in so uncertain, so unrecognized, and so difficult a field. What may be more surprising, however, is the extent to which this appreciation is shared by a large audience among the lay public that is widely distributed around the world. One concrete evidence of this widespread interest is found in the readiness of the public press, the magazines, and the book publishers to accept accounts of the researches for publication. And this readiness on their part has in turn been an important factor in maintaining the interest itself and thereby supporting the research. These agencies have, in fact, been the principal means by which research results have been brought to public attention.

What is it, then, about these studies of psi phenomena that brings the research this vitally needed public interest and support? It is, I think, the fact that the concept of psi expands rather than contracts the boundaries of human life; it extends rather than re-

stricts the vision of man's place in nature; it suggests wider rather
than narrower potentialities for human personality and, finally, it
gives support from science itself for the concept of a spiritual
force in man, and that, of course, is the concept on which the
social values and institutions of mankind were founded.

It is the bearing of psi on an understanding of the nature of
human beings that forms the core of the interest people have
shown. Probably with most of the members of parapsychology's
clientele this interest is not very explicitly formulated. For many
it may be a dim, half-unconscious impression, a mild suggestion, a
slender hope, a faint flutter of encouragement to offset the depressing conception of man that is inherent in the atmosphere of
this mechanistic age. But for most of these individuals, whether
explicitly realized or not, I think it is this concern over the basic
nature of human beings that inspires the response of the parapsychology audience to the research developments of the field.

In a word, the motivating impulse of the interested public
appears to be of the same character, generally speaking, as that
which has activated the workers themselves from the beginning
of the scientific study of psi. It is due to the fact that they are able
to see in the subject a great potential meaning for the understanding and guidance of human life.

The above description would not fit everyone, it is true; there
are always some dissenting voices. They are heard even on the
question of whether parapsychologists ought to *talk* at this stage
about the meaning of their results. One of these more conservative
fellow workers insists that we "let the facts speak for themselves."
"Why not," he urges, "leave all the speculation and interpretation
until we know more about what we have got? By overloading what
we have at this tentative stage with claims of significance for this
and that, scientific groups that might otherwise pay serious attention are certain to be repelled."

Sincere words, yes; but hardly practical advice. It is doubtful if
the spirit of knowledge-for-knowledge's sake, however much it may
inflate the vanity of erudition, has ever initiated and supported a
really difficult pioneer venture in science. Even if facts about psi
could speak for themselves, it is their meaning, their significance,
their possible value that accounts for the interest of the public

that must be relied on to support and encourage them. And that support is imperative for the continuation of the work still to be done. If this meaning were to be classified as secret until all the facts are in, it is hard to see how there could be any sustaining group, any friends to support the struggling young branch of inquiry. To say, "Let the facts speak for themselves," is about as sensible as to say, "Let the research do itself!"

It is clear, however, that facts do not speak for themselves. All facts require interpretation. They are all likely to have different significances for different people for, of course, people vary and have different degrees of understanding and preparation for the appreciation of them. The friend quoted above agrees that the psi researches are important. But for what are they important? Importance always has reference to some viewpoint, some larger context. Are these findings just so many statistical or behavioral data to be considered apart from any bearing on human situations? If that were all they are, most of the researchers would not be interested.

In the beginning of parapsychology it was no general diffuse enthusiasm over any so-called facts for facts' sake that inspired the founding fathers. The larger significances of psi phenomena (to religion, for example) were definite in their minds and in their writings. Read, for example, Chapter I in Frederic Myers' *Human Personality*. He and his associates, faced with a threatening materialism, wanted to find out whether it is the correct theory of human life. This very real need led them to inquire into the claims concerning psychic occurrences for the plain reason that these phenomena appeared to transcend the familiar principles of science from which materialism had been derived. Today it is still the appreciation of this same larger bearing of psi on the concept of human nature that has enlisted the support of a lay public and thereby maintained the researches through the years. The point is, then, that in reality the facts emerging from these researches were spoken for long in advance. There was no waiting for them to speak for themselves.

There is usually some such need, intellectual or practical, back of the systematic inquiries in science. In fact, most scientific fields are frankly utilitarian in their research objectives, as for example, the branches of science connected with medicine. Nowadays a medical discovery is almost always announced while confirmatory tests are still in progress, and physicians eagerly await its release for dependable use. How ridiculous it would be to say to such a science: "It is forbidden to look ahead to interpretations and applications. Just let the facts speak for themselves in order to avoid antagonizing anyone."

The answer, then, to the question of what the real reason is for keeping on with the psi research program is that the facts are needed today by humanity. If there were not a strong sense of this need, I am sure that with all the uncertainty involved most parapsychology workers would not have the time or the will to pursue them. But if there is a good prospect that the discoveries, past or future, of this branch of inquiry can help mankind with the burning, crushing problems of life today, few indeed of the inquirers want them to be concealed. Rather, they all want them made as available, as understandable, and as useful as they can be. And, finally, if talking about their potential value will quicken interest and bring needed cooperation from those who share the interest, then it is a pity it is not possible to talk more, or more effectively, about psi than has ever yet been done. Surely there is no rational need to be silent. Careful, yes; and ever aware that logical application has need of essential empirical check. But any factual findings bearing on problems so fundamental to man that have met the tests and survived the attacks the psi researches have, ought to be heralded instead of hidden.

But if the facts about psi are needed by humanity, there are certain areas of need that are more obvious than others. It is in man's deepest or most vital relations that the importance of knowing his own makeup is best realized. It is in considering a person's larger adjustment to life and society, moral and religious—the spiritual aspect—that it would be very important to know what his true nature is. There it should matter most whether a human personality is, as psychology assumes, a physical system and nothing more. Three of these larger areas of adjustment will be considered in relation to the psi research. It is from these three areas of relationship that most of the sustaining interest behind the inquiries derives its inspiration.

Chapter **7**

IMPORTANCE TO

THE WORLD OF RELIGION

■ The religions were all founded upon some
concept of truth, upon what their founders believed to be the
truth. Whatever else this truth concerns, it deals with the nature
of man's relation to the universe—past, present, and future. Every
religion provides through its doctrine what its founders and followers believe are the answers to the great question of what man
can do about his destiny, and of how he can best live his life. On
these general points the followers of any religion, and even the
nonreligious, will likely concur, even though they do not agree on
the specific answers given by the various religions.

It is, in fact, a common feature of all religions, including yours
and mine, that they have to do with real human problems. These
problems are not only real; they are very important ones as well.
It is the attempted solutions of these problems, the finding of
such answers as have been found, that have given the various
concepts of truth to which I have just referred. The ways in which
these problems have been solved, the means by which the truths
have been established, are obviously of great importance.

Generally speaking, the truths of religion have come from unusual forms of experience believed to have been inspired. The individuals through whom religious truth has been channeled have
usually received it as a revelation of wisdom and teaching deriving supposedly from agencies outside and beyond the recipients
themselves. Such experiences, generally called mystical, may have
been in the form of a waking vision or a dream, resembling in a
general way the more typical forms of psychic experience and,
like them, usually spontaneous. This method of arriving at truth
is radically different from those by which knowledge is obtained in
general. These mystical experiences are not verifiable; there is
no way of checking up on them; and varying as they do, there has
resulted a great variety of widely differing beliefs as these experiences become sound doctrine and truth to those who are able to
accept them as divinely revealed knowledge.

Now, of course, the reliability of what is taken as acceptable
fact depends entirely upon the methods used to find out about it.
Indeed, the method would be as important in religion then as the
great problems themselves with which it deals. As a matter of
fact, when men can agree on the adequacy of the methods in an
inquiry they can usually concur on the results. Reliable method,
then, is the thing; and it is the more crucially important, the
greater the problems involved. And since the comparative reliability of the truth-seeking procedures developed in the sciences
is well known, the question arises as to why equally powerful and
dependable methods would not be in demand and in use on such
significant problems as concern religion. The more familiar one is
with the steady progress of inquiry in all the various fields in
which scientific ways of thinking have penetrated, the more ready
one is to ask: Is there not further inquiry possible into the field
of religious knowledge? Must one believe that everything that
there is to know about man's spiritual nature and spiritual world
has been found out by the old methods that preceded science?

Those who have surveyed the progress of religion itself through
its period of recorded history have seen that it has been a growing,
expanding system of concepts. The progressive adaptation of doctrine to the needs and learning of the changing times indicates
that religion has been, to some extent at least, alive and fluid, not

dead and frozen. The founders of the religious systems were themselves explorers, pioneers, revolutionists! And they used the methods of inquiry of their day. Can we imagine them living and working in our day and not making use of the present methods of inquiry, those methods of science by which have been built the great systems of knowledge so useful to men's other needs?

If today, then, it were possible to catch the *spirit* of these founders and equip ourselves with the truth-finding methods of our own day, we might, for example, be able to advance the spiritual aspects of Jesus's contribution as much as the healing side of His mission has been advanced by those same methods. That spirit is important; medicine itself would still be where it was in the first century B.C. had it not been that the progressive, inquiring individuals in the profession prevailed over the conservative, backward-looking membership. The same struggle goes on in every department of human affairs. The spirit, the will to find out, the driving force, comes first. But the methods, the ways by which problems are solved, are the wheels of progress in knowledge and understanding. They must be well tested and sure, but especially must they be suited to the factors and phenomena with which they have to deal.

I shall now ask about religion from the viewpoint of parapsychology. In *The Reach of the Mind* I suggested that parapsychology is to religion what biology is to medicine or physics to engineering. Is such a suggestion reasonable? If parapsychology deals with all personality manifestations that are beyond explanation by physics, then by definition it should claim the entire spiritual order of reality. Whatever problems in nature arise that lead beyond the boundary of physical operations would be pursued by the "instruments" of parapsychological methods. They would, of course, be adapted to the specific needs of that realm of inquiry; the methods of the physical sciences would not suffice.

While the general way of considering and going about the solving of a problem can be much the same whatever the field, psychology, agriculture, bacteriology, or astronomy, the specific techniques and methods of experimenting must be as different as the subject matter itself. The same reasoning human mind is the main instrument of inquiry in each case, but the specific tools to be geared onto this basic instrument are as different as is Nature in her various aspects. One must not allow his concept of science, then, to be limited to the more familiar fields such as chemistry or physics. These are only the most popular and objective of the sciences. Scientific method is the generalized form of what scientific inquirers do in solving their problems, whatever their field. If they go into the realm of spiritual reality, their techniques will have to be very different indeed from those of the familiar physical sciences. Yet it will be no less a scientific venture if its logic and its standards of evidence are equally as good as those that have produced results in the other fields.

It is not to be expected, however, that the established religious organizations will initiate such research. The principal roles of human organizations of any kind are those of conservation and perpetuation. These functions are, of course, as necessary as progress itself, but are they ever combined with progress? It is a noteworthy fact that the great religious advances have come as heresies, reformations, or schisms under the stress of great need and of glaring inadequacy in the existing situation. There is no use wasting time speculating on the possible initiation of any progressive step in any religion under its established leadership.

The experience parapsychology has already had with organized religion is an example in itself, though a small one. In the seventy-five years of research activity in parapsychology no notice has been taken of the research field by the official religious world. A few individuals from religion have been interested, it is true, but the numbers of these have not been large as the professions go. However, as I have said, the religious revolutions of the past have not come about by official action of the ruling body. If, then, the findings of parapsychology can be of any value to the advancement of religion, the established organizations must not be expected to be quick to recognize it. In the light of the history of ideas, it is clear that any such recognition would have to be compelled by events from without.

Moreover, it would follow that as long as it should seem that religion is succeeding in its mission of saving the world and there is no particular general need felt for anything better than already exists, no change of attitude and no action could be expected. Only if there should be a strong sense of the inadequacy of existing religious truth and the existence of a really critical state of affairs would the significance to religion of the nonmechanistic implications of psi be seriously considered. And yet I submit that religion right now does need and needs desperately all the aid it can get from the best methods of truth finding that it can borrow from the related areas of inquiry on its borders. One of these, and the most logical one, is its own natural affiliate, the science of parapsychology.

Need I even ask if there *is* such a crisis in religion today? Would anyone think that religion is really successfully saving the world? Many people, I know, see things only as they want to see them. Many, too, perhaps the majority, see them the way they are told to see them. They are content to read or hear only slanted versions of the world outlook. Such people, of course, will not realize the critical state of affairs confronting religion today. But for those who see clearly and independently, the failure of the world religions in achieving their great social purpose of producing peace, fraternity, and the full realization of man's potentialities must be all too distressingly apparent. To make such a harsh judgment even more pointed and specific, I will ask whether the collapse of the vast religious organizations in country after country where communism has come in is not something of a grade mark in itself of the inadequacy of these religions for the people and for the times?

It is customary to say that communism comes in only where the people are hungry. Even if that were true, and it does not seem strictly to be so, a still more difficult question stares us in the face: Would the people be hungry and miserable and desperate in a country in which an adequate religion was guiding their thoughts and lives? In other words, is religion succeeding in its great mission when, after it has dominated the life of a nation for many centuries, it allows a situation to develop that invites communism? Rather, is there not in such a religious system just the sort of frustration or manifestation of weakness that demands improvement even at the cost of revolution?

The expansion of communism, however, is but one of many

present-day evidences that might be cited as pointing to the need for more powerful religious guidance among men. Peace on earth is still far from a reality. War is more of a calamity than ever before. Religious rule over morality is hardly more complete than it ever was. Is it unrealistic, then, to assume that religion needs strengthening and support from some source, however unaware of the fact its own following may appear to be?

Before turning to consider what may be the bearing of the results of the study of psi on religion, a serious doubt should first be removed; it is one that has helped to bar progress on the matter for a long time. It is the question of whether science can deal with anything so intangible as spiritual problems, operations beyond the direct reach of the objective instruments of physics.

It is a question, however, that can be answered easily, once and for all. It is the same as asking whether or not there can be a science of psychology. Except for a few extreme behaviorists, most psychologists now at least halfway recognize that as part of their data they are dealing with the conscious experiences of the persons they work with. Even though a physicalistic assumption may require that they view these subjective states as some sort of physical brain emanations, they realize that they are intangible to physical instruments by direct measurements. Psychologists know they cannot measure *directly* the mental operations of a person under observation by another. Nevertheless, there already is such a science of psychology. And whatever its accomplishments or failures, it is now established and its personnel is expanding at an enormous rate. But how are psychologists to study the mental experience of the individual? The answer is: It must first be converted into action. A subjective process must be written, spoken, or converted into some other objective form that can be registered and appraised. After all, that is the method by which most of the physical world itself is today reached by the scientists. The science of physics, for example, began with observations that could be made directly by the senses, but it was soon discovered that there were operations beyond the range of the senses and even beyond those instruments for extending the senses, the telescope, microscope, and the like. Then, of course, even the physical scientist had to devise methods of converting the effects of imperceptible activities into effects that could be perceived. Now the light that human beings *cannot* see and the sounds they *cannot* hear are caught by instruments that are able to convert them into readings which can be seen and heard.

It is the same in parapsychology. It would never have been known that there were any psi processes if their operations had not been converted into other effects. In PK the objects that are influenced can be observed. In ESP the subject gets knowledge he could not otherwise have got and it is converted into significant measurable responses.

In the same way, personal agency of any kind, if it is convertible into effects that can be seen and studied, can be detected and the agency that produced these effects can be determined just as the scientist indirectly works out to the hidden causes of registered effects in all the various sciences that deal with effects beyond the senses. Thus, so far as methodology goes, the procedures of natural science could just as well be set to work on the question of whether or not there are invisible beings such as spirits, as it has done already on the question of whether there are invisible genes or intangible cosmic rays. Any effect that reaches any man, from any source, and shows any regular relationships whatever, will reveal itself by its own operation when the properly inquiring study is made by an observer qualified to interpret the results. By the very nature of the universe, especially its causal character, one cannot get an effect *without* a cause; and this cause is potentially discoverable through the study of its consequences and the conditions under which they occur.

Nothing that is real in religion, then, or in any other realm of experience is beyond the range of investigation. Only an occurrence that would leave no trace or effect which, however indirectly, could bring it within the focus of man and his instruments, could be said to be beyond the reach of the inquiring mind. The existence of such an unobservable element of nature would indeed, be beyond discovery and, hence, a subject of pointless speculation. I profoundly suspect with all the skepticism of my nature any claims whatsoever to *unapproachable* truth. Parapsychology, itself, like many other fields, extends well out into realms far beyond the senses. Human reason, armed with the methods of experimental design and the instruments of mathematics, has a very long reach indeed. It can reach around the universe.

Such bearing as parapsychology may at present have on religion is only a humble beginning. Rather, it is religion's need for help that is great. This beginning, what there is of it, can be regarded as having two components, one of them a much-needed new method of approach to the problems of religion. By that method religion should be able to expand and strengthen its foundations of accepted truth, as many other fields of truth-seeking have done before with its help. Indeed, if nothing more could be done by the psi investigations for the time being than to call attention effectively to the fact that the problem area of religion is not beyond the range of sound inquiry and that its most important problems are actually within the reach of easily adapted or easily designed methods of scientific inquiry, it would at last bring the Renaissance to the field of religion itself.

A major advance, however, has already been made and that is the second of the two components of the psi contribution. When it is recognized it should serve to exemplify what science can do in a concrete way for religion. This advance consists of the fact that it has now been established by scientific means that there is an extraphysical element in man.

It would certainly appear that the chief enemy of religion, at least in the Western world, has been the philosophy of materialism. Whether one goes back to the philosophical materialism of the French Revolution and its rule of reason, whether one centers attention on the emergence of Marxian materialism in the Bolshevik Revolution in Russia, or whether he tries to interpret the present-day loosening of religion's hold on the philosophy of life, the same trend of thought would appear to be responsible. With that trend nature, including man himself, has been increasingly brought into the domain of lawful cause and effect and out of the range of the supernatural. Natural law has come to be taken as synonymous with physical law.

Now, by the application of strict scientific method, the same method by which physical laws have been established, the age-old problem of whether man is wholly mechanical has been approached. Not only that, but an answer quite contrary to the one prevailing in science today is indicated, for it has been shown that in certain subjects under suitable conditions mental processes take place that are not explainable by physical law as presently understood. The conclusion is inescapable that there is something operative in man that transcends the laws of matter and, therefore, by definition, a nonphysical or spiritual law is made manifest. The universe, therefore, does not conform to the prevailing materialistic concept. It is one about which it is possible to be religious; possible, at least, if the minimal requirement of religion be a philosophy of man's place in the universe based on the operation of spiritual forces.

What may lie behind these fleeting effects already discovered the scientist must restrain himself from attempting to say at present, but it would at the same time seem absurd to suppose that these flashes which have been experimentally encountered are the sum total of this kind of operation in nature. On the analogy of discovery in all other fields, these glimpses should only lead to the suspicion that there must be a great hidden system of operations behind these transient phenomena. If such be the case, then this new world of the mind, represented and perhaps only suggested by the psi operations already identified, may very well, through further exploration, expand into an order of significance for a spiritual universe beyond the dreams of religion's own prophets and mystics. It has been so with the other great areas of exploration. No one ever foresaw in his wildest imaginings the wealth of revelations that science in any domain has in time brought forth.

But the work in parapsychology does more than refute materialism. It is more, too, than a new method of solving problems. There are, at least, still other definite implications and possibilities. Since this new science has penetrated the physical barrier that has hidden man's true nature from the scientists of the past, it has become literally the science of the spiritual aspect of nature. Beyond this boundary lie some great questions regarding the spiritual powers of man, questions fundamental to the problems of the religious world. For example, what do spiritual capacities represent in the individual? That is, how much of a man is transphysical? Some kind of spirit double or incorporeal personality, capable of post-mortem survival, has figured in the common beliefs of mankind through the ages. Is there sufficient evidence of a spiritual self to justify raising the further question as to whether a separable spirit personality is conceivable?

This question of spirit survival, difficult to attack though it is in our present state of ignorance concerning the psychology of the living personality, is a perfectly good scientific problem. As many in parapsychology have been recognizing in recent years, the final solution of this question of the possible survival of the personality is awaiting further psychological knowledge of the spiritual aspect of the living man. Unfortunately, the direction in which psychology has been going in the past with its preoccupation with animal behavior and sensory physiology is such that it would seem unlikely ever to get around to the question of what, at his very best and biggest, a person really is; of what there is in him that could conceivably transcend and even survive the destruction of his nervous system.

The question, however, is one that most probably could, in time and with the proper methods, be answered. It is not one that must indefinitely be left entirely to unthinking faith. There is no reason why it should not be admitted that the answer is at present unknown. If so admitted, an attempt to learn the truth would assuredly be made; faith is a bar to inquiry. As later pages will show, the question is still a live one in parapsychology, if nowhere else.

There are other religious topics that could make good problems for experimental study, once the inquiring mind is turned loose on them. One of these is the question of prayer. If prayer *is* effective and if the thoughts of men *do* reach out to other personalities in the universe beyond the range of the senses, it must be through the medium of extrasensory perception. If, originating in any personal agency anywhere, celestial or mundane, there is an effect produced upon the physical world in answer to prayer, it would have to be a psychokinetic effect, a psi phenomenon. Psi, then, would be the scientific concept of the operations underlying any demonstrable spiritual manifestation involving either cognitive or kinetic effects. If this is true, then it would be obvious wisdom to study the "mechanism," the conditions affecting its operation, and the purposes to which its use may be extended. There is the belief, of course, that a divine personal agency exists to which prayer is directed. The cooperation of this agency itself could in all sincerity and propriety quite well be included in the research plan. In fact, the older world religions were supposedly founded with the aid of miracles, that is, cooperative demonstrations by divine agencies.

This leads to the question which most devout religious minds consider the greatest one of all: Is there a universal mind or divine personality? Like any universal negative, to prove conclusively that there is not would indeed be difficult. It would take a very, very long and exhaustive research program indeed to establish a reasonable likelihood that there is not a universal mind.

But if such a universal personality exists, those who believe the hypothesis a reasonable one can perfectly well, with proper thought and ingenuity, design a research program that would establish its presence and operation. Such a project of scientifically proving the thesis is the only one consistent with the approach that has been made to the natural universe in the past and the approach that has led to the discovery of all the natural laws and principles that now fill the treasure house of science. All that manifests itself in the universe, even God, reveals its causation in the effect it produces. Science works back to causes from effects, interpreting the former from the latter. By studying the conditions under which effects occur, scientists learn how to produce them when sufficient discovery and understanding have been reached, if they are of the reproducible kind; or they await their recurrence and try to explain their nonrecurrence if, like tidal waves or glacial ages, they are beyond the experimenter's control.

Naturally, most theologians, of whatever religion, have ready-made for them a quite different viewpoint as to the method of finding the truth from the scientific one I have outlined. Also, since it is human not to want one's beliefs challenged, they may prefer to continue to think and teach that some things are beyond the range of human inquiry. That teaching, however, though it might do for children and for the childhood of the race, will no longer suffice in the present age, for after men have been educated to check things for themselves and when they realize all the inconsistency and uncertainty and failure that goes with the blind acceptance of unverified claims, they will increasingly demand that these great questions of religion be brought under scrutiny by the same methods that have so successfully conquered the mysteries of the physical aspects of the universe.

Such small fragments as the psi inquiries have produced must not be expected to be impressive in themselves. Rather, they may well be only as a small fringe of islands representing a continent of spiritual reality. Leuwenhoek, in his first glimpse through the microscope, saw only the merest fragment of the vast world of microbiology. It was but an infinitesimal part of the electrical universe that Gilbert or Franklin came upon in his discovery. What a small fragment of a new world of energetics it was that Becquerel found in that first radioactive element! The analogy leaves one awe-struck. What if these traces of psi effect are comparable to those earlier traces that ushered in new worlds in the past, and it is only a matter of time and continued research to reveal the mainland it seems there must be behind these reefs of new reality already encountered. Perhaps it is just as well that the imagination fails in such an effort at conjecture.

As I write these words I am fully aware of the visionary aspect they must have for many readers. Knowing, as we all do, of the slow, apathetic response such possibilities as I have pictured are likely to get from professional groups, how, indeed, could one feel that all this talk of new support for religion—at least in this century—is anything but an idle dream?

There is, however, a reason for taking it seriously, a compelling one, a crisis. There are, happily, many people who cannot supinely wait for the crushing impact of the tide of materialistically fostered destruction to advance and put an end to all inquiry and to all hope of it. There are some who are already awake to the realization that the instruments of defense, even of prevention, lie at hand ready to be developed. The basic issue underlying the clash of ideologies in the world today is a theory as to the nature of man. Most thinking people know that blind faith in dogmatic revelationistic religion cannot counter the claims and promises of communism. It is, in fact, all too plain from the history of communism's gains that it has thrived best where authoritarian religion has had its longest and strongest control over the lives of the people.

Neither is there hope that the physicalistic psychology that now prevails in this country can answer the menace of the philosophy of communism to our way of life. For, as I have pointed out, that psychology is still timidly clinging to the same materialistic philosophy of man that, in the nineteenth century, gave communism its great intellectual boost and still sustains it, accrediting it with the authority of science and lending to it a dignity equivalent to what the doctrine of divine right meant to an ancient monarch.

Communism, then, is forcing the issue. And it is doing so in a way that the comparatively quiet, unspectacular discovery of psi could never have done. It has already put pressure upon our national culture in other than ideational ways. It has helped to alter isolationist tendencies, has forced an international "altruism" toward less fortunate peoples in order to keep them from turning communists, and has appreciably improved racial tolerance in this country! It may not be too much to expect, then, that this same pressure will drive home the realization that communism has its roots in ideological deficiencies, too, as well as in physical hunger. It may force a realization of the need to push research on the spiritual armament against communism to its logical scientific limits. After realizing how many battles with communism have been lost by those armed only with blind faith, more of those responsible for the leadership of religion may feel the necessity of being armed with firmly established fact instead of authoritarian dogma.

This pressure from communism could accomplish in a short time what the slow progress of education might take a century to bring about. If so, a religious world, harassed by the threat of communism to its hold on mankind, may accept Tennyson's injunction of a century ago and let religion "arm herself with the instruments of her time." That would mean calling in scientific method. But I am certain that only from such outside influence, such pressure as is being exerted by encroaching Communist ideas, can the internal resistance of established religion to inquiry, and its fear of change and distrust of science in spiritual matters be overcome.

Could mankind, even under pressure, be led into taking a step that involved such a change in its religious philosophy? Would there be the insight, the gumption, the resolution to carry it through? There is ground for hope. There will, of course, be stiff resistances based on misguided loyalties and other fine sentiments. Such misplaced feelings have always stood in the way of every major advance. The point to be most clear about is that this acceptance of psi's contribution of a new approach to religion would be a constructive step. It would be not an attack but a defense. It would be not a tearing down but an underpinning of the structure of spiritual relationships in human life. Let those who can only follow wait for the results; they will relinquish then whatever must give way to a new understanding as they gave up the horse and buggy or the tallow candle. But, I must repeat, there is no ground for anticipating this great advance in religious truth seeking unless and until the full reality is finally forced upon the world, the awful truth of just what an unprogressive religious leadership, however benevolent, can do to its followers.

Such a change conceivably could, it is true, be brought about in a more satisfactory way. It should not be necessary for religion to be *forced* by communism into taking such a step if only the proper questions would be asked of the religions and reliable answers insisted upon. What are the proper questions? The starting point should be: How sound a basis of knowledge has any given religion on which to support any given tenet? One by one every important doctrine needs to be thoughtfully re-examined as to its foundation. Does anyone really yet know, for example, what extrahuman help a human being can call upon and count on in the guidance of his life? What sound and tested teaching is there to prepare a man to face such a final fact as death? On what kind of evidence does this teaching depend? If one asks these and similar questions, and insists on frank, definite answers, an appalling situation comes to light. It is that no one knows or pretends to know, in a way he can prove, the answers to these or any other of the greater questions of religion.

Finally the truth dawns that to these central questions even the most consecrated scholarly leadership in all the religious systems simply does not have answers that would satisfy the ordinary standards of evidence of everyday life in the bank or the court or the market place, let alone in the sciences. In the face of that realization, dogmatic religion comes to assume the shape and proportion of a gigantic group delusion, cutting itself off deliberately from the tests of reality by which its position could be verified and by which its course toward greater positive knowledge could be directed. For in this old attitude is an almost complete abandonment of realism, a surrender to a system of unverified fantasy that, in a single isolated individual, would be diagnosed as psychotic.

As a people, we are not so unrealistic in other matters. We would not leave our loved ones in the hands of surgeons who operated on the unverified authority of ancient manuscripts, deciding with such guesswork as to where the organs on which they were going to operate were located. Mankind has got very much further than that with its veterinary medicine, for example, or its agriculture, or even with its plumbing. What magic spell has kept us all stymied so long in religion? What enchantment keeps the world chanting formulas that may be mostly rubbish for all it knows? *Think* of all the good man-hours of prayer spent through all the centuries by all the billions around the globe, with no one throughout these ages taking the obviously sensible precaution of checking up! For no one ever tried effectively to answer the question of whether the overall yield is worth the effort. Yet during these same ages in which religion has been left comparatively static, its attention fixed on ancient authority, man has efficiently advanced in other less vital areas of interest, utilizing the methods of science to acquire the basis of the knowledge needed.

So many millions of people, so much of the world's value system is involved, that it becomes a stupendous issue. If anything is to be done about it, it is necessary to see it in all its global enormity. Would there be any more monstrous kind of slavery in the world, no matter with what stupid benignity it be practiced, than that which confined people to a narrow primitive religious belief through endless years of blind groping, a slavery of whole peoples that kept them forever missing the richer, more adequate life that might be theirs if they could only be liberated from a fear-inspiring, horizon-lowering theory of the world in which they lived? If it is good and fraternal and blessed to feed them and save them from malaria and cholera, would there be any words to describe what a noble gift it would be to open their eyes to a happier, more complete way of living their lives; a saner, more courageous way of facing and solving their problems on the spot instead of projecting them unrealistically beyond their own reach into another promised world that might, for all anyone has taken the trouble to find out, be only a vain, misguided, enslaving fiction.

These are not negative, anti-religious thoughts. They are the positive, constructive challenges of impersonal facts. There *is* ground for hope. Religion can yet save the world, save it from its misery and fear and confusion and strife, if it can save itself from becoming completely a relic of the past; if it can capture and hold leadership in the knowledge of man's place as a spiritual being in a universe that is, we now know, at least not devoid of spiritual forces. Such a challenge is not for those who cannot change, nor is it for those who cannot think for themselves. But the world would hardly be worth saving if there were not also those and many of them, who want religion to be equal to all of mankind's needs, who are willing to wait and work with all their wits, instead of with mere credulous faith in authority, to help to develop such a saving force for themselves and their fellow men.

Let me summarize. What I am trying to say is that one *can* look with an inquiring mind at the great problems of human life that are grouped under the heading of religion and actually make progress in the solution of them. We have now gone far enough to know that much. Whatever can be found out by sound methods of inquiry will, of course, be part of the same natural universe to which we all belong, and we shall not have to worry about old (and rather useless) distinctions of supernaturalism and the like. The important thing is that the knowledge accepted must be sound. If one demands certainty in connection with the gadgetry of daily living as in engineering and medicine, he certainly cannot afford to do less with the discipline dedicated to the peace and good will and enduring happiness of mankind.

The intellectual leadership of the West will have to clear these matters up if it is to keep an adequate grip on the wheel in the guidance of human affairs, even of its own. The welfare of men everywhere is a problem for mankind at large; the global viewpoint has at last emerged. In our country we are now reaching out (with some element of sincerity beyond political expediency, no doubt) to the aid of the less fortunate, whether suffering from starvation or catastrophe or epidemic or whatever it may be. What utter inconsistency it would be if, now, on the larger matter of a religious philosophy of life, an understanding of the world itself so essential for the charting of a properly satisfying way of life, we were to say, "That is no business of ours."

There are hundreds of millions around the world whose whole outlook on life, whose cramped and distorted vision of the world, is guided, confined, controlled by a faith that is, by the standards of the scholar, an unverified clutter of ancient storytelling. Yet it is more binding upon their lives, more determinative of the total joy or misery of living that will be their lot, than anything else can be for them.

What can be done for them? Well, what do we ourselves know that is so much surer, better, and more useful to live by? The first problem, then, begins at home. At the same time, knowing how much hangs on the outcome, what nobler undertaking can man set for himself than to find out what is true, what is reliable, what is usable and safe and inspiring and sustaining and beautifying as a concept of man and nature.

If discoveries are made by sound methods, no missionaries will be needed to distribute them. Verified knowledge is not easily contained; it crosses boundaries unrestrictedly and as the facts become established and known they penetrate even iron curtains. If it is a truly sound exploration of man's whole personal makeup, of the forces that work within him and in his interrelations with the universe, the result will be one good enough to supplant both the materialistic philosophy of communism and the decaying structures of the old religious organizations which communism itself has been supplanting.

No one can yet say what will survive such a search into the fundamental principles underlying all the problems of religion. That many of the ideological stocks in which mankind has invested are worthless is obvious enough. There is no good in clinging sentimentally to them because they were once of high market value. If due investigation should find no evidence of any or all of the "other worlds," heavens, summerlands, happy hunting grounds, nirvanas, and such, that have been taking men's minds off their present world through the ages, it might lead to an extremely healthy shift of human effort and attention to the problems of the present life. Life would take on a larger area for having its boundary defined.

If, on the other hand, some kind of world of independent spirit agency can be discovered, as there is reason to think may be possible, its establishment would manifestly bring to religious life an incomparably greater meaning and potency. The discovery would do for religion something like what the germ theory did for medicine. It would open the range of religious exploration to horizons beyond all present conceptions. It has always been so when new areas are discovered.

But if one reflects on the direction taken by other fields of research in the past, he will not then expect that Nature in this new world of the mind will prove to be much like tradition and speculation have pictured her. Rather, she has usually proved to be far more interesting, much more useful to mankind when properly understood, and always more "reasonable," of course, than the speculative guesses made about her in advance of fact.

Surely there is no need to be anxious in this instance. No matter how unrefined and unexplained the raw research findings are as they come from the pit of exploration, the eventual processing of the new contributions to knowledge has always permitted the "laws of nature" to emerge triumphant. In that assurance of history lies the promise of an *orderly* new world of spiritual reality, whatever it may be like otherwise. That is a comforting assurance to have as one goes further into the vast unknown areas that remain.

But we may count on more than order. If such an emerging new world is to make sense to our rational minds out of the little we already know, it will have to reveal to us some very strange new principles we have not yet the understanding even to identify. Nothing in the least familiar is going to explain such phenomena as consciousness, love, insight, precognition—to name a few great mysteries. Great surprises, then, await us too. And will they be any the less revelations for our having good reason for being sure about them? Will their guidance value in life be any lower for all the certainty? We shall at last, even in religion, be putting first things first; first-rate problems with first-rate methods of solving them.

Chapter **8**

RELATION TO

THE HEALTH OF THE MIND

███ In considering the relation of psi to mental health the discussion returns to the ground of undisputed natural science. But while there is no longer any involvement of questions of supernaturalism in professional psychiatry (which I shall loosely extend to include mental hygiene in general), it has much in common with religion. Like religion, too, it has a basis of more or less generally accepted truth, even though this is obtained by a very different type of fact-finding method. And there is also the same general social purpose in both, what might be impartially termed the goal of perfecting the long-view adjustment of humanity to its environment with the most complete, balanced, and satisfying life attainable for all. Central to both, too, therefore, is the question of the fundamental makeup of human personality. To the psychiatrist, as to the pastoral counselor, it is of real concern to know what sort of creature it is to whom he gives his services. He must have some answer to the question: What is it in the patient that gets unhappy, goes wrong, upsets his life, and has to be mended? Is it something entirely covered by physical law or something uniquely mental or spiritual with peculiar principles of its own? The answer to this question would affect the whole approach of the psychiatrist, as it would that of the minister.

The problems of parapsychology are not entirely strange to psychiatry. Some of them have been to a large extent historically associated with the study of mental illness. As far back as the time of Franz Mesmer and his followers phenomena such as are now included under extrasensory perception were not uncommonly encountered incidentally in healing practices. Mesmer himself and some of his followers such as Puysegur, Esdaile, Elliotson, and Liebeault mention exceptional powers which in the eighteenth century were simply taken to be part of the mesmeric effect itself. A hundred years or more after Mesmer, in the last quarter of the nineteenth century, a period identified with the investigations of Pierre Janet, Charles Richet, and other European physicians, mesmerism had become hypnotism, and telepathy and clairvoyance had begun to be isolated as phenomena apart from the hypnotic trance; they were then left to the societies for psychical research that were being formed during that period for their study.

Now, again, this time in the twentieth century, and purged completely of the association with hypnosis, telepathy has found a place in the new psychiatry of the psychoanalytic schools. The most outspoken of these analytic leaders in his attention to telepathy was Wilhelm Steckel, although Sigmund Freud and a number of his followers, more or less incidental to their own theories, took some interest in the matter. Among the analytical psychiatrists, however, it has been C. G. Jung who has paid most attention to psi phenomena, although it was not until comparatively recent years that this attention has emerged in explicit form in his writings. His latest book, however, *Naturerklärung und Psyche* (with W. Pauli), puts Jung in the forefront of psychiatrists giving attention to parapsychology.

But interest, especially in telepathy, is widespread among psychiatrists. Active attention to the phenomena of telepathy by psychoanalysts is evident in the publications of Jan Ehrenwald, Jule Eisenbud, E. Servadio, Geraldine Pederson-Krag, Nandor

Fodor, and quite a number of others.[1] This interest has not, however, been confined to analysts or to psychiatrists of any one school. Among independent psychiatrists who have written on the subject in recent decades, to select only a few from western Europe, are the late T. W. Mitchell, William McDougall, and William Brown, and among the living, Hubert Urban, Laurence Bendit, Alfred von Winterstein, Alice Buck, and John Björkhem. In the American Society for Psychical Research in this country there is a Medical Section made up largely of psychiatrists.

There are other indications of professional interest in the field. Among these are the many invitations extended by psychiatric groups to parapsychologists to present their research findings, the readiness of psychiatric periodicals to publish work on parapsychology, and the general participation of the profession in the discussion of the psi research. All in all, the indications are that the psi researches have received a comparatively fair hearing from at least this one of the professions.

There is even an opinion poll to be cited on the matter. In 1948 an American neuropsychiatrist in New York, Dr. Russell MacRobert,[2] made a survey of current attitudes of his American colleagues and reported the returns in the December issue of the *Journal of Parapsychology* for that year. In the 723 replies he obtained to the questionnaire sent to 2,500 psychiatrists, Dr. MacRobert found a distribution of responses quite different from those obtained by Warner from the psychologists. Thirty-one per cent claimed familiarity with results of the ESP researches, 68 per cent considered that the ESP researches should be sponsored, and 23 per cent even considered that they had personally observed ESP occurrences in their own practice or experience; 17 per cent more were uncertain.

This distribution of attitudes seems quite different from that of the psychologists. Why should there be such a difference? For one thing, psychiatrists, faced with the urgency of having to find cures for their patients, have always been more venturesome than psychologists. They have, in fact, in many instances been forced to become research psychologists themselves and find out from their own studies much of what they have needed to know of the psychological makeup of the people they were trying to serve.

Looking back down the history of psychology one can see that most of its greatest achievements, especially those relating to the deeper structure of personality and the ways of studying it, came from such pioneers on the medical frontier of psychology. Evidently orthodoxy is not quite so rigid in the psychiatric branch as in the other branches of the human sciences. In whatever field exploration is still active the fellow explorer is least likely to encounter resistance to his own discoveries.

How deep does the relation between parapsychology and psychiatry go? Is it only historical, an incidental association? Or does it rest on a more fundamental linkage? There was a time when ESP effects were associated with hypnosis so closely that they were considered derivatives of it. Hypnosis, in turn, was at that time thought to be closely involved with hysteria. Accordingly, a suggestion was planted in the thought of the last century (and to some extent still persists) that there is something abnormal about telepathic and clairvoyant experiences and that persons prone to hysteria are more likely to have them.

Parapsychology and psychopathology do have much in common. The phenomena of both are, as a matter of fact, deviations from the normal in the sense of being exceptional. Furthermore, as I have pointed out in Chapter Three, many of the occurrences typical of both fields are, on the surface, almost identical. Certain types of spontaneous psi experiences, for example, are removed from classification as pathological only because they are veridical, which means that actual knowledge which the subject would not normally have had is somehow received. The experience of the person who has recurrent dreams of the death of a friend may well be considered morbid unless, as in a case cited earlier, it turns out that the death actually occurs under circumstances similar in sufficient detail to rule out coincidence.

Or, again, an individual who sees an apparition at his bedside may wonder if he should consult a psychiatrist. If, however, some other person also sees the same apparition, the problem may shift at once from the psychiatric to the parapsychological realm, at least for further investigation.

A considerable range of cases that show little dissimilarity on the level of the subjects' experiences could be drawn from the two fields. Indeed, it is a common thing for a person reporting a psychic experience to begin with the expression: "I wonder if I am in my right mind," or, again, "My husband thinks I am a bit crazy to have had these experiences," or the more indirect statement, "I have never had any signs of mental disorder in my life." Even the general public has not missed the similarity of the subjective side of some of the psi experiences and some of the abnormal ones. In Louisa E. Rhine's analysis of psi experiences,[3] the fact was that the subjective forms in which they commonly came are typical of experiences people ordinarily have, whether psychic or not and whether abnormal or not. They are simply forms that are common to both.

Such resemblances, however, are really on the surface. The one clearly conjunctive feature which parapsychology and psychiatry share that is not superficial is their primary involvement with *unconscious* mental life. This is an identifying characteristic of these two fields and, perhaps, of these two alone.

It is an important one, too. If psi capacities were not obscured by their unconsciousness, they would doubtless be so easily recognized that they would have been on record as early in history as Aristotle's psychology. On the side of psychopathology, as Freud had the genius to appreciate, it is the relegation of maladjusted desires to unconscious levels that enables them to endure and eventually to endanger the adjustment of the individual. This fact, of course, was of the first importance to psychiatry.

And it is this vast psychology of unconsciousness with all its peculiar properties, devices, and functions, how many of them still to be discovered no one can say, that is the main feature of the common background for these two branches of the study of man, psychiatry and parapsychology.

The relationship of psi to psychiatry is still, however, a definitely limited one. The most important question is: Is there any essential causal interrelation between the two fields, between ESP and the pathological devices of the mind that it seems to approximate? Are psi phenomena themselves abnormal; or, on the other hand, are mental illnesses produced by psi? A beginning on the answering of this important two-way question may be made by reviewing here the approaches to the problem that have already yielded results.

First, studies of ESP ability by card-test methods have been conducted in mental hospitals. None of these, however, has yet revealed a causal connection between pathology and ESP. Although many paranoid patients claim they are being telepathically persecuted, there is no record to show that any of them possess any special ESP ability. Even from a wide range of spontaneous cases, no relationship of ESP with mental disorders has been suggested. The impression given is rather that the people who have spontaneous ESP experiences are no less likely than others to be normal, healthy individuals.

The personality studies of Stuart, Schmeidler, and Humphrey tend, with some reservations, to suggest that the better adjusted the individuals the more likely they are to show positive deviations from chance averages in their ESP data.[4] In Schmeidler's work with ESP combined with Rorschach tests, the well-adjusted subjects stood out as the group producing the large deviations, both positive and negative; and the size of deviation from the "chance" mean should be the best measure of amount of ESP effect.

Doubtless if there were any basic connection between mental illness and psi capacity, the early psychiatrists would have encountered many more psi phenomena than they did, and parapsychology likely would never have become an independent branch of inquiry. Also, were there any common causal connections, the psi investigators would by this time have learned to concentrate upon the mental hospitals as the most profitable area for the pursuit of their inquiries. A review of the results of hospital tests made with standard methods and safeguards (awaiting publication, by Esther Foster) shows that while ESP has been demonstrated on different groups of patients, there has been no outstanding performance either by individuals or by any one classified group.

Altogether, there is no good reason to think of psi phenomena as abnormal or of mental disorders as favoring the manifestation of psi effects. Although the two kinds of occurrences have enough in common for many important interrelations, so far none of these appears to be determinative; neither produces the other. Like any other ability, psi can become involved in pathological thinking and can even become the conspicuous feature in it. Also, the similarity between certain psi experiences and pure hallucination often leads to grave errors of judgment by the subject who has the experience, errors that can, if overemphasized, be seriously unhealthy.

There is, for example, a friend who, following the tragic death of her daughter, began to hear the girl's voice reassuring her of her survival. Following that, the mother began to receive guiding counsel and forewarnings that impressed her and her scientist husband as genuinely psychic in nature. (I, too, was impressed, although the case was not one on which I could draw conclusions.) As the experiences she reported increased, there was no way of knowing how far it would be wise to let them go. Finally, however, it became obvious that the mother's mental health was being endangered, and then it was necessary to treat the case as if it were a psychiatric one. It was clear eventually that if psi had been involved it had been utilized as a neurotic device. But there is no reason why it should not be so misused, just as vision or memory or any other normal function can be used in a pathological form and degree. It is rare, however, that psi appears in such an abnormal blend.

Nevertheless, there is need for collaboration between psychiatrist and parapsychologist. Even if no fundamental interconnection is ever found between the major phenomena of their fields of study, there are other grounds of common interest that can make cooperation worth while. For one thing, the psychiatrist is in an advantageous position to do something about psi problems. By the very nature of his work he has an extremely good opportunity not only to encounter psi experiences but also to see them in their psychological setting in the patient's life history. Those who make special use of dream material, as all the analytical schools do, often find instances of ESP, particularly cases suggesting telepathy, emerging in the course of the analyses. Many of these instances have already been reported as incidental material in the literature of psychiatry. Whether the telepathic character of an experience will be noted when it appears depends, of course, upon the interest range of the individual psychiatrist. But no other professional man has an equal opportunity to explore psi experiences at first hand.

The psychiatrist has another advantage, especially if he has hospital connections. There he has groups of classified patients that, to some extent at least, are already grouped from the point of view of certain characteristics of personality, if only from the pathological aspect. The opportunity to observe any psi effects that may occur against this patterned background of classification is a most valuable one.

In the course of the therapy, too, there is a similar leverage. The psychiatrist has the opportunity to study any unique development, such as the tendency to have psi experiences, against the developing pattern of states and stages through which the therapy carries the individual. He could even give comparative psi tests incidentally as the treatment progresses. This opportunity was first utilized by Dr. Hubert Urban[5] at the Neuropsychiatric Clinic at Innsbruck, Austria, when he initiated clinical comparisons of ESP in card tests before and after shock treatment. In this pioneer effort he had to cope with the necessary adaptation of laboratory methods to the clinical situation, and it is not surprising that some problems developed that have delayed interpretation of the results. It is, therefore, still undecided whether shock treatments affect the ESP capacity of the subject in an appreciable way and degree. But at least an attack has been made on the problem, and enough progress has been made to show that the testing methods can now effectively be used at the bedside without unduly lowering the standards of precaution. For that matter, psi tests may very well fit in as incidental to any therapeutic procedure and the whole course of the patient's recovery be accompanied by a record of test performance for purposes of comparative study.

And now to reverse the question, what do the psi researches contribute that may be of interest to psychiatry? A part of the answer can be given in terms of actual findings already obtained, but there are some possibilities still undeveloped which I shall briefly review first. One of these is the question of whether a useful telepathic mode of rapport can be developed between psychiatrist and patient. While it will seem to some professional people a ridiculous fancy, the fact is that many psychiatrists are confident that flashes of telepathic insight sometimes play a part in their own professional work and experiences. As yet such impressions are only clinical, but it is plain enough that if they can be experimentally validated the result would be important to psychiatry. Let it be kept in mind that a scientist is one who raises questions while there is still doubt about the answers. Anyone can do so at the later stages.

A second possibility is the suggestion that psychokinesis may be a factor in psychosomatic medicine. The idea is still tentative but it seems entirely logical. If the mind can operate ever so little on objects such as rolling dice, it seems reasonable to suppose that it should be able to influence the matter of its own body. A number of psychogenetic or mentally produced effects on the body frequently baffle the medical scientist. Among these are some called stigmata, organic lesions or wounds such as those reported to have occurred to Therese Neumann of Germany. In this well-known but still uncertain case the human body is reported to have taken on at regular intervals an imitation of the wounds of Christ. The effect was supposed not to have had any organic or physical cause. In all such unverified cases, of course, one has to withhold scientific judgment. There are, too, effects called dermagraphia or skinwriting, like that of the Parisian Madame Kahl[6] who is reported to have reproduced on her skin the visible outlines of drawings telepathically received.

One of the most frequently demonstrated effects of a mental state on a body condition is that of the formation of blisters at a designated spot as a result of hypnotic suggestion. In some cases the report shows that there was continuous observation throughout the period of the production of the effect. Spontaneous cases, especially when well observed, can also contribute something and are often much more striking than experimental ones. ¶For example, a psychologist whom I have known for many years once told me that one night he had a terrific nightmare dream in the course of which he thought he was being beaten on the back by steel rods. In the dream he was suffering terribly. His groans and moans awakened his wife and she awakened him. Since he could still feel the painful results of the beating, his wife turned on the light to examine his back. Amazingly enough, it was striped with plainly visible red and white welts. Nothing about the bed or his pajamas could have produced the effect. It was, he was convinced, a psychosomatic effect. Of course, this psychologist cannot explain how his own mind could have given him that beating. . . . But if PK is a factor in any or all of the types of cases mentioned, it must have much greater potentiality than the dice tests have yet brought out. That should not be surprising, however, since never in the past have the first traces of a discovered principle revealed its full potential.

There are similar puzzles, too, in certain reported types of cures. The best examples are those called faith healing. With all due allowance made, some of these are completely baffling . . . §In my home town is a home economics teacher, wife of a psychologist, whom I have known for twenty years. She told me that one day in her class in cooking a child spilled boiling fudge over both hands and then ran screaming home to her millworker father, who was reputed to be a "fire blower." The teacher, of course, followed the child home, where she found the father had calmed the child and was already "treating" her. The girl was soon over the pain, and the fudge could be washed off her hands without any ill effects, although the teacher had feared the scalded skin would come off with it. The next day the child had not even a blister, but the other girls who had merely been spattered had blisters wherever the scalding fudge had fallen.

There are a great many, and a great variety, of such unexplainable effects to be found around the fringes of medicine—that is, if one looks for them. The psychophysical mechanisms that must be involved in such puzzling phenomena as the removal of warts by suggestion or the sudden graying of hair from wholly psychical causes are still a mystery. Yet nowadays no well-informed medical man denies that such things do sometimes occur. I am only adding here that the PK hypothesis may help to explain these strange organic occurrences. At any rate they are at present inexplicable, even by all the branches of medicine taken together.

Some psychiatrists appreciate the development of systematic

methods and standards in parapsychology which aid in distinguishing between true psi-experiences and abnormal hallucination and delusion. Many have, for practical purposes, wanted to know the techniques of testing for psi in order, for example, to check up on the psi-delusions that certain patients have. The telepathy test has already found its place in the psychiatrist's armament in treating the individual whose fears of telepathic persecution require the factual type of demonstration that he can see for himself. These beginnings doubtless will expand, too, as scientific knowledge and skills in parapsychology develop.

Among the new findings that are likely to be of importance beyond the borders of parapsychology is the already discussed psi-missing factor that works so subversively in producing negative deviations even when the subject is trying his best to produce scores above the chance average. This effect could also be important for psychiatry and for the psychology of personality in general. In psi-missing (be it recalled) the subject unconsciously makes errors so consistently as to produce the appearance that he is really avoiding instead of trying to hit the target. But the missing that results is not, it now seems, caused by unconscious negativism. In most cases, as I have shown earlier, unconscious negative motivation can be fairly definitely excluded by an analysis of the evidence. Yet here is a tendency toward a wrong-going device deep down in human nature that can, even with the very best of intentions on the part of the individual, really subvert his conscious desires.

Now, would anybody think that such a "derailing" factor is effective in the deep unconscious mental levels only in the psi tests in which it has been discovered? Probably not. It doubtless affects a number of the individual's unconscious mental operations, much as it does the psi process. Of course, no one would ever know it if it did. In any case, it would seem worth while for psychiatry and psychology to find out how general such a perverse factor in personality may be in its hidden operation. And this might not be an overly difficult matter to discover. For this psi-missing "mechanism" may belong to a less profoundly and irrecoverably unconscious level of mental life than psi itself and operate in the shallow stratum of subconsciousness with which psychiatry has mainly to deal, a level from which elements may be brought in to conscious experience.

But the major contribution of psi to psychiatry is on the thought-brain relation; that is, of course, something that is fundamental to psychiatry. It is hard to see how the psychiatrist can ever really know quite where he stands on the proper method of practice until this neuropsychic relation has been figured out in terms of sound scientific principles. How, indeed, can one be expected to arrive at a way of treating a patient until he knows just what it is he is treating, a mind or a body, or both?

Most psychiatrists, it is true, have followed the mechanistic trend of thought of medical science in general. Since the physiological or somatic side of the patient is so much better known and, therefore, so much more dependable and usable than the psychological, the natural tendency has been to place more and more emphasis and reliance on the former as against the latter. The result, of course, has been the mechanistic philosophy of human personality. Professional groups and especially those in public practice, like the psychiatrists, tend toward conservatism, and it is conservative to follow the more established, better developed physical sciences.

Such conservatism would be all right if only it led to a fully effective practice. But no psychiatrist has been able to build a useful and successful psychotherapy on a consistently mechanistic theory of human personality. The physics of the nervous system just does not give him the entire picture of his patient's personality. The psychiatrist knows that he cannot understand his patient's unhappiness in terms of any kind of known physical law. The effect of his mechanistic outlook, however, is shown in his tendency to think mainly of physical techniques, much as in any branch of engineering. The exploratory ideas coming from this source tend to direct effort to therapeutic methods involving the destruction of some critical section of the nervous system. By reaching in here and there with scalpel, needle, or electric current, the psychiatrist tries to see what a little tampering will do to knock out the patient's troubles.

In the profession in general, therefore, one can notice a dearth of over-all theory or guiding idea. The effort seems largely an empirical groping in the dark to find the urgently needed cure as quickly as possible, trusting that the explanation will come later. And as the evidence shows, some of these "tamperings" do bring a cessation of aggravating symptoms; they are illustrated well in various methods of shocking the underlying machinery by means of chemical or mechanical interference from without. This limited measure of success has been taken as supporting the mechanistic approach; and, of course, whatever else there may be in a human organism, there is a tremendous lot of mechanism.

It is this success of physical methods and the lack of anything adequate to challenge the prevailing philosophy that has produced a psychiatric rationale almost exclusively physicalistic. Happily, however, as we have seen, it has not closed the minds of the profession to possibilities that challenge this philosophy. Psychiatry has been so close to human nature and its urgent problems that it is less dogmatic than some of its neighboring professions. It has also been venturesome enough in its own research spirit and sufficiently hard-pressed by its own therapeutic limitations as to make its professional group comparatively open-minded. More than that, psychiatry has been close enough to the facts of parapsychology to appreciate them better, perhaps, as a part of man's total nature, than any other profession.

When and as the implications of the psi discoveries really penetrate psychiatric thinking and theory, the resulting changes should be as revolutionary, perhaps, as any the field has seen. With such a development psychiatry will doubtless continue to hold its advanced sector on the frontier of the sciences concerned with personality, for, without losing the unity of their psychosomatic concept, psychiatrists will have to deal with the fact that genuine differentiation actually exists within the larger unit of personality. Recognizing this basic differentiation within the totality of the individual would bring to an end the fruitless, wasteful seesaw of emphasis that characterizes the history of the profession; for, in the past, psychiatric theory and practice have swung back and forth from psycho- to mechano-therapies without ever reaching a peaceful, workable settlement. This zigzag has, alas, often left an unhealthy conflict within the individual psychiatrist himself when he attempted to unify his own thinking into some semblance of a consistent rational system.

It could mean a great deal to psychiatry to realize that there is a firm ground of mental reality within the natural order of things; and that it is not necessary to force the whole interpretation of its professional operation into the limited patterns of mindless physical law. On this broader basis, psychotherapy could be liberated to work out its own laws. Those laws no longer have to be subordinated to the code of physiological or chemical or physical principles. The ultimate coordination can be, *has* to be, left as a much more remote research objective.

A number of psychiatric explorers have, it is true, attempted to take this very stand but, with the dominant philosophy of psychiatry being one of physical monism and with psychiatry itself as a branch of medicine only emerging from its period of trial, these adventurers have been isolated. They lacked, too, the body of experimental facts such as are now at hand in the psi discoveries. Such individual psychiatric explorers have been very definitely in the minority.

If the implications of psi do break down the resistance due to the influence of mechanistic thinking in psychiatry, and it is at least likely to happen there before it does in academic psychology, the operations of unconscious mental life will come to mean something beyond the viscera, the ductless glands, and the functioning of the autonomic nervous system. While leaving it to future research to discover the underlying interconnections that must, of course, exist, the psychiatrist can at least take the psychical elements of personality as primary realities in themselves. He will no longer be forced to demand of them that they first make sense physiologically. He is going to insist, and this is the nub of the whole shift of emphasis, that, first of all, they make psychological sense. By that I mean that they make sense with a psychology that *begins* with the verifiable subjective realities of personality.

It is the fact that the underlying principles of mental life are still unknown that makes the entire foundation of mental disorder so debatable and obscure, and leaves the whole battery of therapeutic measures resting largely on a trial and error basis. It is not even known on what level of reality to attack the problem.

It is an advance, then, to have established the existence of a genuinely *mental* level of personality. That accomplishment at least makes it reasonable now to attack mental problems on that distinctive level, for, of course, one does not attack or even consider an area unless he believes it exists. Now, however, with that point established, there should be some new ground for hope for a basic principle of psychotherapy. It is not unreasonable, surely, to suggest that *psycho*therapy needs some sort of psyche; but a psyche fits a physicalistic type of psychology about as well as romantic love would apply to a couple of electric calculators. With experimental proof now on record that the personality of man has nonphysical and hence distinctively psychical principles, psychiatrists ought to be better braced to orient their course toward a less physicalistic philosophy of their patients and their practice. The result should be stiffer resistance against a surrender to a wholly materialistic concept of therapy.

There is another implication arising from the psi researches that may be significant for psychotherapy. As I have said before, these studies have provided a basis for a possible concept of volitional freedom. This concept frees the human will from the bondage of materialism; and to the therapist the bearing of this freedom is obvious. Without free will in his patient and without some solid ground for accepting the notion, the psychotherapist would be nothing but a rubber stamper. In fact, the whole concept of all the counseling professions hinges on a shift of position on this basic issue. The conception of a psychotherapy assumes in the patient a free-willing personality with a system of truly psychical (and nonphysical) functions upon which its art may be developed and practiced. That kind of psychotherapy could be developed on the basis of the new knowledge to which the psi researches have contributed.

It would be too much to say that the shift in viewpoint which the implications of the parapsychological findings could bring will throw *immediate* light on these major problems. This is far from the point I am trying to make here. Rather, the point is that an adequate recognition of the fact that the mind does some things in a way that proves it has a nature of its own, and not a physical one—that fact could bring about a great shift of thinking in psychiatry. It could be more than a mere turning away from an emphasis on mechanistic theories and techniques; it could be a positive drive for new principles peculiar to personal as contrasted with material concepts. With such a new turn of thought, the way would be open for consideration of new hypotheses as well as new explorations into borderline problem areas which at present are comparatively closed. This would happen, too, without necessitating the abandonment of any of the principles and practices based on the organic and physical aspects that have been proved efficacious. It would, in a word, open the windows on a new and wider prospect for this important professional service, one that from their present outlook only a portion of its members have been able to see.

Chapter 9

BEARING ON

THE CONDUCT OF LIFE

■ There is still left for discussion the supreme need of human society. Surely the salient need of today and of all time is for a better way for men to live together, a more effective moral code, an adequate ethical philosophy.

"Man's inhumanity to man" is causing immeasurably greater mourning today than ever in the past. This generation has known more slaughter, military and civilian, than any other in recorded history, and we live in dread apprehension that we have not yet seen the worst. We have seen one of the greatest, most Christian, most cultured, most law-abiding of the nations of the earth swept far off its base of ethical values to the practice of deliberate genocide and to the use of the torture chamber. The world is tormented now with the hideous thought that another great people, its system of moral values already subverted, seems to be following a somewhat similar course. Over a large section of the earth's population the ethical gains of centuries have given way to the code of the Communists and the inhuman practices of their secret police.

This critical situation is not wholly confined to distant scenes. In our own country we may think we are far from a national genocidal impulse, but we have by no means solved our problems of racial hatreds; and for all our too much vaunted progress and strength, our nation can offer little evidence of advance in the quality of that greatest of all national traits, moral fiber. In many different aspects of our national life there are indications that the measure of self-discipline is not holding up to the standards which progress in other fields would lead us to expect.

For example, only an extremely partisan observer could think that the years of misconduct in government that have been exposed at almost wearisome length is either a transient matter or a partisan one. Those who are most thoughtfully affected by the revelations of the Kinsey reports on the sex life of Americans are more disturbed by the difficulty of knowing what to do about the situation than shocked by the revelations themselves. Whether one turns to the comparative growth of gambling, organized crime, drug addiction (including alcoholism), character assassination by committees of truant lawmakers, or whatever point of ethical concern in the national scene, the picture is much the same. Those who have defended the world of sports as a school of character building par excellence can find little excuse for the low status to which athletic morality has in too many instances fallen. Whether it be in the life of the individual, the family, or the nation, or on the global scene itself, there is clear and urgent need for the discovery of better ways of guiding human behavior. The conduct of human beings in the present era is not good.

Just how much worse or how much better our times may be in this or that regard from some other particular period in history is not the major issue. Just how much good could be said for the situation and the fact that there are always qualifying explanations for consideration are equally out of the present range of discussion. The point is, people have not yet solved these problems of how to treat each other, how to manage their lives, and how to behave in their group relations in such a way that happiness instead of misery, peace instead of fratricidal destruction, a complete life instead of one of suffering and frustration, can be the lot of men everywhere.

That society does, then, desperately need more effective guidance, is a fact beyond debate and a starting point for the discussion to follow. Whatever the codes and commandments and theories and beliefs and traditions may be by which men have been guided for better or worse in the past, they are not adequate to the world of today. Mankind needs a more effective code of living and needs it badly. The question for careful consideration now—and probably the most important question of this book—is that of what effect the findings of parapsychology and their fullest implications could have on this manifestly urgent need of humanity.

Actually, the direct, immediate, tangible effect would be a limited one. These new discoveries offer no broad entrance to this vast, ethical area. They do not even represent a gate to the entrance. They are more like a key to unlock the gate that has long been barring progress on the problems of ethical behavior.

This is the essential point: Psi is the only phenomenon of human behavior which natural science has been able to study by controlled experiments and quantitative tests with regard to whether or not it has nonphysical properties. That makes it a key phenomenon and its investigation a key research project. Memory or emotion or learning or some other mental process might have served equally well in attacking the fundamental question of the physical versus the spiritual factors of human life if any one of them could have been subjected to controlled quantitative tests. But, as I have said, *psi is the only mental capacity that has lent itself to this crucial test.* For that reason its phenomena were picked up with interest in the first place by explorers who were concerned to find some evidence of nonphysical properties in man, by scholars who were loath to give up easily the concept of spiritual reality.

The science of psi, therefore, unlocks the gate of a materialistic philosophy of man and human behavior and admits to acceptable scientific reality the presence of factors in human life that are not mechanistic. In order to unlock this gate a scientific finding, rather than a corrective philosophy, was necessary. Rationalistic argument had not the force to turn a lock so rusted with long disuse. Nothing but the powerful leverage of empirical, well-confirmed, and incontestable factual discoveries could operate it.

There is, in fact, no other instrument in sight to open that lock. No religious leadership is sufficiently progressive and inquisitive to turn from ancient sources of moral guidance and search for new principles for bettering human relations. Such a gateway would never feel any pressure from orthodox religion, for religion has never equipped itself with the tools of inquiry needed to deal with these issues on a par with the sciences.

Psi need not, however, be *directly* involved in the problems of ethical living to be of importance to them. The point is not that such capacities as ESP and PK have any direct relation whatever to moral values. Rather, the bearing of psi is primarily in the fact that it is a mental process that can be pegged as a genuine causal operation over and beyond the boundary line of physical law. The findings force the repudiation in the name of experimental science of the materialistic philosophy that has shaken the foundation of the ethical systems of the past. While not specifically confirming any traditional ethical system as such, it destroys the principal menace, the one common counterphilosophy, of all ethical systems. The way is thus opened for a reconsideration of what is best for the moral needs of mankind.

The entire argument depends, of course, on this second point: Moral values definitely are not relevant to a physical world. No one thinks of raising questions of morality in dealing with the functions and properties of matter and the energetics of the space-time-mass universe. Accordingly, if there were no evidence of a psi function and there were no demonstration of extraphysical factors of any kind in human personality, there would be no ground for entertaining and maintaining moral values of any kind. If such a physicalistic view came eventually to dominate the lives of men completely, ethical values would be forgotten like any other old outmoded folk belief. Human relations would become, as a matter of course, organized on a sound, intelligent engineering basis.

The discovery of a *non*physical element in personality, therefore, makes all the difference in the world to ethical values. It authorizes the social scientist to deal with the values of moral life in terms of his own principles. It frees him entirely from the necessity of first finding a physical explanation before he can admit human values into the category of scientific data. Now, in short, the world of value may be explored in its own right. If the personality of man to which value experience belongs has properties and lawful operations of its own that defy mechanistic interpretations, the scientist attempting to deal with that personality has clearance to go ahead to discover what this value psychology is, what evaluative behavior is, considered in terms of psychical as distinguished from physical theory. All this is a consequence of recognizing that a passageway is now open across the old forbidding mythical barrier of belief that a mental process has to be physical to be real.

It is not, of course, to be expected that there will be any great sudden rush through this gateway, even though the key for opening the gate is already in hand. For the most part the rest of the social scientists have followed the psychologists and been deterred by the same barrier of mechanistic thinking; but in any case, such openings as this are at first only for the venturesome few.

Is it too extravagant, then, to say that the psi researches can play a part in making possible an advance, if only a liberating action, toward an ethical program for humanity? Such a part may be considered small or great, depending upon the point of view. It can be crucially important if, as this one seems to be, it is an essential step. A key can be very small and play a part that is enormous.

There is a second way in which the work in parapsychology bears on the problem of conduct: Its proof of a nonphysical property in man allows a logical case to be made for volitional freedom. Without free will the idea of moral judgment would be meaningless. Machines, of course, do not have free wills. When the philosophy of mechanism took over biology and psychology, the concept of volitional freedom dropped out of discussion. It is only in the older textbooks of psychology that any appreciable mention of it can be found. The discovery of a nonphysical factor does not establish the presence or operation of volitional freedom in man; it establishes only a situation that makes free will a clearly logical possibility. As I have stated, voluntarism would not be a possibility within any such homogeneously physical system as under materialism a man is supposed to be.

Condensed to nutshell proportion, this is the argument from the implications of psi to the possibility of voluntaristic freedom in man. It was presented in greater length in the chapter on psychology. There I pointed out that the only true freedom that would make any sense to the modern intellect is the concept of freedom within oneself, a certain independence that a person's central, subjective reactions have from those physical principles with which the personality is closely interrelated. The human individual is now shown to be a heterogeneous system, having in addition to his physical makeup an extraphysical order of lawful operations going on within him. This differentiation within the larger whole allows for freedom of action of one system from the other to whatever extent their distinctiveness of character and complexity permit.

Thus freedom is a relation *between*; just as it takes two to make a fight, so it requires two systems to make a possibility of freedom. The extent of such freedom and the full potential that the subjective aspect of personality exercises over the objective are matters that have to be left to inquiries of the future. Such researches are waiting for the return of psychology to these problems of larger magnitude which, however unwelcome, the psi investigations are one by one recovering from the discard.

In practical life, obviously enough, no one has ever given up the common-sense notion of free will. Anyone who tried to act like an automaton would properly enough be locked up as a hopelessly deluded psychotic. The entire institutional system of the "free world" is manifestly built around the assumption that human beings are voluntary individuals. The moralities and their commandments obviously take for granted not only a feeling for the rightness of a given way of living, but the freedom to choose or reject it. The legislature and the court and the penal institutions are meaningful only if they are dealing with free moral beings. The school takes for granted the free purposive nature of the pupils; the church does the same about its members. Even in the realm of commerce, industry, and the practical services of life the dealings are all based on the assumption that men are free-choosing creatures. Salesmanship, promotion, and work-incentives would be wasted on robots. Only on the supposition that men have free will can these practices make sense; and no one in these representative fields of work would think of acting as though he were dealing with a glorified mechanical doll instead of a super-mechanical personality.

It would be quite a different matter in the camp of communism. There the policy requires the party line to follow a materialistic assumption, and the state philosophy allows only sufficient freedom to the individual to enable him to accept communism. That surrender to the deterministic forces of history and nature is all the voluntarism that is considered necessary.

It is, in fact, the main intellectual challenge of communism that it contests the rather loose Western concept of the personal freedom of the individual and confronts mankind with a philosophical determinism that, like an all-adequate religious creed, envelopes the whole of life. Moreover, it has forced the world to face the basic issue of whether there really is the sort of freedom and personal moral responsibility Western culture has taken for granted. It is, therefore, worth a digression here to look at this challenge squarely, for it is not merely a menace to the economic and political peace of the world; it is a threat to the whole ethical life of mankind. It supplants the entire value system by which the West has civilized itself. As it is, this more subtle but most important aspect of communism is almost completely obscured by the threat of physical conflict, and perhaps our only hope is that this latter may yet alert the free world to the far more insidious danger to the entire moral life of man. This danger inherent in the basic philosophy of communism itself would not disappear with the passing of the threat of war if that should occur. Then, indeed, with all guards down, mankind would be in peril.

It is a curious phenomenon, one that would be amusing to watch if it were not for its horrible consequences, to see this monstrous enactment on the international stage of the Frankenstein story. Here is a creation of the philosophy of Western science that has got away from its controlling institutions and is taking a wild destructive turn in the new setting the Communists have given it, a setting in which its materialistic logic is accepted literally and applied to everything. In the West the scientist lives two lives, and he has two philosophies which he keeps comfortably compartmentalized. One is a common-sense type that assumes a real mind in the individual which he makes no claim to understand. He may even link it with the soul theory and interpret it in a religious framework. The other is a mechanistic one confined pretty well to the academic hall, where it is at least less inadequate than in real life. Only now and then some bold, comprehending, straightforward thinker breaks down the insulating wall and tries to merge the two. (Dr. Edmund W. Sinnott has only recently made a noble effort at such a synthesis in his book, *Two Roads to Truth*.) The coexistence of two conflicting philosophies is possible in the West where no revolution has swept away the old conservative institutions as happened in Russia. And in the West institutions still have more influence in determining conduct than all the force of materialistic thought. Over here the Frankenstein creation is still under control.

But the Russians were suckers for the materialism of the West. They swallowed it whole just as they unblinkingly took over Christianity by edict of Prince Vladimir of Kiev, and as they westernized under Peter the Great. And now the West has something terrific on its hands. This scientific philosophy, that works so satisfactorily in the world of matter, with the physical energies and the whole mechanical aspect of life, builds the same war machines for them as it does for the West, the same destructive bombs, the planes and submarines. The grand drama turns sinister and tragic because the Soviet rulers are, with single-minded logic, consciously and deliberately attempting to make men and their conduct fit these physical images. They have made political gospel of it all, frozen it into fanatic finality. This monstrous creation of a mechanistic state with a mechanistic "morality" now turns on the Western world, whose science created it, and threatens to destroy all that belongs to its maker.

This deterministic way of life, entrenched in the minds of a people and endowed with the manic power of nationalism, would only increase the violence of a military convulsion. Then, too, the mechanistic amorality of the Communist system allows its followers an unhampered scope of action, a license, that the philosophical conflict of its opponents will not permit them to practice. This adds immeasurably to the advantage one must concede to the Soviet program in any contest it may have with the West.

The Russian Communists have another great advantage. It lies in the division of thinking still persisting in such a country as ours. I refer not to the division over isolationism or over economic theories. It is, rather, the fact that the most able and enlightened peoples in the West are badly split over the very issue with which communism started out—the theory of the nature of man and the forces operating in human society. Professional schools within the same university characteristically train and indoctrinate their graduates with conflicting concepts of human nature. Certainly it must not be expected that the medical student or psychologist in the United States will be very harshly critical of the Soviets for their efforts at consistently applying accepted textbook knowledge of the very same kind they are learning themselves. After all, on this side of the Iron Curtain exactly the same effort is being made in an educational way to force man into the mechanistic mold that is taking place on the other side. Is it not significant that Western scholars have not been attacking communism on the level of its root ideas?

Surely there is no need to argue for the value, even in physical conflict, of a unified spirit among the people involved. In the present world struggle of ideologies the West cannot afford to let its people remain half physicalistic and half idealistic (that is, spiritualistic) in their philosophy. The moral force of a country can well be the deciding factor in a struggle and that force depends upon how sure its people are of the rightness of their stand. In terms of effectiveness over cost, unified group attitude is probably the best kind of armament there is. Plainly, then, Western leadership needs to get to the bottom of its intellectual issues with communism. If the communist ideology is phony, then clearly the facts that show it to be so ought to be revealed, reinforced, and exploited to the full. Nothing, however, but the authority of science at its best could carry world conviction—and hold it—on such a point. Can enough of the right people see this causal dimension of the communism problem and do so in time to spare mankind its costly course of learning by trial and error?

This discussion may appear to have wandered far afield. But no, the whole ethical integrity of the world is at stake in the moral challenge of communism. If communism is not a new and distinctive way of treating fellowmen in the mass, what *is* it? The first and great question about it, then, should be: Does it have a sound premise of incontestable facts? The evidence from parapsychology flatly contradicts it. What is more, that is the only science that does so in a rigorous and unequivocal fashion. Here, then, is at least a beginning of the intellectual conquest of communism, ready for those who are concerned about its underlying logic. A broad program of sound research on the nonphysical aspects in man *could* become a new unifying influence in Western life, a central factor of understanding around which better human relations could be woven. It could at least unite our own house that is divided, our own hearts that are not whole, toward this root issue of materialism of which communism is only one bitter, prickly fruit.

The weakness of the West is, however, not only in its divided concept of the nature of man. It consists of far more than a difference in ideology or philosophy. There is now going on around the world as much of a realistic practical contest for the hearts and minds of men, indeed, as ever occurred in the sixteenth century with sail and sword for the conquest of the unknown areas of the globe. And while today the Communist leadership may have for its real motivation only the power-seeking impulse to world subjugation, the ostensible propaganda program is a very positive one for the social and economic betterment of mankind. There is no disputing, either, that this promised program of economic betterment, whatever its sincerity or its true value, has been a weapon of tremendous power in the hands of Soviet leadership. One of the surest evidences is the fact that it is manifestly driving other nations, chiefly our own, to expensive, unprecedented, and unwilling competitive generosity.

The irony of this cold war of "altruism" is that the very religions that communism has been supplanting are expressly dedicated to the salvation of man, and the founders of these faiths were not oblivious to his social welfare. They evolved an ideal and a code of conduct so uplifting to mankind that it was considered divine in its origin. Yet after a trial period of many centuries the success of these religions in leading their followers to a satisfying way of life has been so slight that, in the current clash of ideologies, desperate, unhappy, fearful, frustrated masses have been turning to this new promise of a better kind of salvation. Even though we may know that the Marxian promises are hollow, the fact is indisputable that they have been convincing to great groups of people. Could the reason for that be found, perhaps, in the hollowness, the lack of sound foundation underlying the doctrines with which these people have lived their lives in the past? Have these dogmatic claims proved so inadequate as a guide to satisfactory living that even the Communist way seems better?

At least, no one should fool himself by thinking that it is only desperate, illiterate, unthinking masses to whom communism has appealed as a last resort. As we all know, it has persuaded some of the most brilliant scientists of the West, and that in spite of the large element of brutal Russian power-seeking that has obviously polluted the stream. Why, indeed, should it not persuade them? I ask the dominant scientific leadership of the West what, indeed, is keeping the rest of those who are as materialistic in their philosophy as the Communists from following the same logical course?

I do not know what could be healthier than to recognize frankly the weakness in the existing ideology of the Western democracies in facing this challenge of communism. It is not enough to label it and to preach against it. It is not safe to identify it only with Russia and rely on superiority in weapons. It is dangerous to wait for a collapse of Communist regimes or counter-revolution. If scholarship, if science, if intelligence means anything in this matter, we should not be satisfied with anything less than a searchingly honest analysis of the main principle from which communism draws its intellectual power. Everything else is mere "treatment of symptoms." With such an analysis, if it is not too late, there is hope of a social awakening to a rediscovery of man—a man the sciences have never known.

It is, unfortunately, not only an economic gap that communism is filling. Nor is it merely a political innovation, winning its way by new devices of trickery. It is a growth, whether normal or abnormal, that is taking over a great ethical void in the world today, and unless it can be seen in that light I doubt if the Western nations, even with technical superiority, will either save themselves or save the world from communism; for the vacuum is not by any means to be found only in countries already Communist. The same soft spots are apparent almost everywhere. What is this deficiency, this disease, this social pathology that invites an invading organism?

It is a weakness resulting from the clash of great ideas. Civilization has through the centuries developed a high order of social and religious idealism, its origins and traditions going back to Palestine and India, enriched and systematized by European interpretation. The way of life resulting from this heritage gave a noble structure of idealism, of notions of freedom of thought, of fair play, of the golden rule, the philosophy of the good neighbor, world brotherhood, and altruism in general. That these ideals became real forces in life, influencing even, to some degree and in some instances, the heads of state, and reaching down into the lives and conduct of men, there is no need to argue. Indeed, few people, whether or not because they are products of this culture, have ever intellectually questioned the acceptability of these ideals for the conduct of men. It is trite to say that everyone knows that all would be better off if everyone lived by such ideals. (And, be it conceded, it is these same much abused religions that have fostered and conserved these ideals through the ages.)

Why is it then that with all these guiding sentiments intermingled with the educational structure and interwoven into the value system of our lives, the world is still the sorry place it is for the great masses of humanity? The first point is that these values were built on untested (and today outdated) theories of the universe, of life, and of man's nature. They have, therefore, lost power as the educational habits and thoughts of men have shifted more and more toward scientific methods of inquiry and scientific standards of truth. Only the very credulous can attach great force to the finality of ancient writings purporting to be divine revelation, if there is no modern verifying demonstration to support the ancient doctrine.

The second point is that around these ancient doctrines have grown up organizations that have had great power over human life, over education, over thinking, and they have often unwisely overreached their proper role and influenced even the political life of men and their freedoms. They have become strongly entrenched and exceedingly well experienced in the ways of controlling the conduct and the philosophy of man. Every one of these organizations clings tenaciously to its own sacred teachings, to its own version of truth, and is ready to fight with a very effective battery of weapons any effort to change this truth, to improve on it, to test it, or to adapt it to the changing needs of an advancing world. Such organizations have been effective dams across the streams of human progress and they have been most effective on the streams that are most vital in human life. The only thing that breaks such dams as these is explosive revolution or, of course, the slow erosion of time and disuse.

There is in science itself a third factor that widens this gap so inviting to the growth of Communist ideology. The methods by which man has slowly improved his ways of living have, in general, come to be known as science. Under science, to cite an example, he has developed a better agriculture. He has learned to keep himself healthy through the science of medicine. Through the science of engineering he has improved his methods of transportation and communication. But in his way of behaving toward his fellow men, there has been no such growth. It is not only the fact that the problems have been held off in a sacred corner by themselves, covered by supernatural doctrines, left to the domain of the church; it is more than that. The problems of behavior are necessarily more difficult. There are limits to the kind of experimentation possible, although these are often unnecessarily exaggerated limitations; still, as can easily be seen, a human being is a vastly more complex thing to work with than a chemically pure substance or even an isolated bit of tissue. There are too many variables to be controlled to make experimentation nice and easy.

But even this does not explain the lag, even in combination

with the other factors mentioned. Anti-religious and anti-metaphysical reaction that has prevailed strongly amongst those working with the behavior of man has tended to make them as loath to attack the larger problems of human relations and ethics as the leadership of religious organizations has been loath to give them up. Take an example that brings the whole relationship of this fourth factor into focus: Religious ethics has for ages and for many of the peoples of the globe been oriented toward a life beyond the grave. Some sort of spirit survival or immortality of the soul is a basic dogma in most religions, and men are asked to live their lives with this heavenly orientation for their guidance. Yet no orthodox church organization has ever undertaken to get the matter of a future life investigated scientifically as other human problems have been. The theological formulations are even worded so as to appear to make such investigation unnecessary if not undesirable. Religion's answer to the question of man's end is supposed, therefore, to be taken on faith; the kind of faith that does not think. We must not forget, however, that religion once was just as certain about man's origin as a species.

But the point is the sciences as such have been fully as negligent as religion concerning man's destiny after death. It is a very rare individual among the social scientists who has indicated any interest in the investigation of such a problem. The very few, like William James or William McDougall, who undertook to initiate some inquiries on the scientific problem, gained no stature thereby in their profession.

This gap is just the kind into which communism now finds its way unimpeded; it is an area between a religion that is afraid to make inquiry as the sciences have done, and a science that is afraid to inquire into problems like those of religion. It is not that the Communists are working out scientific answers to the question of personal survival after death or the problem of human conduct; it is not that they have stepped in actually to solve any of the problems that the church and Western science have neglected; it is, rather, that communism takes the initiative and meets with no effective opposition because Western institutions have done almost nothing themselves about these crucial matters of life and death. The void is there, and, of course, it takes no great strength or pressure to fill a vacuum. Between the neglect from the old religion and the failure of the new science, space has been left to which it is only natural that there should be some such growth or parasitic intrusion as communism, with its facile claim to a sound basis in the philosophy of history and of science. It is offering to bring to mankind the answers to its crying needs for food and shelter and security and health and peace and education —all the great values that other institutions too long have somewhat vainly promised. In a choice between the new, untested promise and the old, disproved claim, the former should be expected to win.

The diagnostic picture, then, reduces to this: The Marxian philosophy was a product of the times, and the growth of communism was a consequence of the fact that the greater problems of life had been neglected. The world has allowed its backward-looking institutions to have too much to say about what shall be explored, what new advances shall be made for the guidance of men. It has allowed its departments of psychology to be too busy with the small, peripheral problems of its field, letting the world go to the dogs while it is waiting to go to heaven.

Whether or not there is a moral philosophy that can save the world, it is not easy to think of a world worth saving without one. But it needs to be a positive ethics and not the "thou shalt not" variety which has mainly been the type so far inflicted upon our culture. As far as society has any record it seems likely that this negative ethics has been a derivative of the fact that most of the ethical systems of the religions came from the ruling centers, those combinations of church and state that dominated the ancient, the medieval, and even part of the modern world. But now, with the individual point of view more to the fore and the concept of democracy at least in mind, it is necessary to develop an ethics that is oriented not only from the point of view of keeping a person in his place but also that of helping him to find his place. We want a way of life that is good for the people who live it and not good only for some superior individual or governing body or ruling class.

But a positive ethics means more than that. It means one in

which the goal of the most fully perfected vision of living domi-
nates the formulation of policy and practice and standards. Not
some goal that is to be reached, then conventionalized, fixed and
secured for all time, but an advancing, progressive, adaptable concept that moves on ahead of man's growing capacity to appreciate the great potential of his experience. It should, indeed,
be a creative vision, an aspiration projected far out beyond our
immediate realization as our heavenly reach has ever exceeded
our grasp. It should be an ethics so charged with the vital com-
pulsions of our most fully discovered nature that the joy of each
is comprehended in the good of all and yet a goal that, by its
nature, never lags, but continues to challenge newer inquiry with
each advance in understanding.

Just a dream, yes; now. The concept of fluid, creative ethical
ideals is too new for ready realization. What should one expect?
Every ethical advance in the past was boxed around immediately
by the forces of conservation, codification, and defense against
heresy. It still goes against the grain of our Western culture to
tamper with moral standards; most people think such things had
better be let alone. The very idea of instituting a program for
broadening the basis of the enjoyment of life would, somehow,
seem improper. It would, of course, entail the shifting of some old
conventional standards. Few, perhaps, would go so far as to say
it was of the devil, but many would label it ill-advised, and for
most it would be something to go slow about.

All right, then; it may be necessary to let the Communists
crowd us a bit further. The closer they get, the more our "generosity" is quickened, not only with regard to provisions and loans
but even in our acceptance of new ideas. Such enforced liberality
has been in practice for years now, as, for example, in the area
of racial tolerance. The need for African air bases helps the people
of African origin to be better treated in the country that needs
the bases for defense against the Russians.

In time, however, even without the stimulus of Communist
encroachment, it is to be hoped that Western culture may lose
its backward inclination and adopt a progressive, inquiring attitude toward making the most of life. Perhaps, then, there will be
a beginning made on the fundamental research that is needed.

Man's third "inalienable right" would then be thawed loose from its long immobilization under the ice cap of orthodoxy and, blossoming, produce an Alpine meadow of fulfillment of life's potentialities. For certainly, the "pursuit of happiness" is no less sacred or right for man for all the narrow theology by which most of the joy of living was projected to a compensatory heaven beyond death.

Actually, the research needed to develop a better foundation for making the most of life would not be especially difficult. It would so closely parallel other researches into complex social behavior, other psychological studies, that it would not be the difficulty of the research that would retard progress on the project. The real difficulty will be in even getting anything started on so novel a project. It will not be a primarily parapsychological research, although some of the methods of parapsychology will be useful, for example, on the further investigation of the problem of freedom.

This question of freedom, its nature and extent, is, of course, of great importance in any ethical program, but especially one with a positive objective. If there is anything like free volitional choice there are doubtless greater or less amounts of it, depending upon something as yet unknown. It would certainly be imperative to discover that unknown factor and endeavor to control it. The moral power of the human race in itself is, of course, a highly variable factor from individual to individual and even within the life of a given personality. Many of the factors involved are known, but the question that is basic to the whole issue is that of how much truly creative freedom the individual does have. The more, of course, that can be learned about the differential thought-brain reaction, the more we shall be able to understand what is going on in conduct and do something really effective about it. How that reaction can be free, as well as how far it is free, will be something most important to know.

There will be still other possible bearings of the psi investigations, even though they are not primary to the main ethical project. As experimenters in this field continue to search out the extent and depth of the differential lawfulness between psi processes and the physical world, it is hoped that the outlines of the whole psychical makeup of personality will emerge. It would be a great undertaking to add to our usable knowledge of the spirit of man, what it is, what its nature and its brain relations are. It is a research that ought not to have to wait.

If the Russians were not now rocking the boat it would, no doubt, take a long time for this fantastic idea of a science of ethics to penetrate the mind of the conservative educator. It took time of the order of a century for the poetic insight of Burns and Tennyson and other literary seers for world brotherhood and the "parliament of man" to reach some degree of fruition in a general assembly of the United Nations. It also took two world-shattering wars. If now events go teeter-tottering on for a time and do not move too fast down the irreversible path of cataclysm, the Western world may break yet more of the bonds that have been enslaving the human mind to a blind commitment to the past on such vitally urgent issues. If such should develop, even the slender opening already made, offering its glimpse of richer personality attributes, may have a significant place. And to what greater conquest could man aspire than to a movement to capture something of the driving energy and compulsion that has impelled so many to seek the wild and bitter solace of communism in their desperate rejection of the past—capture it and turn it into a constructive search, a scientific research? For it is likely that most such potential searchers aspire with us all to an extension of our ideals of how to live, how to make life good, how to face up fully and bravely to its demands, its temptations, even its eventual termination, in the most satisfying way that sound inquiry can discover.

An ethics so forged in the fires of validating practice should give man victory not only over himself but still further extend his triumph over nature. It should do even more. It should help him to meet that far better test of one's moral armament, the separations of death. It would be one mark of a good and adequate ethics that it enable one to measure up fully to the challenge of William Cullen Bryant's lines from "Thanatopsis":

> "So live, that when thy summons comes to join
> The innumerable caravan, which moves

To that mysterious realm, where each shall take
His chamber in the silent halls of death,
Thou go not, like the quarry-slave at night,
Scourged to his dungeon, but, sustained and soothed
By an unfaltering trust, approach thy grave,
Like one who wraps the drapery of his couch
About him, and lies down to pleasant dreams."*

Whatever it be to which such an unfaltering trust may rightly be given, it is something to which thinking men are entitled as they look at bereavement and death. The essential truth itself, and the fortifying evaluations and disciplines that integrate it with life are all needed to bear humanity on, looking forward with joyful anticipation to every dawn, yet never regretting the toll each day exacts, and keeping books with life that balance to the end.

* William Cullen Bryant, "Thanatopsis."

Part **IV**

THE PROSPECT
FOR FURTHER EXPLORATION

■ Parapsychology is a science for the future. It has not had much time, as the sciences go, to acquire a past of very great magnitude. But if it is to have a proper future, it will have to have and maintain an effective research program and the laboratories and personnel to carry it out. It is, therefore, one of the main experiments of parapsychology today to find out whether a laboratory entirely devoted to the field can maintain itself and achieve some sort of permanent, official status with assurance of continued support. While one such laboratory has existed and functioned for more than twenty years at Duke University, it has had throughout that period, and still has today, no assurance of continuation covering more than a few years ahead.

There are, on the other hand, some reassuring considerations. The research activities in parapsychology have in recent years actually become very widespread geographically. There is in this field today a network of active research interrelationships over the world such as never before existed. There is a certain amount of contact and collaboration between experimental workers extending over Great Britain, Australia, Sweden, Holland, South Africa, Germany, Austria, Chile, India, Norway, France, Italy, and Japan. These connections indicate a spirit and vitality in the research that is general and international and in no sense localized. Without such an active urge to inquire as these researches indicate, no amount of security and support and guarantees for the future would accomplish anything. In the past it has been the actual research findings and their implications that have won such support as the field has had. This broadly extended research activity is, then, at least some justification for the expectation of continued advancement and continued support.

Parapsychology is not, however, for impatient people. Some of the fainter hearts who venture into this difficult field become discouraged when they find that, after what seems to them a great many years, we have still not succeeded in getting control of these skittish phenomena, and that they still have to be caught with the elaborate dragnet of statistics. It is depressing to them that on this point there is not even a sure prospect for the future; no one knows whether or not there will be any way to get reliable control over psi capacity. So long, then, as no one can plan on a development program for practical application or even for a sure-fire demonstration, the whole future of parapsychology would seem to be uncertain and the field full of risk for the explorer.

But such easily discouraged folk see only half of the picture. All that is now known about psi definitely ties it in as part of natural science. Elusive though it is, psi responds to the methods of study that have pinned down other difficult and elusive phenomena in nature. It may take a long time to get hold of its underlying principles and get such control over it as nature allows, but there is nothing at all to indicate that such control is impossible. This stage of ignorance about a process is always discouraging, because one cannot estimate how great it is or how long before it will be removed; but there is certainly no reason why we cannot find out what remains to be found out about the psi functions, and when we do we will have the same added power over them that understanding always gives, allowing us to work intelligently instead of blindly with the principles discovered. When work with psi capacities becomes applied science and can be converted into skills and arts, and when experimenters can be trained to deal perceptively with the capacities they are investigating, parapsychology research will be transformed. Of course, everyone would like to know how soon that will be!

It is naturally discouraging to some would-be parapsychologists, that as yet no sure professional future can be promised in that field of research. There are in this country no endowed or otherwise established chairs or professorships in parapsychology permanently set up to provide a full-time career, in either research or practice or teaching. This is a depressing outlook to those who, stirred by the sense of importance of the field, would like to devote their lives to it in spite of its hazards and handicaps.

Yet this, again, is only one aspect of the situation. First of all, this difficulty is a normal one for a new field; and there is always the possibility for the individual with sufficient resolution and hardihood to make a way for himself as most of the past and present workers in parapsychology have done. It requires special adaptability, but pioneering ventures always do. The establishment, just announced, of the professorship in parapsychology at the University of Utrecht in itself is a step forward, even though as yet the incumbent (Dr. W. H. C. Tenhaeff) is supported by funds from outside the university.

Aside from professorships, the most logical basis for the establishment of a parapsychology profession is on the practice of counseling. A number of professional groups, as, for example, the psychoanalysts, established themselves in this manner. There are in the world today, as the parapsychology mailbag shows, many thousands of people who have problems involving psi on which they would like to have competent counsel. These problems may be in the form of anxieties produced by the puzzling experiences of some member of the family—a child who unaccountably guesses the answer too often for the usual explanations; a mother who has recurrent dreams of apparent premonitions concerning her soldier son; a businessman successfully playing hunches all his life now wonders what is behind them; a priest whose experiences appear to include extrasensory knowledge and at the same time worry his bishop; a wife whose husband went down in a plane over Tibet but whose psi experiences at the time lead her to hope he still lives; a husband who wants help in deciding whether the messages and signs he is receiving are from his deceased wife; an artist who wants to develop the fullest possible rapport, including telepathic, with his subject; a poor chap who needs to be helped over the belief that telepathy is being used to hurt him; a young bride whose soldier husband on far distant foreign soil wants to know all about how to test the contact he feels he has with her—the mere listing would fill pages.

When and how successfully a profession of trained and well-qualified counselors could take over this area of responsibility remains to be seen. That such a professional development should come about is, however, almost inevitable, and the sooner such service is taken out of the hands of those not trained or qualified to handle it, the better it will be for these many thousands who consult the various forms of occult advisers available in most of the larger communities of the world.

There is still another drawback in parapsychology about which enough has already been said—the lack of professional recognition. Being cold-shouldered by his fellow scientists is a real handicap to the research worker even if it does not disturb his equanimity. One effect is that it is hard for him to get a share of the available research funds from philanthropic foundations or other normal sources. (Could not at least one foundation be set up to help the more venturesome explorers on the merits of their problems and methods, at the stage when they need it most?) Lack of recognition may also cut him off from natural contacts with scientific organizations, and he may never in an ordinary lifetime have the usual satisfactions and rewards that accompany or constitute the customary marks of recognition. While the seasoned worker may be fairly well resigned to this state of affairs, the younger man or woman is, in some cases, deterred from entering a profession that has so austere a prospect.

However, the matter of recognition has its other aspects, too. In the first place, for any field of work that really has a sound basis the period of illegitimacy is only a temporary state. One needs but to read a bit of scientific history to see that, as a rule, the more a valid discovery is initially resisted, the more attention is accorded it and its contributors when it finally is accepted. And there are signs already that the tide is beginning to turn for parapsychology. The stage of outspoken criticism is nearly over and one hears many fair words spoken in private, and a few are even beginning to appear in print. As usual with new intellectual challenges, there is more interest shown among professional groups of Western Europe than here. Those of Great Britain and the

Netherlands especially are advanced in their reaction to psi. Many of the leading scientific societies and universities there have had official lecture series or conferences on parapsychology. In this country we are not, I think, likely to trail Europe on such matters by more than a decade or two. Even among American psychologists the percentage of respondents open-minded to ESP in Warner's survey (referred to in Chapter Two) was somewhat greater after fourteen years. There are other signs, too, of a greater readiness on the part of the American scientist to have a look at the case for psi.

Again, there has been frequent mention throughout this book that philosophical difficulties have been a serious handicap to the acceptance of the psi investigations. It is even safe to say that if there had been no disturbing philosophical implications inherent in the results of the psi researches (no conflict with materialism) nobody would be unhappy today over the status of parapsychology one way or the other; but there would, I suspect, be little interest in it either.

The future ought, however, to be reasonably bright as far as the philosophy of psi is concerned. Philosophers have never shown so much interest in it as they are doing both here and in Europe today. In fact, one of the signs of progress is the fact that, now that the psychologists have stopped quarreling, at least publicly, over the psi problems, the philosophers have in much greater number begun to take the results seriously. They would not be doing that if the results were still too hot to handle. The philosophers should at least be able to clear up for the psychologists the confusion embedded in their minds over a fancied linkage between psi and a theory of absolute body-mind dualism of the Cartesian order; such dualism holds special terrors for a psychologist.

Nevertheless, with all these bolstering explanations, it is only fair to say that the prospects for parapsychology are far from certain in any respect; no one can realize this so well as those who have been trying to make it a full-time occupation. The work is becoming more technical and specialized and difficult; it needs not only fully concentrated research workers but also teams of such specialists to handle its larger projects. And even though they must all come eventually, there is no assurance of early recognition or support for any of the research developments or of any dependable application of psi ability that would materially alter its status.

On the other hand, the research explorer does not have to have certainty. The odds against him in the parapsychology field are, if anything, declining; the hardest battles are over and possibly, too, the hardest times. At least we can say that dim as it still is, the future looks brighter today than it ever did, that we are closer to the state that every research worker wants, one in which he can go ahead free and unhampered to the highest goals of his research. What is perhaps still the most stable assurance of continued support is the fact that today there is a much larger and better educated public interested in the researches in parapsychology than ever was the case in this country, thanks in great part to the science writers and editors of the daily press and magazines. This audience, more than it realizes, is upholding the arms of the research worker by the fair and open-minded interest it has taken in what he is doing. This public interest is the best guarantee of a future for parapsychology, one of sound, critical, constructive research that will stop on no problems that concern the transcendant nature of personality until man knows himself as fully as he can be known.

The future of parapsychology must depend, however, more upon the good judgment used in choosing and formulating the pertinent problems in the correct order than on any of the secondary considerations I have just discussed, however important they may be in their place. Such choice, if impractical, could almost completely stall an already slow-going advance; or if too far out from the central interests of the supporting group, it could cost the research its never very adequate support; or if not well oriented scientifically it could bog down the research in a welter of confused interpretations and lose the hard-won respect it has gained through the years. It seems, therefore, worth while taking as the subject for the last chapter the question of what problems ought to come first in the research work ahead. Finding the right perspective on the problems and taking them in the proper order is half of the secret of keeping research efforts effective.

Chapter **10**

THE GREATER PROBLEMS

IN THE PRESENT VIEW

■ What should be the principal aim from now on, the major emphasis in the further exploration of this new world? There is, of course, no one problem for everyone; but there can with advantage be agreement on large general areas of interest that center in a problem of greater magnitude. On what larger research objective would parapsychologists of today most nearly agree? Obviously a degree of coordination and a concerted attack should succeed better than a disorderly scattering of effort in all possible directions.

On the other hand, regardless of any such general agreement as to emphasis, many of those who are actively working at present will, and should, go right on doing just what they are and have been doing; for one thing, certain lines of inquiry are well enough established and sufficiently promising that they need to be carried through to conclusions regardless of changes in current interest. In any case, there are factors that enter into the choice of a research project that are often more important to the individual worker than such general considerations as I am about to take up here. His particular interest or fitness for the specific study being made, the initial success he has had on a preliminary research, the degree of opportunity he may have for carrying out his work and perhaps securing some assistance for the program, these and many other considerations are involved, and, of course, it is better for each one in a pioneer field to be allowed to choose for himself which way he will go. The superior incentive that goes with this freedom is in itself very important.

What are these established lines? It seems of first importance that the work bearing on the psychophysical relationship in psi performance be continued. If, for example, it proves possible to measure the energy involved in displacement tests of PK, there should be every encouragement given these efforts. From another starting point on the same psychophysical relation, there is the problem of precognition and the test of its limits. Up to what limit does length of time make no difference in success in tests of precognition? Obviously, the comparison of long-time precognition scoring rates is something that cannot be speeded up. And, in general, the introduction of new methods and new questions rapidly piles up complications that can easily call for a lifetime of research.

The extending of the psi research into biology is also much too healthy a venture to be in any danger of not being continued. The fact is, the anpsi work is sure of being extended far beyond the mere comparative study of psi capacities in different species, on into a consideration of the evolution, heritability, physiology, and localization of the psi function. This branch of inquiry promises to sustain itself, partly because of its novelty and partly because the animal work apparently meets with less skepticism; probably it seems more objective.

There will, too, be certain lines of psychological research continued as a matter of course. There are certain things that interested psychologists can do in combining psi tests with batteries of other measurements. Also, arising out of the psi research itself there are the urgent questions as to what the psi-missing factor (or factors) is, how position effects are produced, what the process of translation of psi-cognition into consciousness may be, and so on.

There are even certain methods and approaches that it would be disastrous to abandon. One of these is the use of classified and interpreted spontaneous psi experiences for the guidance of the research program. Much of the practical guidance of future research may depend upon this rich store of raw material.

There has been in recent years, too, an emphasis on the side of method that it would be fatal to lose. This is the emphasis upon the use of psychological skills in providing a test situation conducive to psi performance. Slowly the impressions, observations, and findings are accumulating from which rules can be tentatively formulated and training instituted that will enable the experimenter to gain a better percentage of correct responses from his subjects. If anything, this emphasis upon the psychological requirements of a proper psi test must be increased rather than lost sight of.

These and other practices and projects too numerous for listing here should continue and probably will. They are all promising enough, and the gamble of taking up a wholly new line has in such cases largely been removed.

The question I am weighing now is that of what the greater, more central aim ought to be, if anything of that order can be formulated. Aside from the mere vague, general objectives such as the desire to add to the knowledge of man or to advance the science of parapsychology, and the like, what is the main research target to be kept in sight at the moment?

For many the first response would be: It ought to be the goal or objective of making some use of psi. Every now and then throughout the history of parapsychology some thoughtful, well-informed student of the field has proposed that, if only the knowledge of psi and the conditions conducive to its operation could be brought to the point where some reliable application of them could be made, all the troubles would be over. Everybody accepts practical results. Some utilization, however unimportant, and even though comparatively inefficient, would bring the research down to earth, down to the world of common sense; and even groups of doubting scientists would be quickly convinced by that kind of practical demonstration.

Even more specifically, it has often been pointed out, and it is fairly obvious, that with an appreciable degree of control extended over any of the psi capacities and sufficiently well demonstrated, unlimited resources of financial and other aid could, in one way or another, be drawn to the support of the psi investigations. It even follows that the needed funds could easily be earned if only an element of control over psi performance were acquired.

No one knows, of course, how many efforts have already been made throughout the world and through the years to achieve just this very objective. We do know they have been many and varied. Some of these efforts have been made by serious investigators; to choose a familiar example, there have been attempts made to subject the claims of the dowser or water diviner to scientific test. (There has for centuries been a somewhat divided popular opinion about these claims.) While these scientific studies cannot be considered to have verified the claims, the results are not without interest to parapsychology; the question is still open, and the practice of dowsing is taking over new adaptations and wide application.[1]

But as of today, there is no properly demonstrated art or practice of any kind that can, on the evidence, be reliably credited to psi capacity. That is the verdict in spite of all the countless attempts to make use of it and all the possibilities that remain. There have been sincere and even some moderately well-planned efforts made to cause psi to operate reliably, and if any of them had succeeded so as to yield dependable, practical results, it seems reasonably safe to think that some one of the many representatives of the branches of science would have come into contact with the findings. This has nothing to do with the question of whether psi really occurs; it does, however, have a lot to do with the readiness of people to accept the scientific results.

At any rate, it is safe to say that until something more is known about psi than has been available to all these inquirers through the ages, the objective of using psi would be almost certainly a waste of time today. Through the analysis of results painfully gathered by the aid of statistical methods, it has become clear what it is these practical seekers after application are up against, and it is something they could hardly have known from their own experiences. It is a simple and adequate explanation: It is the fact that psi is unconscious, that the subject has no introspective guidance to tell him whether or not he is correct, or even when he gets a true psi experience. With this inner blindness keeping the individual in ignorance of his success, his own judgment as to whether he has made a hit is not dependable and may even be little better than guesswork.

It is not, then, that practical objectives are beneath the parapsychologist's dignity or below his research ideals. It is probably true that most of those who have gone into the field as research workers have been impelled rather by an urge to discover more about the nature of man in the hopes of improving humanity's adjustment. But even with all the most idealistic of human objectives, it would still be good policy to attempt a practical utilization of psi, if such were possible, if only to bring the recognition and support the researchers need.

But even though that avenue of approach seems closed by nature, it may be closed only because we do not yet know enough about the capacities we are studying to find a way around this barrier of unconsciousness. In any case, the job of finding out more about them will have to go on. The essential knowledge is still lacking to make utilization possible or even to permit a conclusion as to whether reliable application is an eventual possibility.

Over at the other extreme from the problem of practical utilization is that of designing an over-all theory of psi. Almost as often has it been urged that the field of research needs a good acceptable theory of psi as it has been argued that its most urgent need is some sort of reliable application. It is generally insisted that a theory, even if only an untested hypothesis, would serve an educational purpose in tying together in a rational whole a large order of isolated test results. The argument goes that many logical minds require at least a line of possible explanation before accepting the facts themselves and that facts, such as those from the psi researches, that challenge the accepted theory of materialism are especially in need of a rationale, since they are suspect in advance. In other words, since psi phenomena as they stand will not make sense to the physicalist, it would help if a plausible, logical clarification, even if only on a tentative, introductory basis, were developed.

That would be fine. We would all welcome a theory that fits the facts, and would welcome it as much as, if not more than, an application that works. It is beyond argument that such a theoretical dressing might accomplish wonders in rendering the psi researches more palatable. As a major research objective it would make a strong appeal and to a certain degree would be justifiable. There is, however, an obstacle in this case comparable to that which stands in the way of the utility objective already discussed. In that case, as I have said, the trouble is that no one knows how to overcome the limitation of the unconscious character of psi activity. On this problem of trying to find a general hypothesis, a logical framework for psi, an equally great difficulty arises. It is that there simply are no scientifically tested principles which can be stretched over into this new area to use as hypotheses for psi. If the untested area of religion and the supernatural is omitted, all the rest of the established principles by which ultimate explanations are tested are physical principles. To try to apply unverified supernatural, occult, or mystical hypotheses would be to desert our basic scientific standards. This is not to say that there is nothing in any of these supernatural hypotheses; the point is that in science it is not fruitful to explain one unknown by another, as would be the case if an unverified speculative principle were offered as an hypothesis to explain psi. When the principle used in the explanation of a new phenomenon has itself been established, there is then a sound beginning from which to work. But since we know by this time that we cannot use a physical theory to explain psi, and since there is no established supernatural theory to apply, there is nothing to do but wait; for in the present undeveloped state of orthodox scholarship, these two basic types of explanatory principle are all there are.

In the case of psi, then, the explanation will have to be patterned from the facts as they develop; that is to say again that it is a new world, and old world theories do not apply. The common ground between psi and general psychology does, it is true, afford opportunities for minor application of hypotheses across the borderline, but psychology itself has no general theory of what the individual's own uniquely personal or subjective nature really is. It is true that a theory of psi is bit by bit growing up out of the fragments of facts that have been uncovered. That is the way the present theory of nature has been constructed from the research products and by-products and the generalizations made therefrom.

The advantage which parapsychology has over general psychology is in its ability to pursue its inquiries knowing where the line of physics lies. It deals with processes that can be identified as nonphysical; the general psychologist has no such phenomena and can only classify his nonpsi mental world by an act of faith, or else suspend judgment. But now, from the approach via parapsychology, there is a possibility of working out just what the basic nature of personality is, what and how much it has to operate on in its own right.

The problem of a general theory of psi, then, is beyond us for the present. It will have to wait and develop as the research advances step by step through the years ahead. As things now stand, the working concept of psi is to the psi investigator just the sum total of what has been found, along with a collection of trial views and suggestions that are only dimly discerned. As far as the findings interrelate psi with principles already known, psi becomes partially explained; as its own unique ways of operating reveal themselves in test results the rest of the theory will develop.

During the decade of the forties the most conspicuous research objective was that of finding a psi-personality type, or anything in any way approaching that. We would gladly have settled for a few identifying traits that correlated with an ability to produce a large extrachance deviation in a psi test. As I have said already, this effort failed, even while it yielded some very valuable material. It is easier now than it was then to see the mistake that was made.

The natural line of thought was that psi ability, like any other, should be found to be correlated with at least some other measurable differences among individuals, such as personality traits. That line of thought is more or less familiar in general psychological research. The implicit assumption therefrom led to many years of work by a large percentage of the active experimenters in parapsychology. They were searching for one trait or character-istic of personality after another that might be associated with the operation of psi. There was hope of finding some specific and easily identified type or grouping of individuals who excelled in the psi tests. As it turned out, however, this large section of the research work in parapsychology was only a detour from its main objective. Its chief value lay in its secondary results, for it de-veloped that no psi-personality type or group or trait has been found, and it looks increasingly doubtful that anything of the kind ever will be. It is, in fact, questionable, in view of the be-ginning made on the ESP work with animals, whether there will even be a species limitation.

The error here which can be avoided in the future, if it is recog-nized, is that of choosing the main course of research on lines of thought appropriate to general psychology—a general psychology that has not yet touched on the area with which psi is concerned. It was mistakenly taken for granted that psi functioned at the level of these more familiar capacities and traits. It is now clear that the spontaneous case reports could have warned us away from such a search for correlates. They come from such a wide range of individuals and groups, and they cross so many lines of classification, even those of species, that consequently they sug-gest that there is probably no recognizable associated group char-acteristic or correlated trait. In retrospect, then, one can see the advantage, at least at this stage of the research, in beginning with and following up the raw, unspoiled, natural events them-selves in planning experiments; not starting out with a rational assumption or a too-sweeping analogy that may have somewhere in it an unchecked premise.

By all odds the most popular problem with which parapsychol-ogy has come into contact and the one that has, at the same time, stirred the very deepest interest of them all, is that commonly re-ferred to as the survival problem. The essential question is whether any incorporeal element or part of the personality (any spirit or soul) survives the bodily death of the individual, retains its capacity to experience, and can manifest itself in a way that allows personal identification to be made. It is, of course, one of the oldest of man's questions about his destiny, and it is one of the oldest of the parapsychological problems to have had some measure of scientific attention. The investigation of it as a research problem was initiated by the challenge of the Spiritualist movement which began in this country over a hundred years ago.

The investigation of spirit survival took the form mainly of studying the communications purportedly coming from the spirits of the dead through persons known as mediums. The communications and related manifestations extended over such a wide range of mental and physical expressions and performances that it would be impossible to describe them here; but in one way or another the manifest purpose of the medium was to bring messages of reassurance, identification, or counsel from spirit personalities that were supposedly connected by some tie or other with the living individuals to whom they were sent. The research aim was to discover whether or not these claims of spirit communication and spirit agency could be verified as such and shown to be unexplainable in any other way.

Whatever we may think of its claims today, the Spiritualist movement had a great deal to do historically with the initiation of the investigation of psychic phenomena and the founding of the research societies that took it up during the last quarter of the nineteenth century. During that period and well up into the first quarter of the present century, the reports of the investigations showed sufficient plausibility and impressiveness to engage the attention of many of the leading scholars of Europe and America. Some of these were even convinced that the essential claim of the Spiritualists was valid, and among them were distinguished scholars of different fields. Among the few psychologists who became interested were men such as William James and William McDougall who were as well prepared as any men of their day to weigh the evidence and give serious attention to all the issues; and while James and McDougall suspended judgment, the evidence was strong enough to compel them to keep an open mind on the issue.

In fact, this great question, with its dramatic human appeal, not only supported and swept along with it the interest in other psychic claims of less colorful character; it played a part, too, in recruiting research workers for the parapsychological field and brought to their aid the support they needed for their work. Even today a goodly number of the more active workers would confess to having been brought into parapsychology by interest in the possibility that there was some foundation for the claims of spirit agency.

The outcome of the scientific investigation of mediumship is best described as a draw.[2] Hardly anyone would claim that all the investigations of seventy-five years or more have had the effect of *dis*proving the claim that if a man die he shall in some manner or other be capable of "living again." On the other hand, no serious scientific student of the field of investigation could say that a clear, defensible, scientific confirmation of the hypothesis had been reached. The question was left in such a status that it was possible for a person to follow his own disposition, whether it was to doubt or to believe. Some of the leading scholars involved in the investigation believed the hypothesis had been proved and as many of equal qualifications were convinced, after examination of the evidence, of the inadequacy of the proof. It was just a matter of interpreting and appraising alternatives, the question of deciding whether the messages conveyed by the medium could have had any other origin than that of the personalities to whom they were attributed. Those who were dissatisfied considered alternative sources, such as combinations of ESP with capacities of dramatization on the part of the medium, to be too plausible to permit so momentous a conclusion as that of survival. Those who were convinced felt that the alternatives were too farfetched to be taken seriously. Clearly, that was no way to leave a problem of such importance if there was anything more that could be done about it.

The proper way out of such an impasse was to look into the objections and counterclaims raised against the spiritistic interpretation. What was it that prevented the more critical thinkers from reaching a scientific judgment? It was mainly that there were certain factors that had not been sufficiently well ruled out in obtaining and interpreting the messages obtained from the medium. The spirit theory was not the only possible explanation of the results. What was most needed was a thorough examination of the recognized counterhypotheses of telepathy, clairvoyance, and precognition, since they, too, were extrasensory methods of gaining knowledge such as mediumship implied, and since they had a better foundation of evidence than the mediumistic studies themselves. It was imperative also to arrive at a clear and objective method of appraisal of the mediumistic messages, one that would avoid the natural bias of the strongly affected sitters—as the persons visiting the medium are called—as they passed judgment on the accuracy of the messages.

These preliminary problems called for years of special research effort, but before progress on the solution of the survival problem could be made they had to be solved. They are not, of course, all solved even yet, but enough progress has been made toward their solution to justify a return now to the original problem, re-examining it in the light of present knowledge. In the light of what is known about the psi capacities and with the improvements of methods of appraising such verbal material as mediumistic utterances, how does the survival problem stand? Is it the great problem now that it once was? Is it the major objective for a parapsychological research program?

It is now evident, along with all the complexity resulting from the investigations establishing the reality of the occurrence of telepathy, clairvoyance, and precognition, that the solution of the question of spirit survival is a far more complicated one even than had been recognized. Not only have the psi researches themselves introduced complications of control that make the design of an experiment on the spirit hypothesis more difficult than any of the psi experiments; over and beyond that there are the difficulties of exercising the needed controls in the collection and interpretation of mediumistic utterances. In fact, in trying to think how the old approach to the problem of spirit survival by the methods of mediumship could be modified so that it would provide a crucial experimental test, one is so thoroughly baffled as to turn rather to search for another approach that may offer a simpler procedure and a detour around old difficulties.

But it is an equally serious fact that, while the difficulties of the investigation have grown greater, public interest in the survival problem as a research objective has grown almost proportionately smaller. The advanced age level as well as the scarcity of those individuals who are most ardently interested in the survival question today is another indication of the fact that the problem is fast losing status. This is, of course, precisely what one should expect. In a culture created in great part by the developments of the physicalistic sciences, the very idea of a surviving double or a spirit of any sort has become increasingly incredible with every decade. Anyone taking the normal collegiate and graduate courses in, for example, biology, psychology, or medicine would definitely have to compartmentalize his thinking if he wished to carry with him through college any effective residue of his childhood education on the existence of a soul that is distinguishable from the body.

But just as one cannot credit childhood education on the spiritual nature of man with any scientific status, so, likewise, one cannot weight seriously against the spirit hypothesis the type of unverified assumption that, on the college level, counteracts these religious influences. One needs scientific caution as much in safeguarding his thinking against uncritical rejections and iconoclasms as he does on the side of accepting untested doctrine.

The survival question, then, is still not answered in any way that can be accepted as scientifically reliable. And conclusion, pro or con, based on the present evidence would involve a large element of uncritical belief. Moreover, there has been not only the decline of popular interest just mentioned. Within the research circles of parapsychology itself during the last two decades, attention has been concentrated almost entirely on experimental work with the psi capacities and away from mediumship. Even the psychical research societies, which were formerly centers of research interest in the question of survival, have followed this general shift and have done little or no systematic experimental research on the problem during the last twenty years. Here and there an interesting proposal as to possible new approaches may be found, but there are no reports of research on survival.

Among these proposals is the suggestion of Thouless[3] that living individuals design coded messages that cannot be decoded without the help of the inventor. If attempts during his lifetime are unsuccessful and if after his death the secret is revealed by a medium, or by anyone, the case would support the hypothesis of his continued existence as a personality. Hornell Hart[4] upholds the view that a profitable attack on the survival hypothesis might be opened through the study of shared dreams and the projection of the living individual's conscious self in what might seem like exteriorization or activity outside the body. These are laudable attempts; whether or not they are adequate in design as they stand, they may initiate a development that will succeed through eventual improvements on the original idea. But even at best, these are as yet only hopeful gropings, still at the blueprint stage.

On the whole, therefore, the survival hypothesis is in the most unpromising situation of its history. The earlier mediumistic studies remain inconclusive, and are not likely ever to be repeated. In the score of years or thereabout since the study made at Duke[5] of the mediumship of Eileen J. Garrett, which gave significant evidence of knowledge in the material recorded, as evaluated by the Soal-Saltmarsh method,[6] there has been no further advance, except in minor improvements in methods.[7] There are no research workers eager to get on with the project. There is no adequate support for them if there were. They would likely even meet with considerable disapproval if they jeopardized, by an approach to the survival problem on any of the old lines, the status the field has secured by its experimental results.

The survival question, then, as we have known it in the past, is definitely not eligible to reinstatement as the great research objective for the future. From all indications there is much to recommend, rather, that it be tabled indefinitely and that the more pressing, more promising, and better supported objectives be given first consideration. If there were no other grounds for continuing active inquiry on the survival issue than the results of the studies of mediumship, there would be no great difficulty in leaving the question to the historian, at any rate for the present hard-pressed years that are already so full of problems important enough in themselves.

Yet there *are*, at least in the judgment of some of us in this field, good grounds for allowing the survival question to survive.

These grounds have nothing to do with mediumship or with any cult or creed or practice or philosophy. They are not, therefore, subject to the usual discounting for possible bias due to ulterior motives such as promotion of a cause. These grounds are not yet very extensive and at best we consider that they go only so far as to justify a reopening of the question of personal agency independent of the body. It is probable, however, that the survival question would have been raised by the material I have in mind even if it had never come up before as a cultural inheritance. The idea that it was this same sort of material that originally made man survival conscious has been suggested, but of course that hypothesis could not be proved, and, if it could, it would not *prove* anything concerning survival.

These new grounds can at least be briefly introduced: From the Duke collection of more than three thousand spontaneous psi experiences (which is just one of several on which such a study could be made), about a hundred cases have been selected as suggesting the operation of some kind of spirit agency more strongly than any other explanation. Many of these instances would appear, as reported, to lend themselves to explanation only by discarnate agency, although the possibility is always open that such cases are erroneously reported. While we shall not try to make evidence out of them, we do want to see what it is they suggest in themselves, how repeatedly the suggestion is made from case to case, and over how large a number of experiences it holds.

The type of case that most arrests attention is the one in which the manifest purpose back of the effect produced is so peculiarly that of a deceased personality that it is not reasonable to attribute the agency to any other source. It is still more arresting when the manifestation or expression of the purpose is conveyed through an innocent medium such as that of a child or a complete stranger who, presumably, would be devoid of any spiritualistic philosophy or other ostensible ulterior motivation.

A few examples may clarify the reason for the interest attaching to this approach to the problem of spirit agency through study of the case material (and may, incidentally, encourage readers who know of or have had similar experiences to add reports of them to the collection . . . ʃA woman in a responsible position in a New York City bank wrote: "About six weeks after the death of my friend, Nurse B, I was lying on a sofa in my home. Suddenly I heard Nurse B's voice calling me by name and saying, 'Do not be alarmed. This is Nurse B speaking, and I have come to warn you. You are pregnant and in grave danger. Go to Dr. H. (full name was given) in Brooklyn not later than Saturday. I warn you, do not delay; you are in grave danger!' The next Saturday I went to see Dr. H. and to my surprise she said she had been expecting me but did not tell me why. I learned that she and Nurse B had been very close friends. She examined me and said that there was no pregnancy but that I did have a fibroid growth attached to the uterus and backbone. She called a surgeon, the diagnosis was confirmed, and a successful operation was performed. Time proved, however, that both doctors were wrong in saying there was no pregnancy. Less than nine months after the examination my baby was born. I believe that God allowed Nurse B to come back and warn me." . . . The suggestion is that some purposive agency was behind the warning given the woman and the preparation of the physician who said she was expecting her. We could not prove that Nurse B had anything to do with it, but she was surely the most appropriate connecting link.

Sometimes these experiences are accompanied by physical effects that seem to be connected and that cannot be considered as hallucinations. These physical manifestations are, however, so dramatic as to tend to force one on the spot to look into the character and credibility of the witness before going on. For that reason, I select from the folder of cases in Louisa E. Rhine's collection one given me by an old friend and a respected professor, even though I have mentioned the case briefly in an earlier book. I give it now, still somewhat condensed, but in Dr. Ralph Harlow's own words . . . ʃ"My sister, Anna, was psychic from early childhood. We had an agreement that whoever passed over first would attempt to give the other some signal of survival. My sister died unexpectedly and her passing was a great loss to me. We had been close friends from early childhood. On my return from her funeral, I entered my office at the college where I was to hold a conference with a senior on the subject of William

James' *Varieties of Religious Experience*. It was a warm, sunny afternoon in mid-October. As the student sat down in the chair by my desk I suggested that I tell her something about the religious experiences of my sister. The moment I uttered the word "Anna" there was a report as though a small pistol had been fired, and the inkwell was cut down through the center. The student, apparently in great fright, arose and backed away, asking what had happened. She was so upset that she asked to be excused and allowed to return another day. I took the inkwell and washed it. Returning to the office, I had a vivid experience which I have had but twice in my life. A voice said distinctly, "Is this clear-cut evidence?" Then I recalled that I had said to my sister in years past, "If you ever give evidence of survival, make it clear-cut." There were no slivers of glass. The inkwell was cut so cleanly that I rubbed my hand against each side. Taking it to a professor of physics, I asked him to explain the break, not telling him anything of the incident. He said that he had never seen glass fracture in that way and that I must have brought a knife down suddenly on the inkwell. In my opinion one could not cut through the glass without many attempts, and then certainly not without splintering the glass." . . . Since I am not trying to prove something with this case, I shall not go into the possibility and probability of spontaneous fracturing in glass and of hallucinations occurring to a bereaved individual, and the like.

A professor at Northwestern University received the following case from one of his students . . . ʃ"One evening when I was a boy of four, before I knew anything of school or the alphabet, my mother was working at her desk in our hotel and I got hold of a call pad and was busy making marks on it. This kept up for three or four small sheets of paper when mother, noticing what I was playing with, told me to stop and play with something else. I put away my pencil, folded the papers I had written on and stuffed them in my mother's mailbox and went away, the incident forgotten. The next morning mother found the papers in her box and was about to throw them away when the day clerk, who had taken shorthand at night school, told her they looked like shorthand. Mother explained that they were just my scribblings, but the clerk insisted on taking the papers to a teacher for examination. They were shorthand. The entire scribblings made sense and there was not one mistake or extra mark on the papers. It was written in the old-fashioned square-type shorthand, something of which I had never heard, let alone having the slightest idea of how to write. It was a message to my mother. It started: 'Dearest Beloved,' and spoke of a letter that had not been posted. It was an urgent letter concerning my father's safety-deposit box in the East. My father had died two weeks before. He had died in New York while mother and I were in Oregon. His death had been sudden and mother had not known the location of that box. Moreover, my father had always called my mother 'Dearest Beloved,' and while he was a young man he had learned shorthand the old-fashioned method. Mother still has those pieces of paper and the message has been translated by other people and is actually there. It was years later, when I was old enough to understand, that Mother told me the story and showed me the papers." . . . The apparent use of the child as a medium is of special interest, though this is not unique. A report like this does not need to be of proof value; it puts ideas into our heads that can be tried out.

Such cases do suggest personal agency of a kind that no living individual would be expected to provide. They do raise the question whether any nonliving or spirit behavior is possible. What is more, they furnish ideas as to what might be done toward setting up a project for the purpose of finding out about whether such agency is possible. Here there are no mediums with professional motives or cultist affiliations involved. Here, too, is a wide variety of manifestations with an extraordinary range of percipient subjects extending from animals and children to highly sophisticated adult human beings such as scientists and professional men and women of various fields. The experiences are not predominantly stereotyped. It is true that a great many instances are reported in which clocks are stopped, glass objects broken, pictures dropped from the walls, doors unaccountably opened or closed, and objects pulled off the mantle or table or desk. There are queer and significant knockings, lights, voices, musical sounds, and such, but few of these look like cultural artifacts. There seems to be a fairly manifest purpose of breaking the shock of tragic news by a warning experience or event or of conveying some news itself of great significance to the loved ones concerned. The motivation is usually plausible enough; it is the agency and the means that are mysterious. In any case, the first step in making a major research project out of this material is a perfectly safe undertaking and a good thing to do on general grounds. That would be to collect and study all of the experiences of these types that can be obtained with the time and means available and try to see what ideas they furnish that could be followed up by a more experimental method of study. The worst that could happen would be to discover that the approach is a blind alley; and it is hardly possible that all this material means nothing for parapsychology, even if it is not what it seems.

However, merely having a fresh approach and a new stimulus to research on the question of personality survival is not enough by any means to justify making it a main research objective. Whatever the merits of the spirit hypothesis and however detached one may be, or determined to see that the question is kept alive, there is the altogether serious fact that, for the reasons already given, this is not the time to launch a large-scale investigation on that problem. In fact, anyone who attempted it in parapsychology today would likely soon find himself comparatively isolated, at least during this period of recovery from the reaction to the failure of the survival research based on mediumship. Such an undertaking must be to some extent sustained by the intellectual setting from which it takes off, and on the other lines as well it would, in order to achieve its purpose, need stronger assurance of continued support than it would get today.

So far as the survival question goes, then, it has a rather limited choice of alternatives, either that of going underground figuratively or of being buried rather more literally. If it is not soon to become a dead and buried issue, it will have to lose its identity, merge with other interests, and become part of a more feasible major research objective. To accomplish this identification, however, it needs only to be turned over or about so that it presents its various similarities to other parapsychological problems. When taken as a full program, the problem of spirit survival is little more

than a focal point on which centers a whole range of parapsychological research questions.

There has been, I think, little or nothing accomplished in the
psi researches that a thoroughgoing survival research program, if
there had ever been one, would not have had to include. For
example, all that has been discovered showing that there is something in man that has a wholly different set of properties from
those of his physical body is basic to the survival hypothesis. In
fact, it is this finding that makes survival logically possible. Furthermore, any sort of spirit agency would obviously have to depend
on psi as a method of operation. Any transfer of thought from
one discarnate personality to another, or to an incarnate one,
would have to be on telepathic lines or else work indirectly
through a psychokinetic effect of some kind. Certainly the sensorimotor system that was destroyed with the death of the body would
no longer be of any help. What else would there be but psi for
a spirit to use?

The spirit hypothesis seems to integrate so fully with the
whole organized program of parapsychology that has shaped itself
up through the years that with this degree of congruency there
is no reason to make a separate issue of it. In any thoroughgoing
survival research program it would be necessary to find out first
whether there is any independence or separability of the subjective self from its *living* physical organism; only if there should
be could a reasonable case be made for the probability of survival
of bodily death. But there are other urgent reasons for wanting
to know this degree of subjective independence; for example, the
question of the degree of volitional freedom in man depends on
that very same inquiry.

In a well-designed research on spirit survival even the current
program of exploring psi capacities in animals would have to be
included. For it would be only as the full, factual reality of psi
in nature became clear and established that the rational possibility
of spirit agency could take on any real meaning and become more
than a fairytale sort of fantasy. And then it would be only if
psi capacities were found to function in an incorporeal state of
personality that there could be a possibility of any effective spirit
communication or other agency. In fact, as most spiritists have

been too impatient to realize, all the psi investigations could just as well have been labeled studies on the ways and means by which spirit personalities, if such there be, live, move and have their being.

Absorbing the survival question in full would make little difference to a well-balanced psi research program. This can be realized by considering what a broadly conceived psi program would really look like. Parapsychology can hardly do less than make a straightforward inquiry into the entire extraphysical nature of personality. Whatever it may involve, that is the defined area of the field; and it is definite enough to be a grand research objective in itself. The first stage has necessarily been a determination of the differential relation of personality to the physical world. The progress already made thereon is, of course, only a beginning. Until we find the basic underlying and unifying psychophysical interconnections that one must infer are present in spite of all the distinctions that have been drawn, we shall still not understand the nature of personality with regard to the physical world. To say that certain operations of personality are not physical is just one important step; to discover how they interoperate with the physical system of the body and its environment now becomes even more important. With this view, too, the intelligent spiritistic explorer would have to agree, since his hypothesis of incorporeal personal agency involves this same problem of the how of psychophysical interaction. He, just as much as any other psi explorer, needs to know how a spiritual function could react with a physical one.

The second objective, then, will be to discover the place of the nonphysical part of personality in the world of living things. This will incidentally mean the discovery of whether the personality includes an extrabiological as well as an extraphysical component, whether it has within it anything more than the processes of life. To trace out the relationship of these nonphysical factors in personality to the life processes of the organism is to probe into the basis specifically needed for judging the possibilities of postmortem survival. It would merely be a case of dealing with the two sides of the same question.

Third and most advanced of all would be the question of

the place of the individual personality in that still largely unknown but enormously baffling new world of natural operation that has been touched upon in the psi explorations. The glimpses already envisaged indicate an order of reality one has neither the imagery nor the symbolism to describe, a level of causality that seems to drop only a transient spontaneous effect from time to time into the human range of perception and when pursued can be caught only by the finest net of statistics and the most patient methods of snaring—but still can be caught. It is with such that any study of personal survival would be concerned.

There is good reason, then, for major research emphasis to be placed on the general nature of psi itself, as opposed to its connection to the post-mortem state. By enlarging the question about the destiny of the human spirit from one of whether it survives the dissolution of its organism to that of what it really is *within* its own living totality, *within* its universe of integrating psychophysical interaction, and *within* that uniquely unimaginable new world of influences beyond space and time, there can be no disappointment over the answer, no failure of the research. The researches are bound to be successful in some way, whatever the answer turns out to be, if the inquiries are oriented from the viewpoint of asking what a man *is*. If the question is only, Is man thus-and-so? the research perspective is limited and the answer loaded in advance. Man may not be thus-and-so. He may be something much better, or, at least, far different; something about which as yet there has not been sufficient understanding to have permitted even the framing of a question. One should not exclude possibilities merely by a narrow or too specialized limitation of the inquiry.

For the larger research objective, then, let us ask for the whole natural history of the spiritual or nonphysical or transcendent aspect of personality, for all that man is as a uniquely personal being, over and above the world of matter. It will be wise not to be limited to a life-beyond-the-grave point of view, just as it would not be profitable to direct the leading inquiry toward practical utility or an over-all psi theory or a psi-personality type, or to any other limited sector of the total perspective.

But is there in the world today sufficient interest in the

field to sustain such an enlarged research project? The answer, I think, is that it is *only* by viewing the program in this larger perspective that one could hope for the inspiration to sustain the research. Only by seeing the problems in their concrete relation to the vital needs of mankind today can a strength of purpose be created and maintained great enough to prevent the weak acceptance of something less than a final, valid, and compelling solution. It is thus necessary to have an objective of magnitude and to keep it in clear focus in order to justify the demands made upon the investigator in the slow, uncertain, and unspectacular explorings, the patiently repetitive researches needed for sure answers. The exploring of this new world simply will not be done at the hard, unrecognized stage by anyone whose purpose is not sustained by some understanding of its meaning for humanity. All along the difficult way are easier turnoffs inviting those who, by exercising an element of uncritical faith, can accept a less exacting standard of significance and conclusiveness, a less rigorous demonstration than is demanded if the results are to be sound and conclusive. There have, fortunately, been some inquirers in the past, and there will be others in the future, prepared to appreciate, to demand, the highest order of reliability in facts about man's own nature. And it is only by such appreciation that individuals can be brought to invest so heavily of their devotion, to endure the long and careful surveying and resurveying, and to carry the burden of suspended judgment required in reaching conclusions on which mankind can safely rely.

To go a step further, unless wider attention can be drawn to the larger meaning for human life which the issues of the psi explorations hold, I do not see how the research can be carried very far beyond its present stage of complexity and difficulty. And it may, of course, be too late for such an undertaking to succeed; the Western world may already have found in the philosophy of the machine a faith that is too easy and satisfying to give up. The almost magical powers of physical nature which have been mastered so efficiently may already have fooled too many into thinking that such power is all there is and that it is enough for men to live by.

But the great hope I see—and it is a real hope—is in that minority who knows that, however useful these physical discoveries may be, they are not carrying man toward the kind of world to which he really aspires and the good life he wants to live with his fellow men. Some few, at least, do recognize the tragedy that, in this vast scientific conquest of physical nature, it is man himself that is being conquered. They realize that not all of the most brilliant physical explorations put together, whether penetrating into the nuclear energies of the atom or reaching far out to the remotest galaxy, have brought man even a short step nearer to grasping the essential mystery of himself as a personality. They know, too, that there are other directions than the materialistic route for the scientific voyager to take to find the fountain of knowledge that will reflect man clearly to himself. But even these few, with their awareness of man's crucial need to solve the ideological crisis of the time by research into the crux of it all, a basic theory of man, can alert the rest if the need continues to grow in urgency and if the menace to world sanity increases. As a spark can start a conflagration, so can a handful of perceptive men and women initiate a movement they could not stop or even guide. What they can accomplish will depend partly on the demand of the times for a scientifically verified basis for a design of life and human relations—upon how great the demand and how soon it comes. This outer pressure of events will be needed. But equally necessary to their success is the growing core of hard fact about man's real nature that the psi researches have produced. The further developed it is, the better the prospect that man will at last recognize himself as his greatest unknown and divest himself of the garments of dogmatism that have prevented thorough examination as a personality.

But whether one sets out on a search for an understanding of man's destiny still bearing the cast of thought molded by his childhood religion; or whether that has been supplanted by a new orthodoxy stamped upon his mind by the materialistic philosophy of a collegiate career; or, whether he has picked up a new outlook from one of the many fringe groups that offer, at patent medicine rates, a full-fledged philosophy of life with whatever mixture of mystery and "proof" you want; however it be, the seeker will be wise to be prepared to adjust his older outlook to the new facts, whatever they turn out to be like. They are likely to bring many surprises and some of them will be disappointing. Not a few of those who have contributed most to the efforts at psi exploration have been depressed by the fact that the shores they perceive dimly rising out of the distant horizon seem not to be those they have specifically sought. But the explorer who is properly prepared for such adventurous inquiry into the unknown of man's nature, into the problem of the unique driving influence in the universe men call the human spirit, will shed no tears if the uncertain shores on which he lands turn out to be, not Cipango with its teas, silks, and spices, but a vast and unexplored continent without as yet even a name. The new worlds of the past have *always* exceeded the wildest dreams of the adventurer. With this realization of the superiority of truth over even the most cherished anticipations, the psi explorer for his reassurance needs no greater promise.

REFERENCES

CHAPTER I: *A Chart of the Areas Discovered*

1. Rhine, J. B., *Extrasensory Perception* (Boston: Bruce Humphries, 1934), pp. 85–86.
2. Greenwood, J. A., "Analysis of a large chance control series of ESP data," *J. Parapsychol.*, 2(1938), pp. 138–146.
3. Rhine, L. E., "Conviction and associated conditions in spontaneous cases," *J. Parapsychol.*, 15 (1951), pp. 164–191.
4. Rhine, J. B., "Evidence of precognition in the covariation of salience ratios," *J. Parapsychol.*, 6 (1942), pp. 111–143.
5. Humphrey, B. M., and J. B. Rhine, "A confirmatory study of salience in precognition tests," *J. Parapsychol.*, 6 (1942), pp. 192–219.
6. Rhine, *Extrasensory Perception*, p. 42.
7. Rhine, J. B., "Telepathy and clairvoyance reconsidered," *J. Parapsychol.*, 9 (1945), pp. 176–193.
8. McMahan, E. A., "An experiment in pure telepathy," *J. Parapsychol.*, 10 (1946), pp. 224–242.
9. Soal, S. G., "The experimental situation in psychical research," *J. Parapsychol.*, 13 (1949), pp. 92–97.
10. Thouless, R. H., and B. P. Wiesner, "The psi process in normal and 'paranormal' psychology," *J. Parapsychol.*, 12 (1948), pp. 192–212.

11. Jung, C. G., and W. Pauli, *Natureklärung und Psyche* (Zurich: Rascher Verlag, 1952).
12. Rhine, J. B., "The psychokinetic effect: A review," *J. Parapsychol.*, 10 (1946), pp. 5–20, and *The Reach of the Mind* (New York: Wm. Sloane Associates, 1947), Chaps. 6, 7, and 8.
13. Rhine, J. B. and B. M. Humphrey, "The PK effect: Special evidence from hit patterns. I. Quarter distributions of the page," *J. Parapsychol.*, 8 (1944), pp. 18–60; *ibid.*, "II. Quarter distributions of the set," *ibid.*, pp. 254–271; Rhine, Humphrey, and J. G. Pratt, *ibid.*, "III. Quarter distributions of the half-set," *ibid.*, 9 (1945), pp. 150–168.
14. Thouless, R. H., "Some experiments on PK effects in coin spinning," *J. Parapsychol.*, 9 (1945), pp. 169–175.
15. McMahan, E. A., "A PK experiment with discs," *J. Parapsychol.*, 10 (1946), pp. 169–180, and "PK experiments with two-sided objects," *ibid.*, 9 (1945), pp. 249–263.
16. Cox, W. E., "The effect of PK on the placement of falling objects," *J. Parapsychol.*, 15 (1951), pp. 40–48; Rhine, J. B., "The Forwald experiments with placement PK," *ibid.*, pp. 49–56; Forwald, H., "A further study of the PK placement effect," *ibid.*, 16 (1952), pp. 59–67.

CHAPTER II: *Claims, Challenges, and Confirmations*

1. Warner, L., "A second survey of psychological opinion on ESP," *J. Parapsychol.*, 16 (1952), pp. 284–295.
2. Warner, L., and C. C. Clark, "A survey of psychological opinion on ESP," *J. Parapsychol.*, 2 (1938), pp. 296–301.
3. Pope, D. H., and J. G. Pratt, "The ESP controversy," *J. Parapsychol.*, 6 (1942), pp. 174–189.
4. "The ESP symposium at the A.P.A.," *J. Parapsychol.*, 2 (1938), pp. 247–272.
5. Kennedy, J. L., "An evaluation of extrasensory perception," *Proc. Amer. Phil. Soc.*, 96 (1952), pp. 513–518.
6. Hebb, D. O., "The role of neurological ideas in psychology," *J. Personal.*, 20 (1951), p. 45.
7. Kellogg, C. E., "New evidence (?) for extrasensory perception," *Sci. Monthly*, October, 1937, p. 332.
8. Pratt, J. G., and J. L. Woodruff, "Size of stimulus symbols in ex-

trasensory perception," *J. Parapsychol.*, 3 (1939), pp. 121–158.

9. "Letters and Notes," *J. Parapsychol.*, 3 (1939), pp. 246–253.

10. Soal, S. G., and K. M. Goldney, "Experiments in precognitive telepathy," *Proc. Soc. Psych. Res.*, 47 (1943), pp. 21–150.

11. Soal, S. G., and F. Bateman, *Modern Experiments in Telepathy* (to be published by Yale University Press).

12. Kahn, S. D., "Studies in extrasensory perception," *Proc. Amer. Soc. Psych. Res.*, 25 (1952), pp. 1–48.

13. "Report of the research committee," *J. Amer. Soc. Psych. Res.*, 46 (1952), p. 71.

14. Estabrooks, G. H., *A contribution to experimental telepathy*, Bull. No. 5, Boston Soc. Psych. Res. (1927), pp. 1–30.

15. Jephson, Ina, "Evidence for clairvoyance in card guessing," *Proc. Soc. Psych. Res.*, 38 (1929), pp. 223–268.

16. Anonymous, "A scientist tests his own ESP ability," *J. Parapsychol.*, 2 (1938), pp. 65–70.

17. Pratt, J. G., "A reinvestigation of the quarter distribution of the (PK) page," *J. Parapsychol.*, 8 (1944), pp. 61–63.

18. Schmeidler, G. R., "Separating the sheep from the goats," *J. Amer. Soc. Psych. Res.*, 39 (1945), pp. 47–49.

19. Schmeidler, G. R., "Personality correlates of ESP as shown by Rorschach studies," *J. Parapsychol.*, 13 (1949), pp. 23–31; Dr. Schmeidler also has a book-length report in preparation.

20. Stuart, C. E., "An interest inventory relation to ESP scores," *J. Parapsychol.*, 10 (1946), pp. 154–161.

21. Humphrey B. M., "Further work of Dr. Stuart on interest test ratings and ESP," *J. Parapsychol.*, 13 (1949), pp. 151–165.

22. Humphrey, B. M., "The relation of ESP to mode of drawing," *J. Parapsychol.*, 13 (1949), pp. 31–46.

23. Pratt, J. G., "The reinforcement effect in ESP displacement," *J. Parapsychol.*, 15 (1951), pp. 103–117.

24. Cadoret, R., and J. G. Pratt, "The consistent missing effect in ESP," *J. Parapsychol.*, 14 (1950), pp. 244–256.

25. Rhine, J. B., "The problem of psi-missing," *J. Parapsychol.*, 16 (1952), pp. 90–129.

26. Jung and Pauli, *op. cit.*

CHAPTER III: *The Present Research Frontiers*

1. Rhine, J. B., "Precognition reconsidered," *J. Parapsychol.*, 9 (1945), pp. 264–277.
2. Soal and Goldney, *op. cit.*
3. Nash, C. B., "Psychokinesis reconsidered," *J. Amer. Soc. Psych. Res.*, 45 (1951), pp. 62–68.
4. Thouless, R. H., "A report on an experiment in psychokinesis with dice, and a discussion of psychological factors favoring success," *Proc. Soc. Psych. Res.*, 49 (1951), pp. 107–130.
5. Reeves, M. P., and J. B. Rhine, "The PK effect: II. A study in declines," *J. Parapsychol.*, 7 (1943), pp. 76–93.
6. Barrett, W. F., and T. Besterman, *The Divining Rod* (London: Methuen and Co., 1926).
7. Bates, E. K., and M. Newton, "An experimental study of ESP capacity in mental patients," *J. Parapsychol.*, 15 (1951), pp. 271–277; Rhine, J. B., "Psi phenomena and psychiatry," *Proc. Roy. Soc. Med.*, 43 (1950), pp. 804–814; Shulman, R., "A study of card guessing in psychotic subjects," *J. Parapsychol.*, 2 (1938), pp. 95–106.
8. Schmeidler, G. R., "Personality correlates of ESP as shown by Rorschach studies," *J. Parapsychol.*, 13 (1949), pp. 23–30.
9. Bond, E. M., "General extrasensory perception with a group of fourth and fifth grade retarded children," *J. Parapsychol.*, 1 (1937), pp. 114–122; Drake, R. M., "An unusual case of extrasensory perception," *J. Parapsychol.*, 2 (1938), pp. 184–198; Humphrey, B. M., "ESP and intelligence," *J. Parapsychol.*, 9 (1945), pp. 7–16; Humphrey, B. M., "A further study of ESP and intelligence," *J. Parapsychol.*, 12 (1948), pp. 213–217.
10. Riess, B. F., "A case of high scores in card guessing at a distance," *J. Parapsychol.*, 1 (1937), pp. 260–263.
11. Rhine, L. E., "Conviction and associated conditions in spontaneous cases," *J. Parapsychol.*, 15 (1951), pp. 164–191.
12. Carington, W., "Experiments with paranormal cognition of drawings," *J. Parapsychol.*, 4 (1940), pp. 1–129; "Parapsychology at Rhodes University, South Africa," *Parapsychol. Bull.* No. 25 (1952); M. C. Marsh's dissertation for the Ph.D. degree, "Linkage in Extrasensory Perception," submitted Rhodes University, 1953.

13. Pratt, J. G., "The reinforcement effect in ESP displacement," *J. Parapsychol.*, 15 (1951), pp. 103–117.
14. Greville, T. N. E., "A method of evaluating the reinforcement effect," *J. Parapsychol.*, 15 (1951), pp. 118–121.
15. Pratt, J. G., "The meaning of performance curves in ESP and PK test data," *J. Parapsychol.*, 13 (1949), pp. 9–23.
16. Foster, A. A., "ESP tests with American Indian children," *J. Parapsychol.*, 7 (1943), pp. 94–103.
17. Rose, L., and R. Rose, "Psi experiments with Australian Aborigines," *J. Parapsychol.*, 15 (1951), pp. 122–131.
18. Price, M. M., "A comparison of blind and seeing subjects in ESP tests," *J. Parapsychol.*, 2 (1938), pp. 271–286.
19. Bechterev, W., " 'Direct influence' of a person upon the behavior of animals," *J. Parapsychol.*, 13 (1949), pp. 166–176.
20. Rhine, J. B., and L. E. Rhine, "An investigation of a 'mind-reading' horse," *J. Ab. Soc. Psychol.*, 23 (1929), pp. 449–466, and "Second report of Lady, the 'mind-reading' horse," *ibid.*, 24 (1929), pp. 287–292.
21. Osis, K., "A test of the occurrence of a psi effect between man and the cat," *J. Parapsychol.*, 16 (1952), pp. 223–256; a second paper is in preparation.
22. Rhine, J. B., "The present outlook on the question of psi in animals," *J. Parapsychol.*, 15 (1951), pp. 230–251.
23. Pratt, J. G., "The homing problem in pigeons," *J. Parapsychol.*, 17 (1953), pp. 34–60.
24. Rhine, J. B., *et al.*, *Extrasensory Perception after Sixty Years* (New York: Henry Holt, 1940), pp. 287–290.
25. Bevan, J. M., "The relation of attitude to success in ESP scoring," *J. Parapsychol.*, 11 (1947), pp. 296–309.

CHAPTER IV: *Nonphysical Reality in Nature*

1. Rhine *et al.*, *op. cit.*, pp. 291–310.
2. Bateman, F., and S. G. Soal, "Long distance experiments in telepathy," *J. Amer. Soc. Psych. Res.*, 44 (1950), pp. 21–33.
3. "Parapsychology at Rhodes University, South Africa," *loc. cit.*; Marsh, *op. cit.*
4. Rhine, J. B., and B. M. Humphrey, "A transoceanic ESP experiment," *J. Parapsychol.*, 6 (1942), pp. 52–74; McMahan, E. A.,

and J. B. Rhine, "A second Zagreb-Durham ESP experiment," *J. Parapsychol.*, 11 (1947), pp. 244–253.

5. Nash, C. B., "Position effects in PK tests with twenty-four dice," *J. Parapsychol.*, 10 (1946), pp. 51–57.

6. Rhine, J. B., "The psychokinetic effect: A review," *loc. cit.*, and *The Reach of the Mind, loc. cit.*; Rhine, J. B., and B. M. Humphrey, "The PK effect: The McDougall one-die series," *J. Parapsychol.*, 7 (1943), pp. 252–263, "PK tests with six, twelve, and twenty-four dice per throw," *ibid.*, 8 (1944), pp. 139–157, and "The PK effect with sixty dice per throw," *ibid.*, 9 (1945), pp. 203–218.

7. Hilton, H., Jr., G. Baer, and J. B. Rhine, "A comparison of three sizes of dice in PK tests," *J. Parapsychol.*, 7 (1943), pp. 172–190; Hilton and Rhine, "A second comparison of three sizes of dice in PK tests," *ibid.*, pp. 191–206; Humphrey, B. M., and J. B. Rhine, "PK tests with two sizes of dice mechanically thrown," *J. Parapsychol.*, 9 (1945), pp. 124–132.

8. Rhine, J. B., and L. E. Rhine, Unpublished work.

CHAPTER V: *The Place of Psi in the Science of Life*

1. Hardy, A. C., "Zoology outside the laboratory," *Advancement of Science* (Brit. Assoc. for Advancement of Sci.), 6 (1949).

2. Matthews, G. V. T., "The experimental investigation of navigation in homing pigeons," *J. Exp. Biol.*, 28 (1951), pp. 508–536.

3. Naether, C. A., *The Book of the Pigeon* (Philadelphia: David McKay Co., 1939).

4. Sumner, F. B., "Human psychology and some things that fishes do," *Sci. Monthly*, 49 (1939), pp. 245–255.

5. Eccles, J. C., *The Neurophysiological Basis of Mind* (Oxford: Clarendon Press, 1953); Hutchinson, G. E., Forthcoming book of essays (New Haven: Yale University Press); Huxley, J. S., "Natural selection and evolutionary progress," *Nature* (London), 138 (1936), pp. 571–573, 603–605; Schaefer, H., "Telepathie und Hellsehen," *Die Umschau*, 19 (1952), pp. 577–578, and "Telepathie und Hellsehen—im Licht der Wissenschaft," *ibid.*, 20 (1952), pp. 611–614.

6. Kramer, G., "Wird die Sonnenhöhe bei der Heimkehrorientierung verwertet?" *J. für Orn.*, 94 (1953).

7. Herrick, F. H., "Homing powers of the cat," *Sci. Mon.*, 14 (1922), pp. 526–539.
8. Schmid, B., *Interviewing Animals* (Boston: Houghton Mifflin Co., 1937).
9. Kramer, G., and U. von St. Paul, "Heimkehrorientierung von Brieftauben ohne Richtungsdressur," *Verhandlungen der Deutschen Zoologischen Gesellschaft* (1951), pp. 172–178.
10. Pratt, J. G., "The homing problem in pigeons," *loc. cit.*
11. Bechterev, *op. cit.*
12. Rhine and Rhine, "An investigation of a 'mind-reading' horse," and "Second report of Lady, the 'mind-reading' horse," *loc. cit.*
13. Osis, *op. cit.*

CHAPTER VI: *Psi, Psyche, and Psychology*

1. Rhine, L. E., "Conviction and associated conditions in spontaneous cases," *J. Parapsychol.*, 15 (1951), pp. 164–191.

CHAPTER VIII: *Relation to the Health of the Mind*

1. Eisenbud, J., "Psychiatric contributions to parapsychology: A review," *J. Parapsychol.*, 13 (1949), pp. 247–263.
2. MacRobert, R. G., "Current attitudes of American neuropsychiatrists toward parapsychology: A survey," *J. Parapsychol.*, 12 (1948), pp. 257–272.
3. Rhine, L. E., "Subjective forms of spontaneous psi experiences," *J. Parapsychol.*, 17 (1953), pp. 77–114.
4. Humphrey, B. M., "Further work of Dr. Stuart on interest test ratings and ESP," *J. Parapsychol.*, 13 (1949), pp. 151–165, and "Introversion-extraversion ratings in relation to scores in ESP tests," *ibid.*, 15 (1951), pp. 252–262; Schmeidler, G. R., "Rorschach variables in relation to ESP scores," *J. Amer. Soc. Psych. Res.*, 41 (1947), pp. 35–64.
5. Urban, H., "Parapsychologie und Psychiatrie," *Pötzl Festschrift*, Dtsche med. Rundschau. No. 3 (Innsbruck, 1949).
6. Efrón, D., "Telepathic skin-writing," *J. Parapsychol.*, 8 (1944), pp. 272–286.

CHAPTER X: *The Greater Problems in the Present View*

1. Barrett and Besterman, *op. cit.*; McMahan, E., "A review of the evidence for dowsing," *J. Parapsychol.*, 11 (1947), pp. 175–190; Rhine, J. B., "Some exploratory tests in dowsing," *J. Parapsychol.*, 14 (1950), pp. 278–286, and "The challenge of the dowsing rod," *ibid.*, 16 (1952), pp. 1–10; Roberts, K., *Henry Gross and His Dowsing Rod* (New York: Doubleday, 1951), and *The Seventh Sense* (New York: Doubleday, 1953).

2. Murphy, G., "An outline of survival evidence," *J. Amer. Soc. Psych. Res.*, 39 (1945), pp. 2–34, "Difficulties confronting the survival hypothesis," *ibid.*, pp. 67–94, and "Field theory and survival," *ibid.*, pp. 181–209 (The three Murphy articles are reprinted in booklet form); Rhine, J. B., "The question of spirit survival," *J. Amer. Soc. Psych. Res.*, 43 (1949), pp. 43–58; Thouless, R. H., *Psychical research past and present*, Eleventh Frederic W. H. Myers Memorial Lecture, *Soc. Psych. Res.*, (1952).

3. Thouless, R. H., "A test of survival," *Proc. Soc. Psych. Res.*, 48 (1948), pp. 253–263, and "Additional note on a test of survival," *ibid.* (1949), pp. 342–343.

4. Hart, H., "The psychic fifth dimension," *J. Amer. Soc. Psych. Res.*, 47 (1953), pp. 3–32, and a sequel, with same title, *ibid.*, pp. 47–79; a third article is awaiting publication.

5. Pratt, J. G., *Toward a Method of Evaluating Mediumistic Material.* Bull. No. 23, Boston Soc. Psych. Res. (1936); Rhine, J. B., "Telepathy and clairvoyance in the normal and trance states of a 'medium,'" *Character and Pers.*, 3 (1934), pp. 91–111.

6. Saltmarsh, H. F., and S. G. Soal, "A method for estimating the supernormal content of mediumistic communications," *Proc. Soc. Psych. Res.*, 39 (1930), pp. 266–271.

7. Pratt, J. G., and W. R. Birge, "Appraising verbal test material in parapsychology," *J. Parapsychol.*, 12 (1948), pp. 236–256.

INDEX